Enterprise Risk Management in the Global Supply Chain

THE GLOBAL WARRIOR SERIES
Series Editor: Thomas A. Cook

Enterprise Risk Management in the Global Supply Chain
Thomas A. Cook (2017)

Excellence in Managing Worldwide Customer Relationships
Thomas A. Cook (2016)

Growing and Managing Foreign Purchasing
Thomas A. Cook (2016)

*Managing Growth and Expansion into Global Markets:
Logistics, Transportation, and Distribution*
Thomas A. Cook (2016)

Driving Risk and Spend Out of the Global Supply Chain
Thomas A. Cook (2015)

*Mastering the Business of Global Trade: Negotiating Competitive
Advantage Contractual Best Practices, Incoterms®
and Leveraging Supply Chain Options,*
Thomas A. Cook (2014)

Enterprise Risk Management in the Global Supply Chain

Thomas A. Cook

CRC Press
Taylor & Francis Group
Boca Raton London New York

CRC Press is an imprint of the
Taylor & Francis Group, an **informa** business

CRC Press
Taylor & Francis Group
6000 Broken Sound Parkway NW, Suite 300
Boca Raton, FL 33487-2742

© 2018 by Taylor & Francis Group, LLC
CRC Press is an imprint of Taylor & Francis Group, an Informa business

No claim to original U.S. Government works

Printed on acid-free paper

International Standard Book Number-13: 978-1-482-22621-8 (Hardback)

Visit the Taylor & Francis Web site at
http://www.taylorandfrancis.com

and the CRC Press Web site at
http://www.crcpress.com

To one of the most beloved persons on our planet: Gillian Rooney.

We and all veterans were blessed to know her and have her

in our lives. Never forgotten and always in our hearts!

Contents

Foreword xiii
Preface xv
Acknowledgments xvii

Chapter 1 Defining the Global Supply Chain and Enterprise
Risk Management.. 1

Overview of Risk Management and the Global
Supply Chain 1
Enterprise Risk Management...................................... 4
Driving Risk and Spending from the Global Supply Chain ... 9
Key Challenges in the Global Supply Chain 10
Risk Defined 11
Managing Cultural Issues in Global Trade............................ 13
Business Culture 14
Considering Cultural Factors................................... 14
Some Interesting Case Studies in Global Risk..................... 18
ARM Manufacturing, Ohio/Kobe Japan, 2011, Tsunami....19
Rathen Industries, New York/Russia, 2014,
Trade Compliance.. 19
Durkee Foods, Netherlands/New Orleans, 2005,
Hurricane... 20
Bering Communications, California/Sudan, 2015,
Political Risk, Kidnap and Ransom, IT Security.............. 21
Global Energies, New Jersey/China, 2016,
Foreign Corrupt Practices Act (FCPA).............................. 22
Deneson Products Corporation, Florida/Venezuela,
2014, Cargo Risk 22
Case Study Summary 23
Training... 24

Chapter 2 Global Risk Management 25

Global Supply Chain Risk Verticals............................ 25

Property, Casualty, Workers' Compensation, Auto,
Fiduciary, etc. ("Supply Chain Focus")..............................26
Political Risk..27
Confiscation, Expropriation, Nationalization,
and Deprivation (C, E, N, and D)....................................28
Contract Repudiation, Default, Currency
Inconvertibility, and Devaluation....................................29
Receivable Management 30
Security and Terrorism..31
Physical Assets..31
Corporate Terrorism Best Practices 35
Foreign Corrupt Practices Act (FCPA) and Antibribery......37
FCPA Corporate Compliance Program............................41
Antibribery 44
Conflict Minerals..46
U.S. Securities and Exchange Commission Guidelines...... 48
Personnel...53
Kidnap and Ransom Exposures 59
Training...60
Areas of Training 60

Chapter 3 Global Trade Risks 61

Technology and Cyber Issues...61
U.S. Government Program for Safeguarding
and Securing Cyberspace...62
CSI, C-TPAT, and ISF: U.S. Customs and Border
Protection's Security Programs 71
Contract Management..77
Financial..82
International Payment Terms 83
Currency 89
Geophysical, Environmental, Sustainability 92
Going Green 94
Corporate Reputation Branding and Marketing 101
Reputational Risk Exposures 102
IPR (Intellectual Property Rights) 103

Chapter 4 Supply Chain and Logistics 109

INCO Terms 109
Sourcing and Purchasing 115
Logistics 119
  Foreign Trade Zones (FTZs) 119
  Bonded Warehouses 120
  Free Trade Agreements 121
  Logistics Bidding 121
  Freight 124
  Reducing International Supply Chain Costs
  without Beating Up Your Carrier or Service Provider ...127
  When a Major Carrier Goes Bankrupt: Managing
  the Aftermath and Future Loss Preventive Measures 129
    Loss Prevention 130
  Global E-Commerce 132
  Trade Compliance 137
    Buying Internationally: Import Supply Chain 138
      Duties and Fees 138
      Harmonized Tariff Classification 142
      Country of Origin Marking 143
      Trade Compliance 143
      Reasonable Care Standard 144
      Customhouse Brokers 149
      Internal Supervision and Control 152
      Supply Chain Security 153
      Invoice Requirements 154
      Bonds 156
      Record Retention 156
    Selling Internationally: The Export Supply Chain 157
      Government Agencies Responsible for Exports 158
      International Traffic in Arms Regulations 158
      Export Administration Regulations 159
      Commerce Control List 160
      Electronic Export Information 160
      U.S. Principal Party in Interest 161
      Schedule B Number/Harmonized Tariff Number 162
      Valuation 163
      Record-Keeping Requirements 163

Denied Party Screening 164
Embargoed Country Screening 164
Breakdown of the Consolidated Screening List..........168
Consularization and Legalization 169
Solid Wood Packing Material (SWPM) Certificates.....170
Preshipment Inspections..170
Free Trade Affirmations...171
Getting Paid...172
ATA Carnets...172
Summary of Logistics Considerations................................173
The Six Steps 173
Choose the Best INCO Term...................................174
Insure the Shipment..175
Chose the Right Freight Forwarder and Carrier 176
Track All Shipments Proactively..............................177
Understand the Total "Landed Costs" 178
Be Trade Compliant!...179
Summary...180

Chapter 5   International Insurance and Global Risk
Management 181

Marine Insurance 181
Geographic Areas Covered...183
Named Insured...183
Modes of Transit Covered 183
Limits of Liability...184
Valuation 184
Underwriting Terms..185
Special Terms...185
War and SRCC Coverage..185
Terrorism 186
Effective Dates...186
Storage/Warehousing..186
Consolidation and Deconsolidation 186
Domestic Transit..187
Interruptions in Transit 187
Exclusions 188

    Loss of Market 188

    Delay 188

    Business Interruption or Consequential Damages 188

    War SRCC 188

    Inadequate Packing...188

   Cancellation..192

   Commercial Insurances Overview.......................................192

   Property Insurance...193

   Liability Insurance...194

   Crime and Fiduciary Liability Insurance 194

   Cyber Liability Insurance Coverage...................................195

   International Directors and Officers Liability

   Insurance...196

   Excellent Resources for International Insurances...........196

Chapter 6   Structuring a Global Supply Chain Risk

     Management Best Practice Strategy............................... 197

   The Ten Step Master Plan 198

    Step 1: Determine a Point Person 198

    Step 2: Obtain Senior Management Support

    and Authorization...199

    Step 3: Create a Committee of Stakeholders 200

    Step 4: Perform an Assessment... 202

    Step 5: Come Up with a Plan of Attack........................... 203

    Step 6: Develop Resources 204

    Step 7: Outreach to All Fiefdoms..................................... 204

    Step 8: Create SOPs... 205

    Step 9: Start Internal Training Programs........................ 206

    Step 10: Ascertain Audit Capability................................. 207

   Resources 211

   Credits 218

Appendix A: Glossary of Business Terms............................... 219

Appendix B: Glossary of Business Contract Terms 229

Appendix C: Glossary of International Trade Terms 235

Appendix D: Acronyms... 247

Appendix E: Cybersecurity..249

Appendix F: C-TPAT's Five Step Risk Assessment...........267

Appendix G: Conflict Minerals Reporting Form...............311

Appendix H: Professionalism Service Managers at U.S. Customs and Border Protection 323

Index...327

About the Author..335

Foreword

Tom's knowledge of reducing risk and spending in the global supply chain always impresses me with his comprehension of contemporary issues, in-depth analysis, and offerings for action steps and achieving high levels of success.

His numerous books in his CRC Global Warrior Series have become a great resource for students and trade professionals to follow to run and master global supply chain management issues.

We utilize all his works in our education and training facilities world-wide, and they have become a staple resource for many executives with responsibilities in international sales, procurement, and operations.

This most recent book on risk management touches an area of growing concern in corporate America, and, as I have become more familiar with its contents, have found it to be a serious resource and information haven for any area in risk, insurance, loss control, and management betterments in global supply chains.

Kelly Raia
President, DragonFly Global

Preface

In the past 30 years, more companies have begun to develop sourcing and purchasing initiatives in foreign markets.

Additionally, U.S.-based export sales have grown to their highest levels. What this growth means is increased exposures. Tied into this increase is a general lack of experience for those executives engaged in global trade with understanding international and supply chain risks and providing cost-effective solutions to their companies benefit.

This book outlines all the critical issues in understanding global risk management and establishes a workable structure, outline, and action plan for corporate executives as a blueprint to follow.

The primary deliverables of the book are

- Comprehension of the risks in global supply chains
- Enterprise solutions
- Cost-effective, functional, and hands-on skill set development to manage risk, insurance, and loss control in international operations, purchasing, and sales
- Addressing the increasing concerns over global security and cybersecurity

Business people need to understand the psychology of risk more than the mathematics of risk.

Paul Gibbons
The Science of Successful Organizational Change: How Leaders Set Strategy, Change Behavior, and Create an Agile Culture

Acknowledgments

Kelly Raia, in particular, for her contribution on the regulatory and trade compliance section and for assisting in editing, formatting, and material gain

Department of Commerce
American Shipper magazine
National Cargo Bureau

If we don't change, we don't grow. If we don't grow, we aren't really living.

Gail Sheehy

1

Defining the Global Supply Chain and Enterprise Risk Management

This chapter sets the tone for the balance of the book in explaining and outlining just what the global supply chain means and the various risks that float throughout its structure and how companies via an enterprise risk management approach can lead to better run companies and more successful supply chain management.

OVERVIEW OF RISK MANAGEMENT AND THE GLOBAL SUPPLY CHAIN

Where opportunity lies, so does risk. For the 40 years of my business career, I have extolled that virtue.

And it is a "true one." Every leading executive and entrepreneur engaged in global trade will tell you that the world is full of opportunity and fraught with risk simultaneously.

The key is to master the opportunities by mitigating the risks. And if we had to define "mitigation of risk," that is where risk management enters the equation. Add in international business, and then combine that with supply chain, then you finally get *risk management in the global supply chain*.

Risk in international trade both mirrors domestic exposures and adds another dimension that has some radical and uncertainty to the mix. For example, political risk enters the equation with exposures like confiscation and nationalization coming into play.

There are also serious financial exposures with little opportunity for recovery. The physical exposures of cyclones, earthquakes, tsunamis, and monsoons are but a few of the global weather events that can wreak havoc on global trade.

Terrorism and security issues emanating from the Middle East pose significant exposures to all business activities both here in the United States, as well as overseas. Cybersecurity issues raise even more serious concerns as evidenced in the presidential election of 2016, where "hackers" entered the Democratic party servers and made attempts at influencing election results.

A huge financial risk is making sure that the global supply chain remains open and is competitive, affording adequate margins and sustainability.

Beginning in 2017, the United States had a new president and administration led by Donald Trump. He has rhetorically announced numerous forthcoming changes to how the country will deal with global trade and the protection of domestic businesses and workers. How this will evolve and impact global trade is an unknown. That "unknown" creates a certain risk as companies plan their international strategies.

In the last hundred years, the United States has slowly dominated global business and international entrepreneurism. The hope is that the new administration will continue those initiatives and keep borders open for trade, supply chains, and favorable international relations.

Until this all gets sorted out, most companies and their executives are moving sheepishly forward to make sure their organizations' best interests are being protected as they expand globally.

The United States in the last 25 years has greatly expanded global sourcing. The main advantage of this effort has been lower costs for most consumer items. The new president has threatened companies who continue to foreign source and build factories on foreign soil. How this will all develop as the administration moves forward on its agenda and in compromise with the American public, business interests, and politics will remain to be seen. One of the worse concerns in all of this is the potential fallout if "trade wars" ensue.

ENTERPRISE RISK MANAGEMENT

Ultimately all the risks must be managed successfully.

Enterprise risk management (ERM) is often defined as a more robust risk management strategy in the process of planning, organizing, leading, and controlling the activities of an organization in order to minimize the effects of risk on an organization's capital and earnings. Enterprise risk management expands the process to include not just risks associated with accidental losses, but also financial, strategic, operational, and other risks. In this book the focus is on the global supply chain.

Factors related to an increase in global risk concerns have fueled a heightened interest by organizations in ERM. Industry and government regulatory bodies, as well as investors, have begun to scrutinize companies' risk-management policies and procedures. In an increasing number of industries, boards of directors are required to review and report on the adequacy of risk-management processes in the organizations they administer.

As gobal supply chains become an increasing critical component of most companies' strategic operations, their success depends on striking a balance between enhancing profits and managing risk.

RIMS (rims.org), based in New York City, explains the following: "Enterprise Risk Management ('ERM') is a strategic business discipline that supports the achievement of an organization's objectives by addressing the full spectrum of its risks and managing the combined impact of those risks as an interrelated risk portfolio."

ERM represents a significant evolution beyond previous approaches to risk management in that it:

1. Encompasses all areas of organizational exposure to risk (financial, operational, reporting, compliance, governance, strategic, reputational, etc.).

It is imperative that we understand that risk is more than property and liability, and extends across every vertical of a company, and can impact both adversely and positively how that company moves forward and survives. You can have the most cost-effective and well-structured domestic property policy on your assets in California, but if a joint venture sourcing manufacturer in Indonesia is impacted by a rogue tsunami and the plant is closed for nine months and you're not protected, the financial impact both in the short and long term could be devastating.

2. Prioritizes and manages those exposures as an interrelated risk portfolio rather than as individual "silos."

The relationships between each company vertical and its operations are all interrelated and what happens in one area can and most likely will impact adjacent corporate silos. For example, if your company decides to build a plant in Mexico, against significant operational savings, existing plants operating in Ohio could receive complications in union negotiations with that labor force. This potentially creates a negative HR (human resources) issue, where a favorable impact in the supply chain was also created. Does the benefit outweigh the risk? Could the risk have been avoided or mitigated? Did anyone even try to analyze and align the issues and determine a better path, which creates compromise and better stability overall?

3. Evaluates the risk portfolio in the context of all significant internal and external environments, systems, circumstances, and stakeholders.

An array of factors must be included in the risk portfolio when evaluating the impact of exposure into the organization. Risk by itself is not a silo. It is an accumulation of factors that impact operations. For example, in the global supply chain, international freight movements create physical risks to the cargo in transit. But having said that, those physical risks are impacted by weather, strikes, terrorist threats, choice of carriers and service providers, and so on, all of which are separate decisions made most likely by personnel operating in other verticals, outside of risk management. But cumulatively, those decisions all impact the risks of international cargo in transit. Loss and damage has multipliers or collaborating factors that impact the nature of the loss or damage, the extent, and the impact. The picture above shows a vessel that hit heavy weather conditions at sea. The heavy weather caused loss and damage to the cargo. But multipliers could be any combination of the following:

- Choice of suppliers
- Location of suppliers
- Choice of carriers or service providers
- Unanticipated delays
- Incorrect shipping methods, documentation, or routing

4. Recognizes that individual risks across the organization are interrelated and can create a combined exposure that differs from the sum of the individual risks.

   In addition to what was outlined earlier, the loss or damage that may or may not be covered under a marine cargo insurance policy could have consequential financial exposures such as:

- Loss of market
- Loss of revenue
- Reputation
- Fines and penalties

   Where and how are these additional exposures evaluated, assessed and managed? Clearly, these exposures impact other verticals and fiefdoms in the company outside of logistics and shipping.

5. Provides a structured process for the management of all risks, whether those risks are primarily quantitative or qualitative in nature.

> **Qualitative** research gathers information that is not in numerical form. For example, diary accounts, open-ended questionnaires, unstructured interviews, and unstructured observations.
>
> **Qualitative** data is typically descriptive data and as such is harder to analyze than **quantitative** data.

Enterprise risk management provides a process where all these risks can be evaluated by all the companywide stakeholders that could be impacted in some way or fashion. The assessment by all concerned and impacted parties leads to a collaborative process of risk management resolution that provides a greater opportunity for success. Risk managers do well by creating a "structure" on how this collaborative process will take place. This requires engagement by senior management who allocates authority, resources, and potential expenditures allowing facilitation.

Keep in mind that in the area of risk management assessment there are very defined metrics and hard data and then there are *sensibilities, experience, and insight* of which both methods (quantitative and qualitative) work in tandem.

Qualitative data	Quantitative data
Overview:	**Overview:**
• Deals with descriptions. • Data can be observed but not measured. • Colors, textures, smells, tastes, appearance, beauty, etc. • Qualitative → Quality	• Deals with numbers. • Data which can be measured. • Length, height, area, volume, weight, speed, time, temperature, humidity, sound levels, cost, members, ages, etc. • Quantitative → Quantity

6. Views the effective management of risk as a competitive advantage.

The author has a book in this Global Warrior Series, *Driving Risk and Spend Out of the Global Supply Chain*, which creates a credible argument on the fact that proactive risk management cannot only protect assets but also create leverage and particularly financial advantages in the global supply chain, the focus of this book.

Risk managers who can add value in their work and initiatives are in a much stronger position than those who just manage exposure.

7. Seeks to embed risk management as a component in all critical decisions throughout the organization.

This can be one of the most important aspects of enterprise risk management in that it sets the foundation for truly corporate-wide and totally encompassing risk strategies throughout the organization. It creates a mind-set on all operating managers and staff to consider direct risks and indirect impacts on all the decisions they make in their daily responsibilities.

I think it is akin to defensive driving of an automobile. You are focused on the road ahead, but you are looking at the side and rear view mirrors. You are viewing the dashboard and seeing how the engine is performing; you are not on your cell and certainly not texting.

It is that all encompassing approach that obtains the best opportunity to avoid pitfalls and problems. And when you have a fleet of cars and all the drivers are interconnected with that defensive mind-set you have an "enterprise solution" that will always work to the betterment overall of the entire organization.

Creating an umbrella over the entire organization by organizing every individual to act with prudence and due diligence in defining and mitigating exposure and risk is a best practice and world class event in any company seeking high levels of growth and profitability along with enhanced shareholder value.

Everyone is a Risk Manager

DRIVING RISK AND SPENDING FROM THE GLOBAL SUPPLY CHAIN

At an RIMS event in 2016 I spoke about Global Risk Management and utilized the following slide:

This slide clearly depicts three areas of opportunity in the global supply chain:

- Foreign sourcing (imports)
- Foreign-owned manufacturing
- Foreign sales (exports)

In a risk management assessment, the following conclusion can easily be drawn: As spending decreases, risk will increase.

In global supply chains the quest was, is, and will continue to be lower cost! And that typically is achieved at a "transactional" level.

Every decision to lower cost in the supply chain will impact risk. Examples:

- Source in a third-world country: lowers cost, increases risk
- Utilize an inexpensive carrier: lowers cost, increases risk
- Cut corners on documentation: lowers cost, increases risk
- Don't insure: lowers cost, increases risk

- Utilize incorrect HTS (Harmonized Tariff Schedule) numbers: lowers cost, increases risk
- Skimp on packaging: lowers cost, increases risk

In all these examples the increased risk scenarios may be worth taking. But have they been duly accessed and thought out? Are there contingencies set up? Are there mitigation or risk transfer options available?

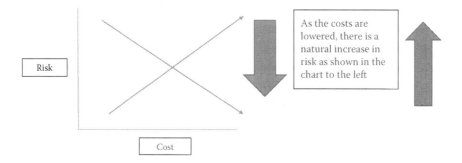

KEY CHALLENGES IN THE GLOBAL SUPPLY CHAIN

There are numerous global supply chain challenges in international business; some are generic and some are specific to particular business verticals and companies.

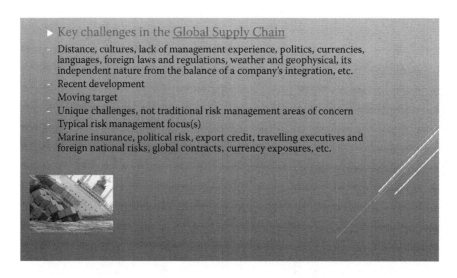

This pictorial outlines a slew of challenges that can easily be described as exposures or risks. The politically correct term is "challenges," as it connotes a more positive tone, something that can be defeated.

These challenges translate to risks. Personnel operating in the global supply chain need to:

1. First acknowledge that the challenges or risks exist.
2. Ascertain and measure their threat.
3. Understand the direct, indirect, and ancillary implications on how these threats may cause loss or consequence to the organization.
4. Comprehend the connectivity between all verticals and interests of the company's fiefdoms and silos.
5. Create a collaborative effort to mitigate the challenges.
6. Take risk management actions.

RISK DEFINED

Risk is the potential of gaining or losing something of value. Values (such as physical health, social status, emotional well-being, or financial wealth) can be gained or lost when taking risk resulting from a given action or inaction, foreseen or unforeseen.

Risk can also be defined as the intentional interaction with uncertainty. Uncertainty is a potential, unpredictable, and uncontrollable outcome; risk is a consequence of action taken or lack of action taken, in spite of uncertainty.

Risk perception is the subjective judgment people make about the severity and probability of a risk, and may vary person to person. Any human endeavor carries some risk, but some are much riskier than others.

It is important to understand what risk is and how it relates to our business responsibilities, as risk management is a growing concern in most verticals and corporations. But it is more important to understand what risk perception is, because that is how business decisions are ultimately made. "Perception is reality" is a very specific truism in all aspects of life, but certainly in risk management and in business.

If senior management perceives a low risk, they will respond accordingly, probably with less zeal. And hopefully, if they perceive a more serious and threatening risk, they will act with more urgency and prudence.

I believe that a risk manager's primary role in communicating risk up to senior management is to close the gap between perception and reality so better decisions can be made. This affords senior management with realistic information flow that allows not only better decision making but also allows better strategies to accept, transfer, or mitigate risk.

With respect to the global supply chain, I believe there are several perceptions that exist that I have found to be troublesome:

- Risks in the global supply chain are minimized as to their relevance and impact on overall business operations.
- Risk managers are not experts in supply chain or in global risk.

- Risks in the supply chain are often transferred to third parties, such as suppliers, carriers, service providers, and contracted intermediaries. Too often the protections that are supposed to be in place are not

where they need to be, leaving serious deficiencies, which are typically not identified until a loss occurs.
- Many risks have convolutions or nuances that become cumbersome to manage or handle, and therefore get overlooked or are not dealt with comprehensively, timely, or responsibly.
- Foreign vendors create an entirely unique and extraordinary set of risks to supply chains that are oftenmisunderstood, and therefore certain and reasonable protections are lacking.
- The purchasing silo impacting imports and the sales silo impacting exports are typically not engaged in any risk management initiatives or strategies in most organizations.
- Western cultures are much more inclined to deal with risk proactively, as other cultures view risks much more insignificantly.

More than 90 percent of those surveyed by the World Economic Forum indicate that supply chain and transport risk management have become a greater priority in their organization over the last five years.

As risk management evolves and engages the global supply chain in an enterprise mind-set there will be a direct betterment in how their international business grows, profits, and sustains.

As you the reader flows through the balance of the chapters in this book, an information transfer will take place to provide a solution to all these changes and a way to move forward in global supply chain management minimizing the impact of risk.

MANAGING CULTURAL ISSUES IN GLOBAL TRADE

Business Culture

There are different cultural factors to consider when launching a product into a foreign market. Some of the cultural differences U.S. companies most often face involve business styles, attitudes toward business relationships and punctuality, negotiating styles, gift-giving customs, greetings, significance of gestures, meanings of colors and numbers, and conventions regarding the use of titles. A useful guide from the U.S. Commercial Service (export.gov) is "A Basic Guide to Exporting."

Considering Cultural Factors

Businesspeople who hope to profit from their travel should learn about the history, culture, and customs of the countries they wish to visit. Flexibility and cultural adaptation should be the guiding principles for traveling abroad on business. Business manners and methods, religious customs, dietary practices, humor, and acceptable dress vary from country to country. You can prepare for your overseas visits by reading travel guides, which are located in the travel sections of most libraries and bookstores.

Some of the cultural differences U.S. companies most often face involve business styles, attitudes toward business relationships and punctuality, negotiating styles, gift-giving customs, greetings, significance of gestures, meanings of colors and numbers, and conventions regarding the use of titles.

The cultural anthropology literature has given us many insights into how other countries do business and how to avoid cultural blunders. To Thai, for example, being touched on the head is extremely offensive. Useful to know? Maybe. But it is hard to imagine in the United States or anywhere else businesspeople meet for the first time or even after several times, engaging in head touching or hair messing. So by all means read the literature and talk with people who know the culture. But don't be intimidated and don't be reluctant to meet people. And do keep these general rules in mind.

Both understanding and heeding cultural differences are critical to success in international business. Lack of familiarity with the business practices, social customs, and etiquette of a country can weaken your company's position in the market.

Understanding local culture can be the difference between making and losing a sale. And, who knows—you may end up loving the local food, movies, and sports teams!

Always answer queries politely and promptly. Don't delay when responding to e-mail, fax, and telephone requests for price lists, quotes, and other information. Build your own marketing list from the contacts. Ask for each customer's communication preferences. The query you ignore today might have been your next best source of future business.

Start with what you know. Try beginning with a business culture and system similar to your own. Canada and the United Kingdom are often good markets for beginners.

Learn from your domestic customers. Apply cultural knowledge you gain from selling to customers from different social and ethnic backgrounds than yourself. Preferences, product usage, and business protocol may not translate perfectly to international customers, but helpful information can be harvested here in the United States and applied to market entry efforts abroad. Be patient. Different cultures have different concepts of time. Few markets have a faster business pace than the United States; many are slower.

Take time to develop personal relationships—especially with distributors or large-volume buyers. Remembering birthdays and other important events is a good intercultural business practice. It's generally not difficult for Americans to be warm, welcoming, respectful, and thoughtful. Be yourself—or even a little more. If you can't, or if the self you know doesn't fit this profile, consider making a trusted employee the primary business contact. Learn the language. A few words of the native language of your buyers or business associates will go a long way. They will appreciate the effort. Words of welcome on your website and maybe a currency converter will further demonstrate your interest in doing business in ways that are mutually respectful.

Something as simple and commonplace as a "thumbs up" may be meaningless—or even offensive—in some cultures.

Get an intern or hire a new employee. As business develops with overseas customers, consider recruiting a student intern or recent college graduate who speaks the language and understands the business culture. Investing in company staffing resources is especially valuable when doing business with customers in Japan, China, and countries in which Arabic is spoken. Attend a U.S. trade show. Find one in your industry that is attended by foreign buyers. You can make good contacts—even sales—and test the waters before heading overseas.

Attend an international trade show in your industry. U.S. embassies abroad often staff a national pavilion where U.S. sellers and foreign buyers, often from many countries in a region, meet. A great way to understand a different business culture is to do business, not read about how others do it.

Get help. Before you head overseas on a business development trip, contact the U.S. embassy and the U.S. Commercial Service. They will line up qualified buyers for you to meet, and they will counsel you on business protocol, market intelligence, regulatory issues, and much more. Not doing so could prevent you from accomplishing your objectives, and ultimately lead to the failure of your exporting effort.

Americans must pay close attention to different styles of doing business and the degree of importance placed on developing business relationships. In some countries, business people have a very direct style, whereas in others they are more subtle and value personal relationships more than is customary in most U.S. business relationships. For example, in the Middle East, indulging in small talk before engaging in the business at hand is standard practice.

Understanding gift-giving customs is also important. In some cultures, gifts are expected, and failure to present them is considered an insult. In other countries, though, the presentation of a gift is viewed as an offense. Business executives also need to know when to present a gift (e.g., on the initial visit or afterward); where to present the gift (in public or privately); what type of gift to present; what color the gift should be; and how many gifts are appropriate.

Gift giving is an important part of doing business in Japan, where gifts are usually exchanged at the first meeting. In sharp contrast, gifts are rarely exchanged in Germany and are usually not appropriate. Gift giving is not customary in Belgium or the United Kingdom either, although in both countries it's suitable to bring flowers when you are invited to someone's home.

Customs concerning the exchange of business cards also vary. Although this point may seem of minor importance, card giving is a key part of business protocol. In Japan, for example, the Western practice of accepting a business card and pocketing it immediately is considered rude. The proper approach is to carefully look at the card after accepting it, observe the title and organization, acknowledge with a nod that the information has been digested, and perhaps make a relevant comment or ask a polite question.

Negotiating is a complex process even between parties from the same nation. It is even more complicated in international transactions because of the potential for misunderstandings that stem from cultural differences.

It is essential to understand the importance of rank in the other country and to know who the decision makers are. It is important to be familiar with the business style of the foreign company, to understand the nature of agreements there, and to know the significance of gestures and negotiating etiquette.

Through research or training, you can acquire a working knowledge of the business culture, management attitudes, business methods, and consumer habits before you travel abroad. That knowledge is very likely to have a positive effect on your overseas travel. Your local U.S. Commercial Service office can provide what you need to make a strong first impression.

Attitudes toward punctuality vary greatly from one culture to another, and misunderstanding those attitudes may cause confusion. Romanians, Japanese, and Germans are very punctual, whereas people in many of the Latin countries have a more relaxed attitude toward time. The Japanese consider it rude to be late for a business meeting but acceptable—even fashionable—to be late for a social occasion. In Guatemala, though, people will arrive from 10 minutes early to 45 minutes late for a luncheon appointment.

Attention to detail can go a long way in making you stand out among the competition.

When cultural lines are being crossed, something as simple as a greeting can be misunderstood. Traditional greetings include shaking hands, hugging, kissing, and placing the hands in praying position. The "wrong" greeting can lead to an awkward encounter.

People around the world use body movements and gestures to convey specific messages. Misunderstandings over gestures are common occurrences in intercultural communication and can lead to business complications and social embarrassment.

The proper use of names and titles is often a source of confusion in international business relations. In many countries (including Denmark, France, and the United Kingdom), it is appropriate to use titles until use of first names is suggested. First names are seldom used by those doing business in Germany. Visiting businesspeople should use the surname preceded by the title. Titles such as "Herr Direktor" are sometimes used to indicate prestige, status, and rank. Thai, however, address one another by first names and reserve last names for very formal occasions and written communications. In Belgium, it is important to address French-speaking business contacts as "Monsieur" or "Madame," whereas Flemish-speaking contacts should be addressed as "Mr." or "Mrs." To misuse these titles is a great faux pas.

Negotiating is a complex process even between parties from the same nation. It is even more complicated in international transactions because of the potential for misunderstandings that stem from cultural differences. It is essential to understand the importance of rank in the other country and to know who the decision makers are. It is important to be familiar with the business style of the foreign company, to understand the nature of agreements there, and to know the significance of gestures and negotiating etiquette.

Through research or training, you can acquire a working knowledge of the business culture, management attitudes, business methods, and consumer habits before you travel abroad. That knowledge is very likely to have a positive effect on your overseas travel. Your local U.S. Commercial Service office can provide what you need to make a strong first impression.

Attention to detail can go a long way in making you stand out among the competition.

SOME INTERESTING CASE STUDIES IN GLOBAL RISK

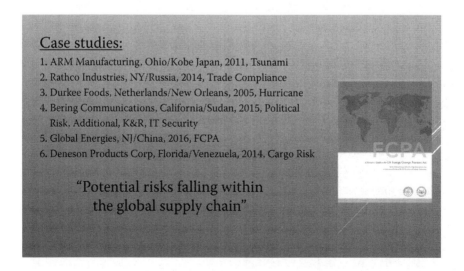

Case studies:
1. ARM Manufacturing, Ohio/Kobe Japan, 2011, Tsunami
2. Rathco Industries, NY/Russia, 2014, Trade Compliance
3. Durkee Foods, Netherlands/New Orleans, 2005, Hurricane
4. Bering Communications, California/Sudan, 2015, Political Risk, Additional, K&R, IT Security
5. Global Energies, NJ/China, 2016, FCPA
6. Deneson Products Corp, Florida/Venezuela, 2014, Cargo Risk

"Potential risks falling within the global supply chain"

ARM Manufacturing, Ohio/Kobe Japan, 2011, Tsunami

ARM Manufacturing moved over a 10-year period all its electronic component manufacturing to a joint venture structure to a city near Kobe, Japan. For 10 years the volume of foreign sourcing continued to grow as greater dependency occurred with this supplier.

When a tsunami hit Japan in 2011, the manufacturing location was rendered completely useless for 13 months and did not come back on line to full capacity for almost 23 months.

This forced the Ohio-based corporation to find alternative sources in desperation, which after 60 days was accomplished but not without consequence. The acquisition costs were higher, some product was off-spec, and the time involved in managing three suppliers—one in California, one in Indonesia, and one in China—was complicated, frustrating, and with a lot of wheel spinning.

Some of their clients found other suppliers and there was a 12% loss of business, with a margin drop of 4%. Overall the costs exceeded $25 million and it took almost a full five years to recover.

The risk management solution included the following:

- Spreading the risk of the company's sourcing model so there was no single supplier representing more than 30% of overall purchases
- Risk assessment on sourcing locations to reduce and/or minimize the probability of certain types of occurrences
- Acquire contingent business interruption insurance in certain business verticals where exposures were better transferred to a third party.

Rathen Industries, New York/Russia, 2014, Trade Compliance

Rathen Industries, a New York-based company, made bulletproof vests typically sold to law enforcement organizations around the world. A new distributor in Europe sold $500,000 worth of equipment to a Russian government agency. The nature of the sale required that the exporter obtain an export license and receive permission to make the export before the sale and delivery was made. The principals of the company avoided any regulatory requirements as they thought that the sale going through a third party would obviate this U.S. government regulatory requirement. This was a serious mistake as Rathen was still considered the USPPI (U.S. Principal Party in Interest) and was still responsible for export trade compliance. A criminal and civil investigation was pursued by authorities leading to jail time and fines in excess of $1 million and loss of export privileges in certain markets for three years.

The risk management solution included the following:

- All personnel were trained in export trade compliance responsibilities.
- SOPs (standard operating procedures) were completed that ensured that trade compliance was integrated into Rathen's sales and supply chain operations.
- Regular audits were and are being done by an external third party to make sure that the company is trade compliant.

Durkee Foods, Netherlands/New Orleans, 2005, Hurricane

Durkee Foods, out of the Netherlands, was into food manufacturing in over 25 locations in the United States, mainly in the Midwest. Sugar along with other ingredients were imported through the Port of New Orleans. A centralized and primary warehousing and domestic distribution facility was located near the port, handling over 90% of over $100 million annually of various ingredients.

When Hurricane Katrina hit, the entire flow of ingredients halted for almost six months. The products that were in their warehouses were 90% lost or damaged. The disruption to Durkee's supply chain was enormous. The overall loss exceeded $650 million directly and estimates of another 100 million indirectly.

Insurances in place covered Durkee for only approximately 60% of its losses. Much of its losses were business-interruption related and their limits were exceeded very quickly. Other losses were plant closings that were unable to keep production schedules with no flow of needed ingredients.

Clients were lost to competitors and never recovered.

The risk management solution included the following:

- A risk management assessment was accomplished and it was determined to split the ingredient inbound gateways over four different entry ports so no one location had more than 30% of the company's requirements.
- The JIT (just-in-time) inventory system was amended to add storage for another 60 days' contingency.
- A proper level of business interruption and contingent business interruption was introduced into the insurance purchasing to provide more serious levels of coverage that may be required.
- Warehousing storage operations were altered to maintain product from being stored on the "deck/floor" with minimum heights of six feet.

(Following Katrina it was determined that at several facilities in New Orleans product was seriously damaged that was stored on the deck/floor and at very low levels in the racking system.)

- A committee was formed internally with support from the insurance brokers and underwriters to establish loss control measures to mitigate future losses that could occur from natural disasters.
- The risk management team was authorized to create a "natural disaster" alert system so proactive steps could be taken before a disaster occurs and not just relying on reactive measures.

Bering Communications, California/Sudan, 2015, Political Risk, Kidnap and Ransom, IT Security

Bering sold mobile communication systems globally directly through international sales representatives (American). One of its sales representatives was kidnapped while concluding a sale to a Middle Eastern client. Along with the kidnapping, his personal computer was stolen.

U.S. Embassy and State Department Officials were notified of the incident.

Three weeks and $250,000 after the kidnapping, the salesman was released, unharmed, but seriously impacted by the occurrence. His computer controlled sensitive product specifications, export licensing, and corporate intelligence.

An agreement was ultimately made between all parties as long as the Californian company adhered to certain practices going forward:

- Train all personal and develop SOPs in export controls.
- Obtain government authorization on all future export sales.
- Create an encryption technology for all personal computers.

The risk management solution included the following:

- Acting aggressively on all the above recommendations from the U.S. government
- Acquire K&R (kidnap and ransom) insurance on all its personnel traveling overseas to provide financial protection and a means to introduce expertise into the K&R process as it occurs
- Train personnel on how to travel overseas and be more diligent and responsible about how they transit and conduct themselves to mitigate the potential of kidnapping or other hostile situations

Global Energies, New Jersey/China, 2016, Foreign Corrupt Practices Act (FCPA)

Global Energies provided technology solutions for energy companies here and abroad. It was successful on bidding on an IT service to a Chinese government agency. The sale was made through a local Chinese agent who explained that he needed approximately $100,000 in advance to create the opportunity for the sale to advance forward.

After Global Energies was successful in the sale, it was prosecuted by the U.S. Department of Justice for a violation of the Foreign Corrupt Practices Act (FCPA). Ultimately a settlement was accomplished after a $1 million fine was levied and FCPA Loss Prevention Training secured throughout the company.

The risk management solution included the following:

- FCPA training for all existing and new personnel, reoccurring annually
- FCPA audits by an independent third party, at least every two to three years
- Sales training on how to manage sales through third-party agents while exercising due diligence, reasonable care, and supervision and control.

Deneson Products Corporation, Florida/Venezuela, 2014, Cargo Risk

Deneson imported perishable flora and fauna from several cooperatives in Venezuela. The terms of purchase were CIF Miami, which laid the responsibility for freight and insurance in the hands of the selling or exporting entities.

Deneson had four years of favorable experience with a particular supplier. But in the fall of 2014, an ocean vessel on its way north hit heavy weather, and several containers loaded on deck carrying Deneson's product were destroyed, creating a loss exceeding $300,000. When Deneson pursued recovery from the supplier, the supplier referred Deneson to the cargo insurance it had purchased as part of the transaction on its behalf.

In a CIF (cost, insurance, and freight) transaction, the seller or exporter arranges insurance on the buyer's behalf and provides a certificate of insurance evidencing the same.

When Deneson put a claim into the insurance company located in Caracas, it soon was very disappointed to learn that the coverage was only in effect if the cargo was stowed in the containers under deck. In other policies, protection was afforded in containers stowed on deck, but this policy was very explicit that the containers needed to be stowed under deck containing the perishable products covered under the policy.

No one read the certificates of insurance, or the underlying insuring terms, conditions, or warranties.

After a year, a settlement was reached between the supplier and the buyer, and business once again moved forward.

The risk management solution included the following:

- The INCO Term utilized was changed to FOB (freight on board), outbound gateway. This gave control over the purchasing of freight and insurance to the buyer.
- Deneson purchased "all risk," "warehouse to warehouse" coverage through an American A+ Bests rated underwriting company that provided the necessary coverages.
- All purchasing, operations, and logistics personnel were trained in INCO Terms, cargo insurance, and how to assess risks in their supply chain and best practices to avoid future issues.

Case Study Summary

In all these cases, which are all based upon real-life and company experiences drawn from our case files, there are common elements:

1. In most cases, there was not bad intent, but mostly uninformed, untrained personnel committing mistakes unwittingly.
2. The dependence on third parties to act in a company's best interest left a lot to be desired.
3. Personnel consistently lacked the necessary international business skill sets, such is in but not limited to:
   - INCO Terms
   - Cargo insurance
   - Export and import regulations
   - Leveraging freight options
   - Harmonized Tariff Codes
   - Managing risk in global supply chains

Training

In all these cases, and many more my firm deals with every day, the key ingredient missing in most personnel engaged in global trade was training. Training is a very critical component of how successfully a company manages its business model in international business.

The National Institute for World Trade (niwt.org) and the American Management Association (amanet.org) are two highly recommended training facilities for companies operating in the global arena. Both have generic public seminars and outreach, and have the ability to handle customized training in-house focusing on specific global supply chain nuances and needs.

Due diligence and reasonable care, two of the stalwarts of regulation, can best be achieved and documented through serious training programs.

Where's the fun in playing with knives if you can't draw a little blood?

Donald Gorman
Paradox

2

Global Risk Management

This chapter looks at several ancillary issues in global risk management such as the numerous risk verticals in most international operations, political, and terrorist risks. Many of these risks will dominate global operations in 2017 and beyond, and many senior executives are paying close attention to these serious areas of concern.

GLOBAL SUPPLY CHAIN RISK VERTICALS

Every company has various fiefdoms, silos, operating groups, and so on, also referred to as "verticals." The following figure shows the many verticals outlining the risks that most companies face in managing global supply chains. The names in various corporations may be different, but they all lead to the same or similar areas of responsibility.

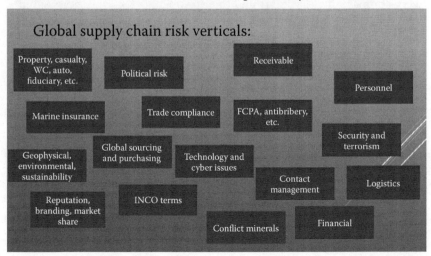

Global supply chain risk verticals:

Property, casualty, WC, auto, fiduciary, etc.

Political risk

Receivable

Personnel

Marine insurance

Trade compliance

FCPA, antibribery, etc.

Security and terrorism

Global sourcing and purchasing

Technology and cyber issues

Geophysical, environmental, sustainability

Contact management

Logistics

Reputation, branding, market share

INCO terms

Conflict minerals

Financial

Most of these areas of risk and concern are covered in great detail throughout the book; a summary is outlined next:

- Property, casualty, workers' compensation, auto, fiduciary, etc. ("supply chain focus")
- Political risk
- Receivable
- Marine insurance
- Trade compliance
- Foreign Corrupt Practices Act (FCPA), antibribery, etc.
- Security and terrorism
- Geophysical, environmental, sustainability
- Global sourcing and purchasing
- Technology and cyber issues
- Contract management
- Logistics
- Reputation, branding, market share
- INCO Terms
- Conflict minerals
- Personnel
- Financial

Property, Casualty, Workers' Compensation, Auto, Fiduciary, etc. ("Supply Chain Focus")

Every company operating around the world will be creating both liability and property exposures. These are covered in Chapter 5 as they relate to their role in understanding risk in global supply chains.

There are a number of key issues regarding standard property, liability, workers' compensation, and automobile exposures in overseas markets:

1. Local culture, laws, regulations, and religious ideals will impact how these risks and related insurances can or cannot be placed.
2. In many countries, insurances have to be "admitted" or purchased in their local economies.
3. Terms and conditions could vary dramatically or even be omitted or nonexistent when compared to broad coverages available in the United States.

4. Not all insurance brokers and underwriters have an ability to insure in all markets globally.
5. Insurance companies have to pay attention to U.S. export regulations in how they conduct their business models overseas and therefore may have certain restrictions in place controlling protocols.
6. Typically, most U.S.-based companies, when having to purchase local insurances, will have contingent and overriding policies placed to ensure comprehensive coverage.

POLITICAL RISK

Political risk is an exposure faced by individuals, investors, corporations, and governments that political decisions, events, or conditions will significantly affect the viability and/or profitability of a business model.

Events over the last 30 years in Iran, Mexico, Venezuela, Nigeria, Sudan, Afghanistan, Myanmar, and many other countries have caused huge financial losses for Western businesses. The reason that we even discuss political risk is not only the concerns, but also political risk can be understood and managed with a risk management approach, foresight, and investment.

Political risk refers to the complications businesses and governments may face as a result of what are commonly referred to as political decisions—or "any political change that alters the expected outcome and value of a given economic action by changing the probability of achieving business objectives."

Political risk faced by firms can be defined as "the risk of a strategic, financial, or personnel loss for a firm because of such nonmarket factors as macroeconomic and social policies (fiscal, monetary, trade, investment, industrial, income, labor, and developmental), or events related to political instability (terrorism, riots, coups, civil war, and insurrection)."

Understanding risk partly as probability and partly as impact provides insight into political risk. Political risk is mostly viewed as a business risk, with the implication that there is a measure of likelihood that political events may complicate its pursuit of earnings through direct impacts (such as taxes or fees) or indirect impacts (such as opportunity cost forgone).

Political risk is both an art and science, and governments, institutions, universities, and private facilities have spent a great deal of time studying the impact and likelihood of the events. Models have been developed to create predictive information flows allowing companies to move forward with various levels of concern and potential loss mitigating actions, or simply avoid certain countries where political instability may be considered unworthy of any level of risk taking or assumption.

There are four primary classifications of political risk coverage: confiscation, nationalization, expropriation, and deprivation.

Confiscation, Expropriation, Nationalization, and Deprivation (C, E, N, and D)

Confiscation, expropriation, nationalization, and deprivation (C, E, N, and D) is political risk coverage purchased by businesses that have an ownership interest in property abroad, to cover loss resulting from government nationalization of the property or other action by the government that effectively deprives the insured of the property or restricts its operations. Coverage may be structured to insure such current assets as bank accounts, intercompany or bank loans, accounts receivable, inventory, retained earnings, supplies, and work in progress. Deprivation coverage, which insures against the risk of a government action preventing use of the asset (such as denying a permit to run a plant), can be added to the basic CNE policy.

In many instances a government does not make the typical swift action of seizure but accomplishes it over a period of time as baby steps, called creeping C, E, N, and D. This may take several years where they slowly encroach their ownership or control. This has been observed in some third world countries as it related to their energy production (oil), where they slowly take over the wells, the production, and supply of the product or resource.

Contract Repudiation, Default, Currency Inconvertibility, and Devaluation

Additional political risk exposures are referred to as contract repudiation, default, currency inconvertibility, and devaluation.

Contract repudiation in international business occurs in the following cases:

1. Repudiation will be established if the conduct of Party A, whether verbal or otherwise, conveyed to Party B demonstrates Party A's inability to perform the contract, or an intention not to perform its obligations.
2. Whether there has been repudiation depends on the objective acts of the parties.
3. There will be repudiation if the conduct of Party A was such as to convey to a reasonable person in the position of Party B, repudiation of the contract as a whole, or of a fundamental obligation under it.
4. Repudiation may occur at any time between the formation of the contract and completion.
5. If Party A repudiates a contract or a fundamental obligation under it, Party B has the election to accept the repudiation and bring the contract to an end.
6. A clear inability or unwillingness to perform a fundamental obligation at a stipulated essential time by Party A is an anticipatory breach, entitling Party B to terminate the contract.
7. If Party A repudiates and Party B elects not to terminate but to affirm the contract, but thereafter Party A continues to repudiate, Party B may terminate on the basis of the continued repudiation.
8. Party B, in order to be entitled to rescind for anticipatory breach, must at the time of Party A's rescission itself be willing to perform the contract.

Default internationally occurs when one party fails to fulfill an obligation, especially to repay a loan or appear in a court of law. Default in some countries is almost impossible to pursue legally successfully.

Currency inconvertibility is a situation where one currency cannot be exchanged for another currency because of foreign exchange regulations or physical barriers. **Inconvertible currencies** may be restricted from trade due to extremely high volatility or political sanctions.

Devaluation means the official lowering of the value of a country's currency within a fixed exchange rate system, by which the monetary authority formally sets a new fixed rate with respect to a foreign reference currency.

RECEIVABLE MANAGEMENT

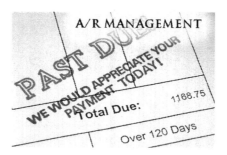

Receivable exposures only exist with export sales activity. Also referred to as trade credit insurance, business credit insurance, export credit insurance, or credit insurance, it is an insurance policy and a risk management product offered by private insurance companies and governmental export credit agencies to business entities wishing to protect their accounts receivables from loss due to credit risks such as protracted default, insolvency, or bankruptcy.

This export credit insurance product is a type of property and casualty insurance, and should not be confused with such products as credit life or credit disability insurance, which individuals obtain to protect against the risk of loss of income needed to pay debts. Trade credit insurance can include a component of political risk insurance, which is offered by the same insurers to insure the risk of nonpayment by foreign buyers due to currency issues, political unrest, expropriation, and so on. It is usually associated with private companies' unwillingness to pay debt obligations.

Export credit insurance allows companies to expand into foreign markets where the "getting paid" is a more serious concern. The insurance does not replace common sense or due diligence but becomes a backstop against financial loss and a leverage for global expansion.

SECURITY AND TERRORISM

This section covers security and terrorist issues as it relates to property and personnel. Information technology (IT) and cyber security issues are covered later.

Physical Assets

Companies engaged in global trade often have both fixed and in-transit assets located all over the world. The exposures to these assets must be assessed and managed. The typical resolve is associated with two activities:

- Transferring to a third-party insurance cover as in property or marine coverages, extended to cover acts of terrorism
- Risk mitigation through loss prevention and cargo loss control techniques

Global insurance brokers such as Gallagher, Marsh, Aon and Willis, along with major insurance carriers like AIG, Chubb, Hartford, and Zurich, all have made major commitments in loss prevention and control to assist their clients in reducing exposures to physical loss and damage due to acts of terrorism worldwide.

The FBI is another resource for fighting terrorism and offers the following advice:

How to Help Prevent Terrorist Attacks

This is a message that bears repeating, no matter where you live in the world: Your assistance is needed in preventing terrorist acts.

It's a fact that certain kinds of activities can indicate terrorist plans that are in the works, especially when they occur at or near high profile sites or places where large numbers of people gather—like government buildings, military facilities, utilities, bus or train stations, major public events. If you see or know about suspicious activities, like the ones listed below, please report them immediately to the proper authorities. In the United States, that means your closest Joint Terrorist Task Force, located in an FBI field office. In other countries, that means your closest law enforcement/counterterrorism agency.

Surveillance: Are you aware of anyone video recording or monitoring activities, taking notes, using cameras, maps, binoculars, etc., near key facilities/events?

Suspicious Questioning: Are you aware of anyone attempting to gain information in person, by phone, mail, email, etc., regarding a key facility or people who work there?

Tests of Security: Are you aware of any attempts to penetrate or test physical security or procedures at a key facility/event?

Acquiring Supplies: Are you aware of anyone attempting to improperly acquire explosives, weapons, ammunition, dangerous chemicals, uniforms, badges, flight manuals, access cards or identification for a key facility/event or to legally obtain items under suspicious circumstances that could be used in a terrorist attack?

Suspicious Persons: Are you aware of anyone who does not appear to belong in the workplace, neighborhood, business establishment, or near a key facility/event?

"Dry Runs": Have you observed any behavior that appears to be preparation for a terrorist act, such as mapping out routes, playing out scenarios with other people, monitoring key facilities/events, timing traffic lights or traffic flow, or other suspicious activities?

Deploying Assets: Have you observed abandoned vehicles, stockpiling of suspicious materials, or persons being deployed near a key facility/event?

If you answered yes to any of the above … if you have observed any suspicious activity that may relate to terrorism … again, please contact the Joint Terrorist Task Force or law enforcement/counterterrorism agency closest to you immediately. Your tip could save the lives of innocent people, just like you and yours.

Contact details: www.fbi.gov; or FBI Headquarters, 935 Pennsylvania Avenue, NW, Washington, D.C. 20535-0001; (202) 324-3000

The Terrorist Initiative Project advocates research to advise on terrorist strategies, at a high level, as follows, as outlined by the UN Terrorism Prevention Branch:

Twelve Rules for Preventing and Countering Terrorism

1. Try to address the underlying conflict issues exploited by the terrorists and work towards a peaceful solution while not making substantive concessions to the terrorists themselves;

2. Prevent radical individuals and groups from becoming terrorist extremists by confronting them with a mix of "carrot and stick" tactics and search for effective counter-motivation measures;

3. Stimulate and encourage defection and conversion of free and imprisoned terrorists and find ways to reduce the support of aggrieved constituencies for terrorist organizations;

4. Deny terrorists access to arms, explosives, false identification documents, safe communication, safe travel and sanctuaries; disrupt and incapacitate their preparations and operations through infiltration, communication intercept, espionage and by limiting their criminal- and other fund-raising capabilities;

5. Reduce low-risk/high-gain opportunities for terrorists to strike by enhancing communications-, energy- and transportation-security, by hardening critical infrastructures and potential sites where mass casualties could occur and apply principles of situational crime prevention to the prevention of terrorism;

6. Keep in mind that terrorists seek publicity and exploit the media and the Internet to propagate their cause, glorify their attacks, win recruits, solicit donations, gather intelligence, disseminate terrorist know-how and communicate with their target audiences. Try to devise communication strategies to counter them in each of these areas.

7. Prepare for crisis- and consequence-management for both "regular" and "catastrophic" acts of terrorism in coordinated simulation exercises and educate first responders and the public on how to cope with terrorism.

8. Establish an Early Detection and Early Warning intelligence system against terrorism and other violent crimes on the interface between organized crime and political conflict;

9. Strengthen the coordination of efforts against terrorism both within and between states; enhance international police and intelligence cooperation, and offer technical assistance to those

countries lacking the know-how and means to upgrade their counter-terrorism instruments.

10. Show solidarity with, and offer support to, victims of terrorism at home and abroad.
11. Maintain the moral high ground in the struggle with terrorists by defending and strengthening the rule of law, good governance, democracy and social justice and by matching your deeds with your words;
12. Finally, counter the ideologies, indoctrination, and propaganda of secular and non-secular terrorists and try to get the upper hand in the war of ideas—the battle for the hearts and minds of those terrorists claim to speak and fight for.

Corporate Terrorism Best Practices

1. Assess areas of the world where you are engaged and terrorism is a likely event. Congruently assess all areas of operation and assess terrorist exposures. Some companies will assign and rank terrorism threats on a 1–10 scale, putting resources and initiatives in place where the threat is most significant.
2. Engage external resources to support your internal information flow and strategies to combat terrorism proactively.
3. Create internal training programs to inform and empower appropriate company personnel in anti-terrorism protocols.
4. Insurance brokers and underwriters are excellent resources for terrorism controls.
5. Conduct a risk management review of all insurance policies and coverages to determine where terrorist coverages exist or not and to what extent. Assess where modifications in coverage need to occur. Working with senior management is important, in this regard to understand corporate policies, tolerances, and their will to deal with these sensitive areas of risk.

Insuran

Appl___ ___ees that by checking this b
he/she is ___ ___ full responsibility of ever
they have ever ___ ne

☑ *You're Covered!*

Key factors:

- Coverage is or is not included, completely or to an extent
- Restrictions by terms restrictions, geographic limitations, definitions
- Limits or sublimits
- Warranties
- Property versus business interruption

6. Develop relationships with all relevant government agencies, here and abroad, such as Customs (CBP), FBI, DHS, and local authorities, and build these contacts into your overall anti-terrorist strategies.

7. Have dedicated personnel assigned to monitor global and domestic terrorist and security events to determine the "best courses of action" for your organization in preparing or reacting to such evensts.

▶ Security and Terrorism

Terrorism ...

- ▸ It is the use of violence or threat of violence in order to purport a political, religious, or ideological change.
- ▸ It can only be committed by non-state actors or undercover personnel serving on the behalf of their respective governments.
- ▸ It reaches more than the immediate target victims and is also directed at targets consisting of a larger spectrum of society.
- ▸ It is both *mala prohibita* (i.e., crime that is made illegal by legislation) and *mala in se* (i.e., crime that is inherently immoral or wrong).
- ▸ The following criteria of violence or threat of violence fall outside of the definition of terrorism:
  - ▸ Wartime (including a declared war) or peacetime acts of violence committed by a nation state against another nation state regardless of leaglity or illegality taht are carried out by properly uniformed forces or legal combatants of such nation states.
  - ▸ Reasonable acts of self-defense, such as the use of force to kill, apprehend, or punish criminals who pose a threat to the lives of humans or property.
  - ▸ Legitimate targets in war, such as enemy combatants and strategic infrastructure that are an integral part of the enemy's war effort.
  - ▸ Collateral damage, including the infliction of incidental damage to non-combatant targets during an attack on or attempting to attack legitimate targets in war.

TERRORISM

FOREIGN CORRUPT PRACTICES ACT (FCPA) AND ANTIBRIBERY

According to the U.S. Department of Justice:

> The Foreign Corrupt Practices Act of 1977, as amended, 15 U.S.C. §§ 78dd-1, et seq. ("FCPA"), was enacted for the purpose of making it unlawful for certain classes of persons and entities to make payments to foreign government officials to assist in obtaining or retaining business.
>
> Specifically, the antibribery provisions of the FCPA prohibit the willful use of the mails or any means of instrumentality of interstate commerce corruptly in furtherance of any offer, payment, promise to pay, or authorization of the payment of money or anything of value to any person, while knowing that all or a portion of such money or thing of value will be offered, given or promised, directly or indirectly, to a foreign official to influence the foreign official in his or her official capacity, induce the foreign official to do or omit to do an act in violation of his or her lawful duty, or to secure any improper advantage in order to assist in obtaining or retaining business for or with, or directing business to, any person.
>
> Since 1977, the anti-bribery provisions of the FCPA have applied to all U.S. persons and certain foreign issuers of securities. With the enactment of certain amendments in 1998, the anti-bribery provisions of the FCPA now also apply to foreign firms and persons who cause, directly or through agents, an act in furtherance of such a corrupt payment to take place within the territory of the United States.

The FCPA also requires companies whose securities are listed in the United States to meet its accounting provisions. See 15 U.S.C. § 78m. These accounting provisions, which were designed to operate in tandem with the antibribery provisions of the FCPA, require corporations covered by the provisions to (a) make and keep books and records that accurately and fairly reflect the transactions of the corporation and (b) devise and maintain an adequate system of internal accounting controls.

For particular FCPA compliance questions relating to specific conduct, you should seek the advice of counsel as well as consider using the Department of Justice's FCPA Opinion Procedure, found at DOJ.gov.

Some of the highlights of the FCPA include:

- The idea of the FCPA is to make it illegal for companies and their supervisors to influence foreign officials with any personal payments or rewards.
- The FCPA applies to any person who has a certain degree of connection to the United States and engages in foreign corrupt practices. The act also applies to any act by U.S. businesses, foreign corporations trading securities in the U.S., American nationals, citizens, and residents acting in furtherance of a foreign corrupt practice whether or not they are physically present in the United States. This is considered the nationality principle of the act. Any individuals that are involved in those activities may face prison time.
- This act was passed to make it unlawful for certain classes of persons and entities to make payments to foreign government officials to assist in obtaining or retaining business.
- In the case of foreign natural and legal persons, the act covers their deeds if they are in the United States at the time of the corrupt conduct. This is considered the protective principle of the act.
- Further, the act governs not only payments to foreign officials, candidates, and parties, but any other recipient if part of the bribe is ultimately attributable to a foreign official, candidate, or party. These payments are not restricted to monetary forms and may include anything of value. This is considered the territoriality principle of the act.

Example cases involving the FCPA include (according to the U.S. Securities and Exchange Commission [SEC]):

- JPMorgan—The firm agreed to pay $264 million to the SEC, Justice Department, and Federal Reserve to settle charges that it corruptly influenced government officials and won business in the Asia-Pacific region by giving jobs and internships to their relatives and friends. (11/17/16)
- Embraer—The Brazilian-based aircraft manufacturer agreed to pay $205 million to settle charges that it violated the FCPA to win business in the Dominican Republic, Saudi Arabia, Mozambique, and India. (10/24/16)
- GlaxoSmithKline—The U.K.-based pharmaceutical company agreed to pay a $20 million penalty to settle charges that it violated the FCPA when its China-based subsidiaries engaged in pay-to-prescribe schemes to increase sales. (9/30/16)
- Och-Ziff—The hedge fund and two executives settled charges related to the use of intermediaries, agents, and business partners to pay bribes to high-level government officials in Africa. Och-Ziff agreed to pay $412 million in civil and criminal matters, and CEO Daniel Och agreed to pay $2.2 million to settle charges against him. (9/29/16)
- Anheuser-Busch InBev—The Belgium-based global brewery agreed to pay $6 million to settle charges that it violated the FCPA by using third-party sales promoters to make improper payments to government officials in India and chilled a whistleblower who reported the misconduct. (9/28/16)
- Nu Skin Enterprises—The Provo, Utah-based skin care products company agreed to pay more than $765,000 for an improper payment made to a charity related to a high-ranking member of China's Communist Party in order to influence the outcome of a pending provincial regulatory investigation in China. (9/20/16)
- Jun Ping Zhang—The former chairman/CEO of Harris Corporation's subsidiary in China agreed to pay a $46,000 penalty for violating FCPA by facilitating a bribery scheme that provided illegal gifts to Chinese government officials in order to obtain and retain business for the company. (9/13/16)

- AstraZeneca—The U.K.-based biopharmaceutical company agreed to pay more than $5 million to settle FCPA violations resulting from improper payments made by subsidiaries in China and Russia to foreign officials. (8/30/16)

In the last five years there have been more than 15 to 20 cases a year, totaling as much as $140 million in fines and penalties authorized by the Department of Justice.

Prevention is best managed by creating FCPA standard operating procedures (SOPs) and internal training programs.

An Overview from the Department of Justice

The Strategy, Policy and Training Unit focuses on combating national and international economic crimes by, among other things:

- coordinating the Section's vast experience in managing complex and multi-jurisdictional cases in order to strategically fight against sophisticated economic crimes;
- developing and implementing with the other Units strategic enforcement initiatives to identify and combat emerging white-collar crimes;
- coordinating inter-agency and inter-governmental enforcement efforts, including with the Financial Fraud Enforcement Task Force and other inter-agency working groups;
- increasing cooperation between domestic and international law enforcement agencies, as well as the U.S. Attorney's Offices throughout the nation;
- advising the Department's leadership on such matters as anti-fraud legislation, crime prevention, citizen correspondence, and public education;
- preparing Section guidelines and policies regarding investigative and prosecutorial best practices;
- assisting prosecutors, regulators, law enforcement and the private sector by providing training, advice and other assistance on white-collar crimes;
- conducting internal training to strengthen attorneys' investigative, prosecutorial, and trial skills;

- advising attorneys on developments in the law and enforcement initiatives; and,
- assisting prosecutors in the evaluation of corporate compliance programs, compliance-focused remediation efforts, and Monitorships, including by overseeing the work of the Section's Compliance Consultant, Hui Chen.

For questions and requests, please use the DOJ contact information below:

Pablo Quiñones
Chief – Strategy, Policy & Training Unit
Fraud Section, Criminal Division
U.S. Department of Justice
950 Constitution Ave., NW
Washington, DC 20530
www.DOJ.gov
(202) 514-2000

FCPA Corporate Compliance Program

In a global marketplace, an effective compliance program is a critical component of a company's internal controls and is essential to detecting and preventing FCPA violations.

Effective compliance programs are tailored to the company's specific business and to the risks associated with that business. They are dynamic and evolve as the business and the markets change. An effective compliance program promotes "an organizational culture that encourages ethical conduct and a commitment to compliance with the law." Such a program protects a company's reputation, ensures investor value and confidence, reduces uncertainty in business transactions, and secures a company's assets.

A well-constructed, thoughtfully implemented, and consistently enforced compliance and ethics program helps prevent, detect, remediate, and report misconduct, including FCPA violations.

In addition to considering whether a company has self-reported, cooperated, and taken appropriate remedial actions, the DOJ and SEC also

FCPA COMPLIANCE PROGRAM CASE STUDY

Recent DOJ and SEC actions relating to a financial institution's real estate transactions with a government agency in China illustrate the benefits of implementing and enforcing a comprehensive risk-based compliance program. The case involved a joint venture real estate investment in the Luwan District of Shanghai, China, between a U.S.-based financial institution and a state-owned entity that functioned as the district's real estate arm.

The government entity conducted the transactions through two special purpose vehicles (SPVs), with the second SPV purchasing a 12% stake in a real estate project.

The financial institution, through a robust compliance program, frequently trained its employees, imposed a comprehensive payment-approval process designed to prevent bribery, and staffed a compliance department with a direct reporting line to the board of directors. As appropriate given the industry, market, and size and structure of the transactions, the financial institution (1) provided extensive FCPA training to the senior executive responsible for the transactions and (2) conducted extensive due diligence on the transactions, the local government entity, and the SPVs.

Due diligence on the entity included reviewing Chinese government records; speaking with sources familiar with the Shanghai real estate market; checking the government entity's payment records and credit references; conducting an on-site visit and placing a pretextual telephone call to the entity's offices; searching media sources; and conducting background checks on the entity's principals. The financial institution vetted the SPVs by obtaining a letter with designated bank account information from a Chinese official associated with the government entity (the "Chinese Official"); using an international law firm to request and review 50 documents from the SPVs' Canadian attorney; interviewing the attorney; and interviewing the SPVs' management.

Notwithstanding the financial institution's robust compliance program and good faith enforcement of it, the company failed to learn that the Chinese Official personally owned nearly 50% of the second

SPV (and therefore a nearly 6% stake in the joint venture) and that the SPV was used as a vehicle for corrupt payments.

This failure was due, in large part, to misrepresentations by the Chinese Official, the financial institution's executive in charge of the project, and the SPV's attorney that the SPV was 100% owned and controlled by the government entity.

The DOJ and SEC declined to take enforcement action against the financial institution, and its executive pleaded guilty to conspiracy to violate the FCPA's internal control provisions and also settled with SEC.

consider the adequacy of a company's compliance program when deciding what, if any, action to take. The program may influence whether or not charges should be resolved through a deferred prosecution agreement (DPA) or non-prosecution agreement (NPA), as well as the appropriate length of any DPA or NPA, or the term of corporate probation. It will often affect the penalty amount and the need for a monitor or self-reporting. The SEC focuses, among other things, on a company's self-policing prior to the discovery of the misconduct, including whether it had established effective compliance procedures.

Likewise, three of the nine factors set forth in DOJ's *Principles of Federal Prosecution of Business Organizations* relate, either directly or indirectly, to a compliance program's design and implementation, including the pervasiveness of wrongdoing within the company, the existence and effectiveness of the company's preexisting compliance program, and the company's remedial actions.

The DOJ also considers the U.S. Sentencing Guidelines' elements of an effective compliance program, as set forth in § 8B2.1 of the guidelines.

These considerations reflect the recognition that a company's failure to prevent every single violation does not necessarily mean that a particular company's compliance program was not generally effective. The DOJ and SEC understand that "no compliance program can ever prevent all criminal activity by a corporation's employees," and they do not hold companies to a standard of perfection.

An assessment of a company's compliance program, including its design and good faith implementation and enforcement, is an important part of the government's assessment of whether a violation occurred, and if so, what action should be taken. In appropriate circumstances, the DOJ and SEC may decline to pursue charges against a company based on the company's effective compliance program, or may otherwise seek to reward a company for its program, even when that program did not prevent the particular underlying FCPA violation that gave rise to the investigation.

FCPA Compliance Checklist

The DOJ and SEC have no formulaic requirements regarding compliance programs. Rather, they employ a common sense and pragmatic approach to evaluating compliance programs, making inquiries related to three basic questions:

1. Is the company's compliance program well designed?
2. Is it being applied in good faith?
3. Does it work?

Although the focus is on compliance with the FCPA, given the existence of anticorruption laws in many other countries, businesses should consider designing programs focused on anticorruption compliance more broadly.

Antibribery

An antibribery compliance program is a system of self-governance established by companies in order to prevent and detect bribery acts and remediate compliance failures. In a global marketplace, an effective anti-bribery compliance program is becoming a critical component of a company's business model.

There are various reasons for why a company should have such a program in place. This section highlights six.

Mandatory requirement. While in most jurisdictions companies are not obligated to have antibribery compliance programs, in certain jurisdictions they may be required to do so. In the United Kingdom, for example, companies can be liable for failure to prevent bribery. Local laws may require companies to have other sorts of compliance programs. In many jurisdictions, anti-money laundering laws, for example, obligate individuals and legal persons involved in certain activities to report suspicious transactions. Failing to do so may subject the companies to sanctions, including significant fines and imprisonment.

Mitigating factor. In many jurisdictions, the existence of an antibribery compliance program is an important mitigating factor that may reduce or, when combined with other factors (e.g., self disclosure and cooperation), exempt the legal entity from liability. This result is illustrated in the Morgan Stanley case, in which U.S. authorities recognized that (in addition to the bank's voluntary disclosure and cooperation with the investigation) Morgan Stanley constructed and maintained a system of internal controls. This system provided reasonable assurances that its employees were not bribing government officials. As a result, the authorities declined to bring any enforcement action against Morgan Stanley for the acts of one of its former directors.

Competitive advantage. Given the risks that indirect payments through third parties present for companies under the FCPA and other antibribery laws, some companies are now requiring that their third parties have antibribery programs in place as a condition of engagement or renovation of contracts. Other companies have gone further and are requiring suppliers as well to have compliance programs in place. In this way, having an antibribery compliance program has become a competitive advantage in many industries.

Attracting investors. Since the consequences of violating antibribery laws may be harsh and expensive, investors are increasingly looking for antibribery compliance programs before investing in companies. Under Brazil's Clean Companies Act, for example, if a company has 10% or more of the shares of another entity (even with no control over that entity), the company may be held jointly liable for a fine and restitution of damages for the violations committed by the invested company. As such, venture capital and private equity firms investing in the country are conditioning their investments on the existence or implementation of an antibribery compliance program that meets certain standards agreed upon beforehand.

Facilitating acquisitions. In recent years, preacquisition antibribery due diligence has become an important component of a company's expansion strategy. Many companies conduct anticorruption legal due diligence before continuing with other areas (e.g., corporate, tax, environmental). This is because, clearing antibribery compliance due diligence has become a condition for proceeding with the transaction in order to avoid successor liability. Companies that have an effective antibribery compliance program in place are better positioned to undergo that process.

Ensuring shareholder value. Another reason for companies to have an antibribery compliance program, as highlighted in the FCPA Resource Guide, is that such a program "protects a company's reputation, ensures investor value and confidence, reduces uncertainty in business transactions, and secures a company's assets."

Based on reasons like the ones stated here, adopting an antibribery compliance program has exponentially grown in importance in recent years. It has evolved from a legal obligation or mitigating factor to now being a key element of a company's business growth model.

A good resource for this material is FCPAméricas LLC (fcpamericas.com).

CONFLICT MINERALS

Conflict minerals consist of natural elements taken from the earth that have caused massive deaths in how the products are mined and brought to market. Basically, it is where slaves and pirates are involved in the movement of raw product to market, through clandestine and illegal activity. It is usually associated with certain African countries where people are brutalized, enslaved, and murdered for commercial advantage to rogue governments, officials and bad commercial interests.

- The mineral trade has funded some of the world's most brutal conflicts for decades. Today, resources from conflict or high-risk areas, such as parts of Afghanistan, Colombia, the Democratic Republic of Congo (DRC), and Zimbabwe, can fund armed groups and fuel human rights abuses.
- These resources can enter global supply chains, ending up in our mobile phones, laptops, jewelry, and other products. It is very difficult for consumers to know if their favorite products fund violence overseas.
- We have already seen significant steps towards change. The United States passed landmark legislation in 2010, known as the Dodd-Frank Act Section 1502, requiring U.S.-listed companies to carry out due diligence on minerals sourced from the Democratic Republic of Congo (DRC) and neighboring countries. Several African countries, including the DRC and Rwanda, have legislation in place requiring companies to undertake supply chain checks. China has recently developed its own conflict minerals guidelines.

Conflict minerals include columbite-tantalite, also known as coltan (from which tantalum is derived); cassiterite (tin); gold; wolframite (tungsten); or their derivatives; or any other mineral or its derivatives.

U.S. Securities and Exchange Commission Guidelines

The following describes the rules regarding when and how companies should diclose use of conflict materials.

Fact Sheet: Disclosing Use of Conflict Materials

In 2010, Congress passed the Dodd-Frank Act, which directs the Commission to issue rules requiring certain companies to disclose their use of conflict minerals if those minerals are "necessary to the functionality or production of a product" manufactured by those companies. Under the Act, those minerals include tantalum, tin, gold or tungsten.

Congress enacted Section 1502 of the Act because of concerns that the exploitation and trade of conflict minerals by armed groups is helping to finance conflict in the DRC region and is contributing to an emergency humanitarian crisis. Section 1502 of the Act amends the Securities and Exchange Act of 1934.

THE RULE

The final rule applies to a company that uses minerals including tantalum, tin, gold, or tungsten.

- The company files reports with the SEC under the Exchange Act.
- The minerals are "necessary to the functionality or production" of a product manufactured or contracted to be manufactured by the company.

The final rule requires a company to provide the disclosure on a new form to be filed with the SEC.

CONTRACTING TO MANUFACTURE

A company is considered to be "contracting to manufacture" a product if it has some actual influence over the manufacturing of that product. This determination is based on facts and circumstances, taking into account the degree of influence a company exercises over the product's manufacturing.

A company is not deemed to have influence over the manufacturing if it merely:

- Affixes its brand, marks, logo, or label to a generic product manufactured by a third party.
- Services, maintains, or repairs a product manufactured by a third party.
- Specifies or negotiates contractual terms with a manufacturer that do not directly relate to the manufacturing of the product.

The requirements apply equally to domestic and foreign issuers.

DETERMINING WHETHER CONFLICT MINERALS ORIGINATED IN THE DRC OR OTHER COVERED COUNTRIES

Under the final rule, a company that uses any of the designated minerals is required to conduct a reasonable "country of origin" inquiry that must be performed in good faith and be reasonably designed to determine whether any of its minerals originated in the covered countries or are from scrap or recycled sources.

If the inquiry determines either of the following to be true:

- The company *knows* that the minerals *did not* originate in the covered countries or *are* from scrap or recycled sources.
- The company *has no reason to believe* that the minerals *may have* originated in the covered countries or *may not be* from scrap or recycled sources.

… then the company must disclose its determination, provide a brief description of the inquiry it undertook and the results of the inquiry on Form SD.

The company also is required to:

- Make its description publicly available on its Internet website.
- Provide the Internet address of that site in the Form SD.

If the inquiry otherwise determines both of the following to be true:

- The company *knows or has reason to believe* that the minerals *may have* originated in the covered countries.
- The company *knows or has reason to believe* that the minerals *may not be* from scrap or recycled sources.

... then the company must undertake "due diligence" on the source and chain of custody of its conflict minerals and file a Conflict Minerals Report as an exhibit to the Form SD.

The company also is required to:

- Make publicly available the Conflict Minerals Report on its Internet website.
- Provide the Internet address of that site on Form SD.

WHAT MUST BE INCLUDED IN THE CONFLICT MINERALS REPORT

Under the final rule, companies that are required to file a Conflict Minerals Report must exercise due diligence on the source and chain of custody of their conflict minerals. The due diligence measures must conform to a nationally or internationally recognized due diligence framework, such as the due diligence guidance approved by the Organization for Economic Co-operation and Development (OECD).

DRC Conflict Free—If a company determines that its products are "DRC conflict free"—that is, the minerals may originate from the covered countries but did not finance or benefit armed groups—then the company must undertake the following audit and certification requirements:

- Obtain an independent private sector audit of its Conflict Minerals Report.
- Certify that it obtained such an audit.
- Include the audit report as part of the Conflict Minerals Report.
- Identify the auditor.

Not Been Found to Be "DRC Conflict Free"—If a company's products have not been found to be "DRC conflict free," then the company in addition to the audit and certification requirements must describe the following in its Conflict Minerals Report:

- The products manufactured or contracted to be manufactured that have not been found to be "DRC conflict free."

- The facilities used to process the conflict minerals in those products.
- The country of origin of the conflict minerals in those products.
- The efforts to determine the mine or location of origin with the greatest possible specificity.

DRC Conflict Undeterminable—For a temporary two-year period (or four-year period for smaller reporting companies), if the company is unable to determine whether the minerals in its products originated in the covered countries or financed or benefited armed groups in those countries, then those products are considered "DRC conflict undeterminable."

In that case, the company must describe the following in its Conflict Minerals Report:

- Its products manufactured or contracted to be manufactured that are "DRC conflict undeterminable."
- The facilities used to process the conflict minerals in those products, if known.
- The country of origin of the conflict minerals in those products, if known.

- The efforts to determine the mine or location of origin with the greatest possible specificity.
- The steps it has taken or will take, if any, since the end of the period covered in its most recent Conflict Minerals Report to mitigate the risk that its necessary conflict minerals benefit armed groups, including any steps to improve due diligence.

For those products that are "DRC conflict undeterminable," the company is not required to obtain an independent private sector audit of the Conflict Minerals Report regarding the conflict minerals in those products.

Recycled or Scrap Due Diligence—There are special rules governing the due diligence and Conflict Minerals Report for minerals from recycled or scrap sources. If a company's conflict minerals are derived from recycled or scrap sources rather than from mined sources, the company's products containing such minerals are considered "DRC conflict free."

If a company cannot reasonably conclude after its inquiry that its gold is from recycled or scrap sources, then it is required to undertake due diligence in accordance with the OECD Due Diligence Guidance, and get an audit of its Conflict Minerals Report. Currently, gold is the only conflict mineral with a nationally or internationally recognized due diligence framework for determining whether it is recycled or scrap, which is part of the OECD Due Diligence Guidance.

For the other three minerals, if a company cannot reasonably conclude after its inquiry that its minerals are from recycled or scrap sources, until a due diligence framework is developed, the company is required to describe the due diligence measures it exercised in determining that its conflict minerals are from recycled or scrap sources in its Conflict Minerals Report. Such a company is not required to obtain an independent private sector audit regarding such conflict minerals.

Squirepb.com, a legal resource, offers the following action steps in preparing your company to manage conflict minerals compliance:

Internal Organization—Designate a working group and develop an overall schedule with deadlines.

Communicate with Senior Management and Board—Make an initial report to senior management and board of directors (remember that the MSA Statements must be signed, so the board will need to understand the process and requirements).

Supply Chain—Develop a slavery and human trafficking policy.

Industry Group Involvement—Determine relevant industry groups and investigate their slavery and human trafficking-related activities.

Assess Risk—Consider the level of risk of slavery and human trafficking based on your products, geographic locations, and industry.

Address Supply Chain Management with IT System Solutions—Inventory existing IT systems and their connection to supply chain and suppliers.

Internal Communications—Alert employees and managers to the slavery and human trafficking requirements.

External Communications—Provide initial responses to customers and understand existing supplier engagement efforts to build upon.

Contracts—Review key supply contracts and inventory supplier codes of conduct.

PERSONNEL

Personnel who travel overseas have exposures just as they do when traveling in the United States. Risk may even be amplified depending on where they travel. They get sick overseas, and are exposed to terrorism, economic and political risks. Our responsibility as employers is to make sure they are protected with their health insurances and worker's compensation coverages, which need to be endorsed to protect the employee in travel abroad.

Additional protections should be offered that provide a higher degree of personnel security while they are on foreign shores. One of the leading companies that engages in providing employee protections while they travel overseas is International SOS (internationalsos.com).

Three examples of the exposure and their solutions are as follows:

Containing a Measles Outbreak on an Oil Rig

OVERVIEW

Measles is highly contagious. Though not usually fatal, serious complications can occur amongst those with compromised immune systems, children, and the elderly. As such, any measles outbreak is considered very serious. During an outbreak on an oil rig, the International SOS rapidly leveraged its medical resources—quarantining patients and launching sanitation, health promotion, and vaccination programs to contain the spread of infections.

Service: Medical staffing

Location: Bohai Bay

PROBLEM

At an offshore oil rig in the Bohai Bay, a measles outbreak already infected three people. In this isolated environment, there was a threat of the virus spreading further amongst the 130 workers on-board— and a potential public health risk when workers left the vessel.

The International SOS doctor on the rig immediately contacted his medical colleagues in Beijing for advice on how to mitigate the outbreak. In the meantime, the local public health authorities threatened to shut the rig down for three weeks until the measles was controlled. Any type of operational hiatus represented a potential loss of $1 million USD in revenue per day.

SOLUTION

The International SOS immediately sent a medical crisis team to the rig comprising a physician specializing in infectious disease and two nurses. They put the rig on high alert. All employees were prevented from leaving the rig, and new employees joining the rig, until the outbreak was mitigated. They quarantined the infected patients in the best way possible despite the tight space on-board.

To prevent infection, the team instigated a robust health promotion program. Employees were educated about proper hand washing and personal hygiene, how to contain the respiratory droplets from coughs or sneezes, and how to fit masks. A stringent cleaning regime was implemented to disinfect all surfaces from contamination by the virus.

Along with the International SOS office in China, the medical team assessed the crew to ascertain who was vulnerable to the measles virus. They checked the vaccination history of the employees, and then carried out blood tests to see which employees had measles antibodies present. Anyone on-board without vaccination records or measles antibodies was given the measles vaccine.

As a result, the company soon adopted a rigorous vaccination and measles health promotion program for other vessels in the region.

The public health authorities were satisfied that the client had taken best efforts to control the outbreak. They let the rig continue its operations while closely monitoring the situation to make sure that the number of infections did not increase.

Two weeks later, the rig was taken off high alert. There were only two new cases of measles after the International SOS interventions and all the infected patients fully recovered.

IMPACT

The company was able to show the authorities that it had credible occupational health policies and procedures that would work in the event of genuine threat to employee health. Their reputation remained intact during a difficult period and they were able to balance Duty of Care obligations with their operational needs.

Japanese Tsunami Response

OVERVIEW

On March 11, 2011 an 8.9-magnitude earthquake occurred off the coast of Japan triggering consecutive disasters.

Service: Emergency response

Location: Japan

PROBLEM

The earthquake caused a tsunami—resulting in the deaths of 12,000 people. Fifteen thousand people were recorded missing. Roads, housing, and communication networks were destroyed. The Fukushima nuclear power plant was struck, resulting in a state of nuclear emergency. The initial natural disaster widened and quickly became a medical-related crisis. Strong aftershocks and rolling blackouts left millions without power.

In Tokyo, the bullet and commuter train services were canceled or delayed. Flights to Narita International Airport were canceled due to radiation fears. During this time of uncertainty, calls to International SOS Assistance Centers increased by 250%.

SOLUTION

We provided assistance, evacuation, support, and medical advice on the radiation threat. Forty-five percent of our global clients who utilize TravelTracker had members affected by the crisis. Via this service, we received and answered many questions on health, safety and the developing nuclear disaster.

The International SOS supported evacuation requests, including movement within Japan: taking calls, and providing medical advice and information on radiation exposure.

IMPACT

Within days after the earthquake, we launched a comprehensive website for our members—kept updated 24/7 in Japanese and English. This provided vital information on:

- Medical risks
- Risk mitigation
- Procurement
- Iodine prophylaxis
- Food and water concerns
- Advice from a radiation epidemiologist

Mali Attack

OVERVIEW

On November 20, 2015 terrorists attacked an internationally recognized hotel chain in Bamako, capital of Mali. They took 170 hostages and killed 20 in a mass shooting. Throughout the day, our crisis management teams in Paris and London provided essential advice to clients. Our unique operations network meant we were able to maintain contact with clients and members affected and coordinate the response accordingly. Control Risks' embedded crisis management resource further enabled the effectiveness of support.

In total we dealt with 29 cases.

Service: Security Assistance: Diplomatic representation of members, flight support, crisis management support

Location: Bamako, Mali

PROBLEM

One member was trapped in her hotel room during the attack. She called us for support. One of our security experts stayed on the phone with her for four hours to help her through the ordeal. This lifeline provided essential emotional support in addition to expert advice.

SOLUTION

During the call, we advised on how to deal with the smoke in the room, life-safety techniques, and what to do in the event of the attackers trying to gain entry.

We supported other members in the hotel who either escaped or were freed by security forces, including:

- On-the-ground security assistance to move people to a lower-profile hotel
- Diplomatic representation for those whose passports had been left in the hotel
- Flight support where needed

Thanks to our social media monitoring, we were amongst the first to find out about the attack. Once the information was confirmed with our provider on the ground, we immediately issued a special advisory to our clients.

IMPACT

Our work did not end after the main crisis was over. We continued to provide updates on the situation, e.g., whether the security environment had materially changed.

Kidnap and Ransom Exposures

Personnel who travel overseas particularly in developing and third world countries are at great risk of K&R and terrorist related exposures.

According to *Wikipedia*, K&R insurance policies typically cover the perils of kidnap, extortion, wrongful detention, and hijacking. K&R policies are indemnity policies—they reimburse a loss incurred by the insured. The policies do not pay ransoms on the behalf of the insured. Typically, the insured must first pay the ransom, thus incurring the loss, and then seek reimbursement under the policy.

Claims and losses typically reimbursed by K&R insurance include:

- Ransom monies—Money paid or lost due to kidnapping
- Transit/delivery—Loss due to destruction, disappearance, confiscation, or wrongful appropriation of ransom monies being delivered to a covered kidnapping or extortion
- Accidental death or dismemberment—Death or permanent physical disablement occurring during a kidnapping
- Judgements and legal liability—Cost resulting from any claim or suit brought by any insured person against the insured
- Additional expenses—Medical care, PR counsel, wage and salary replacement, relocation and job retraining, and other expenses related to a kidnapping incident.

Typical K&R scenarios and occurrences require the need for additional expertise, and the policies also typically pay for the fees and expenses of crisis management consultants. These consultants provide advice to the insured on how to best respond to the incident. Even the most basic training for people traveling to dangerous places is not easily provided or is not obtained by small to mid-sized companies.

Training

Personnel who travel overseas need to be trained in two primary areas:

- How to conduct their business activities without creating undue exposure to themselves or their businesses
- What steps to take if something goes wrong

Both steps can be considered "risk management" in both avoiding exposure and dealing with it when it happens.

Areas of Training

Training has a very direct benefit in avoiding the potential impact of terrorist and K&F threats. It also teaches the staff that have overseas travel responsibilities their best courses of avoidance and what to do if any eventuality occurs.

3

Global Trade Risks

As corporations build their international trade activity they create both opportunity and risk. This chapter views the challenges and exposures associated with technology, cyber, customs security programs, contracts, financial, geophysical, and reputation—all peripheral and potentially consequential, if not proactively managed.

TECHNOLOGY AND CYBER ISSUES

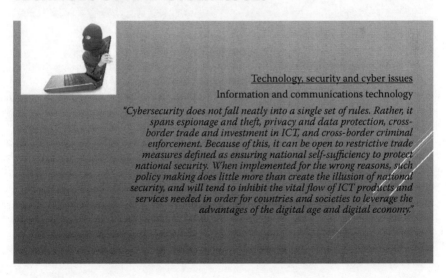

Technology, security and cyber issues
Information and communications technology

"Cybersecurity does not fall neatly into a single set of rules. Rather, it spans espionage and theft, privacy and data protection, cross-border trade and investment in ICT, and cross-border criminal enforcement. Because of this, it can be open to restrictive trade measures defined as ensuring national self-sufficiency to protect national security. When implemented for the wrong reasons, such policy making does little more than create the illusion of national security, and will tend to inhibit the vital flow of ICT products and services needed in order for countries and societies to leverage the advantages of the digital age and digital economy."

Technology and cyber security concerns are dominating issues in everyday life and certainly in businesses that operate globally. The U.S. presidential election of 2016 highlighted the controversial issues surrounding the "hacking" of the Democratic National Committee and the Russians so-called attempts at impacting the election results.

When you contemplate the huge amount of information transfer that takes place between U.S. companies and the world, the exposures are vast and convoluted. The criminals and those with clandestine agendas are always out there. We need to stay one step ahead at all times. Vigilance and due diligence are critical components of any technology and cybersecurity program.

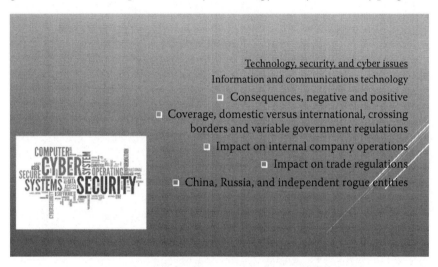

Technology, security, and cyber issues
Information and communications technology
□ Consequences, negative and positive
□ Coverage, domestic versus international, crossing borders and variable government regulations
□ Impact on internal company operations
□ Impact on trade regulations
□ China, Russia, and independent rogue entities

U.S. Government Program for Safeguarding and Securing Cyberspace

The following, from the Department of Homeland Security (DHS), describes the steps the government has been taken to address cyber issues.

> DHS has made significant progress since 9/11 in enhancing the security of the nation's critical physical infrastructure as well as its cyber infrastructure and networks. Today's threats to cybersecurity require the engagement of the entire society—from government and law enforcement to the private sector and importantly, members of the public—to block malicious actors while bolstering defensive capabilities.

Progress Made Since 9/11

Analyzing and Reducing Cyber Threats and Vulnerabilities

- National Cybersecurity Protection System: Developed by DHS as the nation's focal point for cyber activity and analysis, The National Cybersecurity Protection System fulfills a key requirement of the

National Cybersecurity Protection Plan (NCPP) to work collaboratively with public, private, and international entities to protect infrastructure, enhance situational awareness and implement analysis, warning and risk-management programs.

- EINSTEIN—Initially deployed in 2004, this system helps block malicious actors from accessing federal executive branch civilian agencies while working closely with those agencies to bolster their defensive capabilities. EINSTEIN 2 is an automated cyber surveillance system that monitors federal Internet traffic for malicious intrusions at 15 departments and agencies and 4 Managed Trusted Internet Protocol Service providers. EINSTEIN 3 will provide DHS with the ability to detect malicious activity and disable Trusted Internet connections— As part of the Comprehensive National Cybersecurity Initiative, DHS works to reduce and consolidate the number of external connections that federal agencies have to the Internet in order to limit the number of potential vulnerabilities to government networks and to focus monitoring efforts and security capabilities on limited and known avenues for Internet traffic.
- U.S. Computer Emergency Readiness Team (US-CERT)—In partnership with antivirus companies, US-CERT takes proactive measures to stop possible threats from reaching public and private sector partners by developing and sharing standardized threat indication, prevention, mitigation, and response information products with its .gov partners and constituents.

Distributing Threat Warnings

- National Cybersecurity and Communications Integration Center— Opened in October 2009, this 24-hour watch and warning center serves as the nation's principal hub for organizing cyber response efforts and maintaining the national cyber and communications common operational picture. DHS also works with the private sector, other government agencies, and the international community to mitigate risks by leveraging the tools, tradecraft, and techniques malicious actors use and converting them into actionable information for all 18 critical infrastructure sectors to use against cyber threats.
- Cybersecurity Partners Local Access Plan—DHS enhances information sharing with cleared owners and operators of critical infrastructure and key resources, as well as state technology officials and law enforcement officials, through access to secret-level cybersecurity information and video teleconference calls via local fusion centers.

- Information Sharing and Analysis Centers—DHS enhances situational awareness among stakeholders including those at the state and local level as well as industrial control system owners and operators by allowing the federal government to quickly and efficiently provide critical cyber risk, vulnerability, and mitigation data.

Coordinating Response to Cyber Incidents

- Interagency Collaboration—In October 2010, DHS and DOD (Department of Defense) signed a landmark memorandum of agreement to align and enhance America's capabilities to protect against threats to critical civilian and military computer systems and networks while ensuring appropriate levels of privacy.
- National Cyber Incident Response Plan—Developed in September 2010, this plan coordinates the response of multiple federal agencies, state and local governments, and hundreds of private firms, to incidents at all levels. DHS tested this plan during the CyberStorm III national exercise, which simulated a large-scale attack on the nation's critical information infrastructure.

Ensuring Safety of Cyber Systems

- Cybersecurity Workforce Initiative—Since its creation, DHS has increased its cyber staff by 500 percent while working with universities to build the cybersecurity pipeline through competitive scholarship, fellowship, and internship programs to continue to attract top talent.
- Technological development and deployment—DHS is guiding research and development as well as advancements in scientific and technical knowledge to support cybersecurity through targeted grant programs that encourage academic research, private sector investment, and innovation from small businesses.

Public Engagement

- Stop.Think.Connect.—The DHS Stop.Think.Connect. public cybersecurity awareness campaign is designed to increase public understanding of cyber threats and promote simple steps the public can take to increase their safety and security online.
- National Cybersecurity Awareness Month—Every October, DHS and its public and private sector partners promote efforts to educate citizens about guarding against cyber threats.

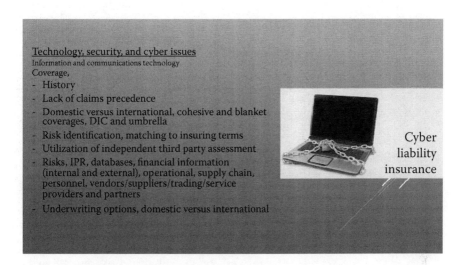

Technology, security, and cyber issues
Information and communications technology
Coverage,
- History
- Lack of claims precedence
- Domestic versus international, cohesive and blanket coverages, DIC and umbrella
- Risk identification, matching to insuring terms
- Utilization of independent third party assessment
- Risks, IPR, databases, financial information (internal and external), operational, supply chain, personnel, vendors/suppliers/trading/service providers and partners
- Underwriting options, domestic versus international

Cyber liability insurance

Cyber and technology insurances are relatively new to the underwriting world. It is evolving as we speak in 2017. The Ohio Insurance Blog reports:

> When you hear the words "data breach" or "cyber attack," what comes to mind? For many people, these words conjure up images of rogue hackers infiltrating secure computer systems to steal valuable or sensitive data.
>
> Although malicious cyber criminals are a real threat, in many cases, data breaches are caused by something much more mundane, like a stolen laptop, misplaced thumb drive, or lost smartphone.

Cyber Liability Claims Examples

While small businesses are increasingly at risk of a cyber attack, unfortunately, this is not the only threat. Here are some of the most common types of incidents resulting in a cyber or data breach claim:

Stolen Laptops

A regional retailer contracted with a third-party service provider. A burglar stole two laptops from the service provider containing the data of over 80,000 clients of the retailer.

Per applicable notification laws, the retailer—not the service provider—was required to notify the affected individuals.

Total expenses incurred for notification and crisis management alone was nearly $5,000,000.

Rogue Employee

An employee learns she may be terminated, and in response, she steals names, addresses, social security numbers, and other personal information from customer files.

She sold the information to her cousin, who used the identities to fraudulently obtain credit cards. *The affected individuals filed suit against the company for identity theft.*

Small Business Hacked

A business is hacked by a local teenager who stole social security numbers and bank account data from customer files. He sold the information to an internet website which used it to create false identities for criminals to use.

The business incurred notification and credit monitoring costs, and the legal expenses as well as the damages from potential lawsuits resulted in more than $500,000 in damages.

Manufacturer Duped

A manufacturer located in northeast Ohio nearly transferred $315,000 to China based solely on an email request to pay for raw materials that appeared to be legitimate.

If you think this couldn't happen to you, or that you would easily be capable of uncovering the fraud, you might be interested to know that the FBI released information indicating that thieves had stolen $215 million over a 14-month period using this exact scam.

Certainly, those businesses that were victims thought it couldn't happen to them too.

Spyware Virus

A man sent an email to his ex-girlfriend hoping to monitor what she did on her computer. She opened the email on her work computer, and over the course of two weeks, the spyware emailed the man more than 1,000 screenshots of confidential data on 150 customers.

The business incurred notification and credit monitoring expenses for the affected customers.

Dumpster Diving

A woman looking for coupons in a large recycling bin found records containing social security numbers and medical histories. The papers came from a local medical office, and included details about more than sixty patients, including drugs they were taking, and whether they were seeing a psychiatrist.

The papers were tossed by an employee with an otherwise long and stellar service record. *The incident constituted a breach of HIPPA, and resulted in governmental fines against the medical office.*

Data Theft or Cyber Extortion

A U.S.-based information technology company contracted with an overseas software vendor. The vendor left certain "administrator" defaults on the company's server and a "hacker for hire" was paid $20,000 to exploit the vulnerability.

The hacker demanded an extortion payment, otherwise he would post records of millions of registered users on a blog available for all to see.

The extortion expenses and payments are expected to exceed $2,000,000.

Why Businesses Need Coverage

The claims examples above only scratch the surface when it comes to the types of claims occurring daily.

Just consider how many ads you see offering to monitor your credit, protect your identity, and spend millions to restore your good name if stolen.

Unfortunately, we're in a whole new world where the physical threats we faced years ago, from severe weather, highly dangerous products, or inherently risky professions such as a neurosurgeon are not the only factors we need to consider.

Historically, the cost of insurance protection generally decreased as your risk of loss diminished. We could all understand this logic, and we could adapt our businesses accordingly.

We could risk manage exposures such as severe weather by selecting higher deductibles, we put quality controls in place to substantially reduce the risk of the products we manufacture causing injury to someone, and we require the best education and put the most advanced technology in the hands of our neurosurgeons to all but eliminate the chances of bad outcomes.

But how do we manage this new cyber and data breach risk?

If our country's largest, most sophisticated organizations deploying the best cyber security protocols can be breached, how can we assume we're immune?

If the data and systems of our government, the IRS, CIA, and FBI can all be compromised, is it realistic to believe that just because we're a small business, we're safe?

Now more than ever, small businesses are standing up and saying "we need help."

And that's exactly what we provide.

Help in managing the exposures a small business faces so we can reduce the likelihood of a breach, and help in securing the most appropriate cyber and data breach insurance to respond when the inevitable breach does occur.

- There is no standard cyber liability policy.
- Cyber is a whole new animal.
- There is no standard policy, no common forms, no historical trends to analyze.
- Each company offering a policy form has developed their own list of coverage options available and exclusions included, which is great for consumers because so many different options exist.

However, it presents a challenge in that no standard cyber policy is available that consumers, insurance advisors, consultants, and even court systems can use as a benchmark.

Cyber insurance is hugely complex, and since each policy is different, only a licensed Insurance Advisor is equipped to assist you in understanding why you need cyber insurance, and then most importantly, helping you develop a specific policy designed to adequately protect your business.

CYBER ATTACK CASE STUDY: AS REPORTED
BY INSURANCE 360.COM AND *USA TODAY*

Sony Pictures Entertainment holds $60 million in cyber insurance with Marsh, according to documents leaked by the group claiming responsibility for the attack on the movie studio.

The documents, covered in detail by Steve Ragan at CSO, say that after sonypictures.com was breached in 2011, Sony made a claim of $1.6 million with Hiscox, its cyber provider at the time. The insurer declined to quote at renewal, so Sony Pictures turned to Lockton, which brokered a $20 million policy that included $10 million in self-insured retention.

Around April 1 of 2015, Sony moved its cyber policy to AIG, when it acquired $10 million in coverage. This policy, effective until April 1, 2015, overlaps with its existing coverage, Ragan writes. In May, the movie studio turned to a new insurance broker, Marsh, which reached out to Brit Insurance, Liberty International Underwriters, Beazley and other carriers to secure upward of $60 million in coverage.

Policy details say that the studio consolidated coverage with Sony Corporation of America, with a $5 million retention at an annual cost of $356,963. The policy includes security and privacy liability coverage, as well as event management, network interruption, cyber extortion, and regulatory action.

The massive hack of Sony Pictures Entertainment's computers has spurred what may be the first lawsuit by former employees. ...

But is $60 million enough coverage? After the hackers ("Guardians of Peace") threatened a terrorist attack on Christmas Day at theaters showing Sony's film *The Interview*, five of the country's largest chains, including AMC and Regal Entertaiment, pulled the movie from their lineups. In turn, the studio canceled the release of the film.

A Seth Rogen comedy about a television crew that plots to kill North Korean leader Kim Jong Un, *The Interview* reportedly cost $80 million to make and market, but the expenditures are growing.

"The cost to Sony from new software and hardware, employee labor to clean up the mess, investigation, lost productivity, and reputational damage, just to name a few, is at least over a $100 million and growing daily," said Hemanshu Nigam in a Bloomberg interview. Nigam founded the cybersecurity firm SSP Blue and has worked with Microsoft Corp. and News Corp.

The cost now includes a lawsuit filed against the studio by two former employees, who accuse Sony Pictures of knowing it had inadequate cybersecurity measures in place and failing to protect the personal information of thousands of workers.

What could have been the film's future earnings—from video-on-demand and Blu-ray/DVD purchases—won't soften the blow. Sony Pictures told *USA Today* Dec. 18 [2014] that it won't make the film available on any platform.

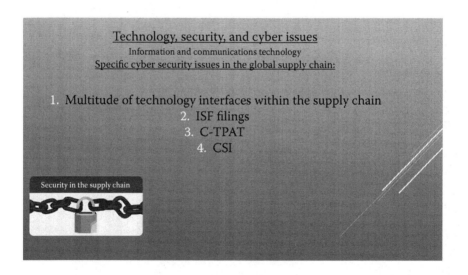

The International Chamber of Commerce (ICC; iccwbo.org) can help with cybersecurity issues. The following outlines its services:

Fighting Commercial Crime

ICC combats all types of crime affecting business, from piracy on the high seas and trade finance fraud to counterfeiting and cybercrime.

New Criminal Threats

The scope and variety of criminal threats facing business grow ever larger, with the methods of commercial criminals becoming increasingly sophisticated. Through its dedicated crime-fighting division (Commercial Crime Services), policymaking bodies and other initiatives, ICC combats all types of crime affecting business, from piracy on the high seas and trade finance fraud to counterfeiting and cybercrimes.

Stamping Out Corruption

Taking the lead among business organizations in denouncing corruption and developing rules to combat it, the ICC Commission on Corporate Responsibility and Anti-corruption puts forth policy recommendations from a global business perspective and develops practical rules of conduct and best practices for fighting corruption.

Commercial Crime Services

ICC's Commercial Crime Services (CCS) division in the UK is a centralized crime-fighting body—one with a global network and a sterling reputation. It draws on the worldwide resources of its members in the fight against commercial crime.

From its base in London, and comprising three distinct crime-fighting divisions, CCS operates according to two basic precepts: to prevent and investigate commercial crime and to help prosecute commercial criminals. CCS works closely with international law enforcement officials, including Interpol, and uses its expertise and network of members to remain one step ahead of the criminals.

Fighting Counterfeiting and Piracy of Goods

ICC's Business Action to Stop Counterfeiting and Piracy (BASCAP) initiative connects all business sectors and cut across national borders in the fight against counterfeiting and piracy.

This global approach is designed to support individual company and organizational efforts and amplify business messages with national governments and intergovernmental organizations.

CSI, C-TPAT, AND ISF: U.S. CUSTOMS AND BORDER PROTECTION'S SECURITY PROGRAMS

CSI, C-TPAT, and ISF are three specific U.S. Customs and Border Protection (CBP) initiatives since the events of 9/11 that have impacted security requirements for businesses involved in global supply chains. The following information about the three initiatives is according to the CBP.

CSI: Container Security Initiative

As the single, unified border agency of the United States, U.S. Customs and Border Protection's (CBP's) mission is extraordinarily important to the protection of America and the American people. In the aftermath of the terrorist attacks on September 11, 2001, U.S. Customs Service began developing antiterrorism programs to help secure the United States. Within months of these attacks, U.S. Customs Service had created the Container Security Initiative (CSI).

CSI addresses the threat to border security and global trade posed by the potential for terrorist use of a maritime container to deliver a weapon. CSI proposes a security regime to ensure all containers that pose a potential risk for terrorism are identified and inspected at foreign ports before they are placed on vessels destined for the United States. CBP has stationed teams of U.S. CBP Officers in foreign locations to work together with our host foreign government counterparts.

Their mission is to target and prescreen containers and to develop additional investigative leads related to the terrorist threat to cargo destined to the United States.

The three core elements of CSI are:

- Identify high-risk containers. CBP uses automated targeting tools to identify containers that pose a potential risk for terrorism, based on advance information and strategic intelligence.
- Prescreen and evaluate containers before they are shipped. Containers are screened as early in the supply chain as possible, generally at the port of departure.
- Use technology to prescreen high-risk containers to ensure that screening can be done rapidly without slowing down the movement of trade. This technology includes large-scale X-ray and gamma ray machines and radiation detection devices.

Through CSI, CBP officers work with host customs administrations to establish security criteria for identifying high-risk containers. Those administrations use non-intrusive inspection (NII) and radiation detection technology to screen high-risk containers before they are shipped to U.S. ports.

Announced in January 2002, CSI has made great strides since its inception. A significant number of customs administrations have committed to joining CSI and operate at various stages of implementation.

CSI is now operational at ports in North America, Europe, Asia, Africa, the Middle East, and Latin and Central America. CBP's 58 operational CSI ports now prescreen over 80 percent of all maritime containerized cargo imported into the United States.

C-TPAT: Customs-Trade Partnership Against Terrorism

Customs-Trade
Partnership Against Terrorism

Sea carriers in the C-TPAT program may now apply to participate in the Advanced Qualified Unlading Approval. The advanced unlading process will be available to sea carriers in 10 seaports throughout the U.S. The process will potentially save time for sea carriers in the C-TPAT program and allow CBP to better focus our resources.

C-TPAT is but one layer in U.S. Customs and Border Protection's (CBP's) multi-layered cargo enforcement strategy. Through this program, CBP works with the trade community to strengthen international supply chains and improve United States border security. C-TPAT is a voluntary public-private sector partnership program which recognizes that CBP can provide the highest level of cargo security only through close cooperation with the principle stakeholders of the international supply chain such as importers, carriers, consolidators, licensed customs brokers, and manufacturers. The Security and Accountability for Every Port Act of 2006 provided a statutory framework for the C-TPAT program and imposed strict program oversight requirements.

A Growing Partnership

From its inception in November 2001, C-TPAT has continued to grow. Today, more than 11,400 certified partners spanning the gamut of the trade community, have been accepted into the program. The partners include

U.S. importers/exporters, U.S./Canada highway carriers; U.S./Mexico highway carriers; rail and sea carriers; licensed U.S. Customs brokers; U.S. marine port authority/terminal operators; U.S. freight consolidators; ocean transportation intermediaries and non-operating common carriers; Mexican and Canadian manufacturers; and Mexican long-haul carriers, all of whom account for over 52 percent (by value) of cargo imported into the U.S.

How C-TPAT Works

When an entity joins C-TPAT, an agreement is made to work with CBP to protect the supply chain, identify security gaps, and implement specific security measures and best practices. Applicants must address a broad range of security topics and present security profiles that list action plans to align security throughout the supply chain.

C-TPAT members are considered to be of low risk, and are therefore less likely to be examined at a U.S. port of entry.

C-TPAT Benefits

C-TPAT Partners enjoy a variety of benefits, including taking an active role in working closer with the U.S. Government in its war against terrorism. As they do this, Partners are able to better identify their own security vulnerabilities and take corrective actions to mitigate risks. Some of the benefits of the program include:

- Reduced number of CBP examinations
- Front of the line inspections
- Possible exemption from Stratified Exams
- Shorter wait times at the border
- Assignment of a Supply Chain Security Specialist to the company
- Access to the Free and Secure Trade (FAST) Lanes at the land borders
- Access to the C-TPAT web-based Portal system and a library of training materials
- Possibility of enjoying additional benefits by being recognized as a trusted trade Partner by foreign Customs administrations that have signed Mutual Recognition with the United States
- Eligibility for other U.S. Government pilot programs, such as the Food and Drug Administration's Secure Supply Chain program
- Business resumption priority following a natural disaster or terrorist attack
- Importer eligibility to participate in the Importer Self-Assessment Program (ISA)
- Priority consideration at CBP's industry-focused Centers of Excellence and Expertise

How Do I Become a Partner?

Participation in C-TPAT is voluntary and there are no costs associated with joining the program. Moreover, a company does not need an intermediary in order to apply to the program and work with CBP; the application process is easy and it is done online. The first step is for the company to review the C-TPAT Minimum Security Criteria for their business entity to determine eligibility for the program. The second step is for the company to submit a basic application via the C-TPAT Portal system and to agree to voluntarily participate. The third step is for the company to complete a supply chain security profile. The security profile explains how the company is meeting C-TPAT's minimum security criteria.

In order to do this, the company should have already conducted a risk assessment. Upon satisfactory completion of the application and supply chain security profile, the applicant company is assigned a C-TPAT Supply Chain Security Specialist to review the submitted materials and to provide program guidance on an on-going basis. The C-TPAT program will then have up to 90 days to certify the company into the program or to reject the application. If certified, the company will be validated within a year of certification.

If you have C-TPAT issues or questions, please contact your Supply Chain Security Specialist, or the Duty Officer of the Day by email at industry.partnership@dhs.gov or by phone at (202) 344-1180. Be advised that the Duty Officer cannot reset your password for you; they assist with general inquiries and questions.

Note: Visit www.cbp.gov/CTPAT for instructions to complete annual reviews, and to view training materials related to common C-TPAT processes. Also, information on new features will be posted to the C-TPAT Public Library.

Note: Technical issues should be reported via telephone to the national Help Desk at 1-866-530-4172 option 4, (after hours at 1-800-927-8729) or via email to ctpathelpdesk@cbp.dhs.gov.

ISF: Importer Security Filing

Bulk and Break Bulk Cargo

An Importer Security Filing is not required for bulk cargo. For break bulk cargo that is exempt from the 24 hour prior to lading timing requirement for 24 Hour Rule purposes, the Importer Security Filing is required 24 hours prior to arrival.

How Will the Rule Be Enforced?

The interim final rule includes a delayed enforcement date of 12 months after the interim final rule takes effect. During this 12-month period, CBP will show restrint in enforcing the rule. CBP will take into account difficulties that importers may face in complying with the rule *as long as importers are making a good faith effort and satisfactory progress toward compliance*. The flexible enforcement period will end January 26, 2010. CBP may issue liquidated damages of $5,000 per violation for the submission of an inaccurate, incomplete or untimely filing. If goods for which an ISF has not been filed arrive in the U.S., CBP may withhold the release or transfer of the cargo; CBP may refuse to grant a permit to unlade for the merchandise; and if such cargo is unladen without permission, it may be subject to seizure. Additionally, noncompliant cargo could be subject to "do not load" orders at origin or further inspection on arrival.

Where Can I Find More Information?

For more detailed information about the Importer Security Filing, please visit the CBP website at http://www.cbp.gov/xp/cgov/trade/cargo_security/carriers /security_filing/. The website includes fact sheets, FAQs, and other public outreach sources. Additionally, questions may be sent to Security_Filing_General @cbp.dhs.gov. Additional assistance may be available from your licensed customs broker, freight forwarders, trade associations and local trade centers.

CONTRACT MANAGEMENT

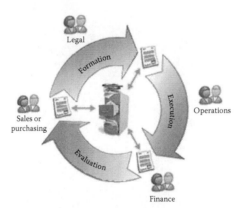

International trade means international contracts. International contracting is very different from domestic contracts because of exposures to

- Cultural differences
- Legal and regulatory variables

- Time and distance
- Convoluted terms and conditions

We offer the following recommendations for companies to follow to reduce the risk of issues developing with foreign entities:

- Understand and act on all the concerns outlined above.
- Obtain expertise not from General Counsel, but from specific legal talent who have experience in the countries and markets you are working in.
- Create defined SOPs and checklists to make sure all the contractual issues are addressed, such as but not limited to:

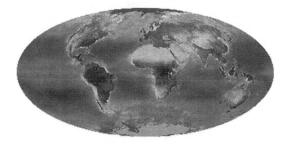

  - INCO Term
  - Dispute Resolution
  - Jurisdiction
  - Payment Terms
  - Currency
- Address all critical contractual concerns upfront and with transparency.
- Make sure collaboration occurs with all key stakeholders.
- Make sure all stakeholders review the contract before finalizing.

The Contract Management Process

Rene G. Rendon

U.S Naval Postgraduate School

The contracting process can be analyzed using a six-phase model. These six phases include Procurement Planning, Solicitation Planning, Solicitation, Source Selection, Contract Administration, and Contract

Close-out (Garrett & Rendon, 2005). Each of these contract management phases provides critical planning, execution, and control of the overall contracting process, and is integral to the success of the resultant contact and contractor performance. This section provides a brief overview of the phases of the contracting process and identifies key areas for consideration for each contracting phase, as well as best practices.

1. *Procurement Planning* involves the process of identifying which business needs can be best met by procuring products or services outside the organization. This process involves determining whether to procure, how to procure, what to procure, how much to procure, and when to procure (Garrett & Rendon, 2005). This phase of the contracting process includes the following key activities:
   a. Determining and defining the procurement requirement (the supply or service to procure).
   b. Conducting market research and/or a pre-solicitation conference.
   c. Developing a preliminary Work Breakdown Structures (WBS) and Statements of Work (SOW), or description of the supply or service to be procured.
   d. Develop preliminary budgets and cost estimates.
   e. Preliminary consideration of contract type, risk assessment, and any special terms and conditions.

   Best practices in procurement planning include the use of outsourcing analysis to assess contract risks and market research to identify supplier capabilities, as well as determine industry practices for describing the requirement and determining contract type. Early supplier involvement though the use of pre-solicitation conferences and industry benchmarking are also considered best practices.

2. *Solicitation Planning* involves the process of preparing the documents needed to support the solicitation. This process involves documenting program requirements and identifying potential sources (Garrett & Rendon, 2005). This contracting phase includes the following activities:
   a. Selecting appropriate contract type.
   b. Determine procurement method (sealed bids, negotiated proposals, e-procurement methods, procurement cards)
   c. Developing the solicitation document (IFB, RFQ, or RFP).

  d. Determining proposal evaluation criteria, and contract award strategy (lowest priced versus best value).

  e. Structuring contract terms and conditions.

  f. Finalizing solicitation Work Breakdown Structures (WBS), Statements of Work (SOW), or product or service descriptions.

  Best practices in solicitation planning include using cross-functional teams for developing solicitations, and identifying contract risks. The use of Statements of Objectives (SOO) and Performance-based Statements of Work (SOW) are also considered best practices.

3. *Solicitation* is the process of obtaining information (bids and proposals) from the prospective sellers on how project needs can be met (Garrett & Rendon, 2005). This phase of the contracting process includes:

  a. Conduct pre-proposal conference, if required.

  b. Conduct advertising of the procurement opportunity, or providing notice to interested suppliers.

  c. Develop and maintain qualified bidder's list.

  Best practices in the solicitation phase include using web-based and other paperless solicitation processes, as well as using draft solicitations as a source industry feedback.

4. *Source Selection* is the process of receiving bids or proposals and applying the proposal evaluation criteria to select a supplier (Garrett & Rendon, 2005). The source selection process includes the contract negotiations between the buyer and the seller in attempting to come to agreement on all aspects of the contract, to include cost, schedule, performance, terms and conditions, and

anything else related to the contracted effort. This source selection process includes the following activities:

a. Applying evaluation criteria to management, cost, and technical proposals.
b. Negotiating with suppliers.
c. Executing the contract award strategy.

Best practices in the source selection phase include using a formal source selection organization with trained and experienced cross-functional proposal evaluation teams, using a weighting system to prioritize the evaluation criteria and using a disciplined approach to following the evaluation criteria stated in the solicitation. Additional best practices include obtaining independent cost estimates to assist in evaluation supplier proposals, and conducting a price realism analysis on each supplier proposal.

5. *Contract Administration* is the process of ensuring that each party's performance meets the contractual requirements. The contract administration process includes:

a. Conducting a pre-performance conference.
b. Measuring contractor's performance, using performance evaluation tools (Earned Value Management, schedule analysis, budget analysis).
c. Conducting risk monitoring and control.
d. Managing the contract change control process.
e. Measuring and reporting contractor's performance (cost, schedule, performance).
f. Conducting project milestone reviews.

Best practices in the contract administration phase include using a formal contract administration methodology with trained and experienced cross-functional team members competent in contractor performance measurement. Additional best practices for the contract administration phase include using an integrated performance evaluation method and establishing a contract change control process.

6. *Contract Closeout* is the process of verifying that all administrative matters are concluded on a contract that is otherwise physically complete. The contract closeout process includes the following activities:

a. Processing property dispositions.
b. Conducting final acceptance of products or services.

   c. Processing final contractor payments.

   d. Documenting contractor's performance.

   e. Conducting post project audit.

     Best practices in the contract closeout phase include designating and empowering a formal contract closeout team, using contract closeout checklists, and documenting contracting lessons learned and best practices.

Assessing Contract Management Process Maturity. Leading organizations conduct an assessment of their contract management process maturity through the use of the Contract Management Maturity Model (CMMM©). The CMMM consists of five levels of maturity ranging from an ad hoc level (Level 1), to a basic, disciplined process capability (Level 2), to a fully established and institutionalized processes capability (Level 3), to a level characterized by processes integrated with other corporate processes resulting in synergistic corporate benefits (Level 4), and finally, to a level in which processes focused on continuous improvement and adoption of lessons learned and best practices (Level 5).

These CMMM assessment results provide a wealth of insight to the organization in terms of which contract management key process areas need to be improved and which program offices to direct its improvement effort. Furthermore, the assessment results will provide the organization with a roadmap of additional needed training and education for improving its contract management process capability. For example, an organization with low maturity level (Ad hoc or Basic) in the Source Selection key process area, will know that it needs to provide additional training or policies and standards in the areas related to the key practice activities for that specific process area. This is the true value and benefit of the contract management process capability maturity model—the continuous improvement of the organization's contract management processes.

FINANCIAL

Every risk we discuss in this book has financial ramifications—both positive and negative. This supports the idea that risk management and finance are two very aligned silos in any organization. Often, we see that risk management becomes a secondary division of finance in many large organizations, because of this alignment feature. In this book my focus on financial risk will be in the area of payment terms and currency exposures.

International Payment Terms

Advanced relationships will always allow payment terms to be extended. Extensions are OK, but they must be managed timely and comprehensively to avoid any payment problems.

The Department of Commerce provides various resources to assist companies on international payment terms, as outlined next.

Cash-in-Advance

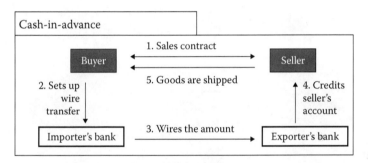

With cash-in-advance payment terms, an exporter can avoid credit risk because payment is received before the ownership of the goods is transferred. For international sales, wire transfers and credit cards are the most commonly used cash-in-advance options available to exporters. With the advancement of the Internet, escrow services are becoming another cash-in-advance option for small export transactions. However, requiring payment in advance is the least attractive option for the buyer, because it creates unfavorable cash flow. Foreign buyers are also concerned that the goods may not be sent if payment is made in advance. Thus, exporters who insist on this payment method as their sole manner of doing business may lose to competitors who offer more attractive payment terms.

Letters of Credit

Letters of credit (LCs) are one of the most secure instruments available to international traders. An LC is a commitment by a bank on behalf of the buyer that payment will be made to the exporter, provided that the terms and conditions stated in the LC have been met, as verified through the presentation of all required documents. The buyer establishes credit and pays his or her bank to render this service. An LC is useful when reliable credit information about a foreign buyer is difficult to obtain, but the exporter is satisfied with the creditworthiness of the buyer's foreign bank. An LC also protects the buyer since no payment obligation arises until the goods have been shipped as promised.

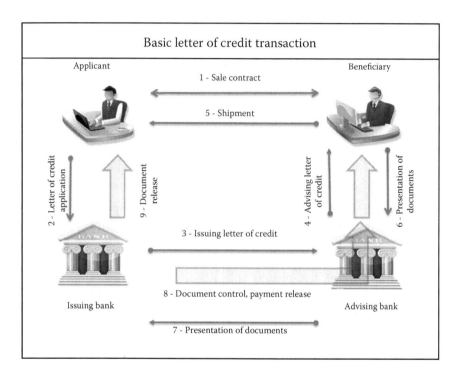

Basic letter of credit transaction

Documentary Collections

A documentary collection (D/C) is a transaction whereby the exporter entrusts the collection of the payment for a sale to its bank (remitting bank), which sends the documents that its buyer needs to the importer's bank (collecting bank), with instructions to release the documents to the buyer for payment. Funds are received from the importer and remitted to the exporter through the banks involved in the collection in exchange for those documents. D/Cs involve using a draft that requires the importer to pay the face amount either at sight (document against payment) or on a specified date (document against acceptance). The collection letter gives instructions that specify the documents required for the transfer of title to the goods. Although banks do act as facilitators for their clients, D/Cs offer no verification process and limited recourse in the event of non-payment. D/Cs are generally less expensive than LCs.

Open Account

An open account transaction is a sale where the goods are shipped and delivered before payment is due, which in international sales is typically in 30, 60 or 90 days. Obviously, this is one of the most advantageous options to the importer in terms of cash flow and cost, but it is consequently one of the highest risk options for an exporter. Because of intense competition in export markets, foreign buyers often press exporters for open account terms since the extension of credit by the seller to the buyer is more common abroad. Therefore, exporters who are reluctant to extend credit may lose a sale to their competitors. Exporters can offer competitive open account terms while substantially mitigating the risk of non-payment by using one or more of the appropriate trade finance techniques. ... When offering open account terms, the exporter can seek extra protection using export credit insurance.

Consignment

Consignment in international trade is a variation of open account in which payment is sent to the exporter only after the goods have been sold by the foreign distributor to the end customer. An international consignment transaction is based on a contractual arrangement in which the foreign distributor receives, manages, and sells the goods for the exporter who retains title to the goods until they are sold. Clearly, exporting on consignment is very risky as the exporter is not guaranteed any payment and its goods are in a foreign country in the hands of an independent distributor or agent. Consignment helps exporters become more competitive on the basis of better availability and faster delivery of goods. Selling on consignment can also help exporters reduce the direct costs of storing and managing inventory. The key to success in exporting on consignment is to partner with a reputable and trustworthy foreign distributor or a third-party logistics provider. Appropriate insurance should be in place to cover consigned goods in transit or in possession of a foreign distributor as well as to mitigate the risk of non-payment.

Illustrative Letter of Credit Transaction

1. The importer arranges for the issuing bank to open an LC in favor of the exporter.
2. The issuing bank transmits the LC to the nominated bank, which forwards it to the exporter.
3. The exporter forwards the goods and documents to a freight forwarder.
4. The freight forwarder dispatches the goods and either the dispatcher or the exporter submits documents to the nominated bank.

5. The nominated bank checks documents for compliance with the LC and collects payment from the issuing bank for the exporter.
6. The importer's account at the issuing bank is debited.
7. The issuing bank releases documents to the importer to claim the goods from the carrier and to clear them at customs.

How to Offer Open Account Terms in Competitive Markets

Open account terms may be offered in competitive markets with the use of one or more of the following trade finance techniques: (a) export working capital financing, (b) government-guaranteed export working capital programs, (c) export credit insurance, and (d) export factoring.

Export Working Capital Financing

Exporters who lack sufficient funds to extend open accounts in the global market need export working capital financing that covers the entire cash cycle, from the purchase of raw materials through the ultimate collection of the sales proceeds. Export working capital facilities, which are generally secured by personal guarantees, assets, or receivables, can be structured to support export sales in the form of a loan or revolving line of credit.

Government-Guaranteed Export Working Capital Programs

The U.S. Small Business Administration and the U.S. Export-Import Bank offer programs that guarantee export working capital facilities granted by participating lenders to U.S. exporters. With those programs, U.S. exporters can obtain needed facilities from commercial lenders when financing is otherwise not available or when their borrowing capacity needs to be increased.

Export Credit Insurance

Export credit insurance provides protection against commercial losses (such as default, insolvency, bankruptcy) and political losses (such as war, nationalization, and currency inconvertibility). It allows exporters to increase sales by offering more liberal open account terms to new and existing customers. Insurance also provides security for banks that are providing working capital and are financing exports.

Export Factoring

Factoring in international trade is the discounting of short-term receivables (up to 180 days). The exporter transfers title to his short-term foreign accounts receivable to a factoring house, or a factor, for cash at a discount from the face value. It allows an exporter to ship on open account as the factor assumes the financial liability of the importer to pay and handles collections on the receivables. Factoring houses most commonly work with exports of consumer goods.

Trade Finance Technique Unavailable for Open Account Terms: Forfaiting

Forfaiting is a method of trade financing that allows the exporter to sell his medium- and long-term receivables (180 days to 7 years or more) to a forfaiter at a discount, in exchange for cash. The forfaiter assumes all the risks, thereby enabling the exporter to offer extended credit terms and to incorporate the discount into the selling price. Forfaiters usually work with exports of capital goods, commodities, and large projects. Forfaiting was developed in Switzerland in the 1950s to fill the gap between the exporter of capital goods, who would not or could not deal on open account, and the importer, who desired to defer payment until the capital equipment could begin to pay for itself.

Key Common Features of Ex-Im Bank's Loan Guarantees and Direct Loans

Ex-Im Bank [U.S. Export-Import Bank] assists U.S. exporters by: (a) providing direct loans; or (b) guaranteeing repayment of commercial loans to creditworthy foreign buyers for purchases of U.S. goods and services. These loans are generally used to finance the purchase of high-value capital equipment or services or exports to large-scale projects that require medium- or long-term financing. Ex-Im Bank's foreign buyer financing is also used to finance the purchase of refurbished equipment, software, and certain banking and legal fees, as well as some local costs and expenses. There is no minimum or maximum limit to the size of the export sale that may be supported by the Bank's foreign buyer financing. Ex-Im Bank requires the foreign buyer to make a cash payment to the exporter equal to at least 15 percent of the U.S. supply contract. Repayment terms up to five years are available for exports of capital goods and services. Transportation equipment and exports to large-scale projects may be eligible for repayment terms up to 10 years (12 to 18 years for certain sectors). Military items are generally not eligible for Ex-Im Bank financing nor are sales to foreign military entities. In addition, goods must meet the Bank's foreign content requirements. Finally, Ex-Im Bank financing may not be available in certain countries and certain terms for U.S. government policy reasons (for more information, see the Country Limitation Schedule posted on the Bank's Web site, www.exim.gov, under the "Apply" section).

Key Features of Ex-Im Bank Loan Guarantees

- Loans are made by commercial banks and repayment of these loans is guaranteed.
- Guaranteed loans cover 100 percent of the principal and interest for 85 percent of the U.S. contract price.
- Interest rates are negotiable, and are usually floating and lower than fixed rates.
- Guaranteed loans are fully transferable, can be securitized and are available in certain foreign currencies.
- Guaranteed loans have a faster documentation process with the assistance of commercial banks.
- There are no U.S. vessel shipping requirements for amounts less than $20 million.

Key Features of Ex-Im Bank Direct Loans

- Fixed-rate loans are provided directly to creditworthy foreign buyers.
- Direct loans support 85 percent of the U.S. contract price.
- Exporters will be paid in full upon disbursement of a loan to the foreign buyers.
- Generally, goods shipped by sea must be carried exclusively on U.S. vessels.
- Direct loans are best used when the buyer insists on a fixed rate.

Fees and Ex-Im Bank Contact Information

- Letter of interest: $50 for online application; $100 for paper application via mail and fax.
- Preliminary commitment: 0.1 of 1 percent of the financed amount up to $25,000.
- Guarantee commitment: 0.125 percent per year on the undisbursed balance of the loan.

- Direct loan commitment: 0.5 percent per year on the undisbursed balance of the loan.
- Exposure fee: varies, depending upon tenor, country risk, and buyer credit risk.

For more information about loans from Ex-Im Bank, visit its Web site at www.exim.gov or call 1-800-565-EXIM (3946).

Currency

Foreign Exchange Risk

Foreign exchange (FX) is a risk factor that is often overlooked by small- and medium-sized enterprises (SMEs) that wish to enter, grow, and succeed in the global marketplace. Although most U.S. SME exporters prefer to sell in U.S. dollars, creditworthy foreign buyers today are increasingly demanding to pay in their local currencies. From the viewpoint of a U.S. exporter who chooses to sell in foreign currencies, FX risk is the exposure to potential financial losses due to devaluation of the foreign currency against the U.S. dollar. Obviously, this exposure can be avoided by insisting on selling only in U.S. dollars. However, such an approach may result in losing export opportunities to competitors who are willing to accommodate their foreign buyers by selling in their local currencies. This approach could also result in the non-payment by a foreign buyer who may find it impossible to meet U.S. dollar-denominated payment obligations due to a significant devaluation of the local currency against the U.S. dollar. While losses due to non-payment could be covered by export credit insurance, such "what-if" protection is meaningless if export opportunities are lost in the first place because of a "payment in U.S. dollars only" policy. Selling in foreign currencies, if FX risk is successfully managed or hedged, can be a viable option for U.S. exporters who wish to enter and remain competitive in the global marketplace.

Key Points

- Most foreign buyers generally prefer to trade in their local currencies to avoid FX risk exposure.
- U.S. SME exporters who choose to trade in foreign currencies can minimize FX exposure by using one of the widely used FX risk management techniques available.
- The sometimes volatile nature of the FX market poses a risk of unfavorable FX rate movements, which may cause significantly damaging financial losses from otherwise profitable export sales.
- The primary objective of FX risk management is to minimize potential currency losses, not to profit from FX rate movements, which are unpredictable.

Characteristics of a Foreign Currency-Denominated Export Sale

Applicability

Recommended for use (a) in competitive markets and (b) when foreign buyers insist on purchasing in their local currencies.

Risk

Exporter is exposed to the risk of currency exchange loss unless FX risk management techniques are used.

Pros

Enhances export sales terms to help exporters remain competitive. Reduces non-payment risk because of local currency devaluation.

Cons

Cost of using some FX risk management techniques. Burden of FX risk management.

FX Risk Management Options

A variety of options are available for reducing short-term FX exposure. The following sections list FX risk management techniques considered suitable for new-to-export U.S. SME companies. The FX instruments mentioned below are available in all major currencies and are offered by numerous commercial banks. However, not all of these techniques may be available in the buyer's country or they may be too expensive to be useful.

Non-Hedging FX Risk Management Techniques

The exporter can avoid FX exposure by using the simplest non-hedging technique: price the sale in a foreign currency in exchange for cash in advance. The current spot market rate will then determine the U.S. dollar value of the foreign proceeds. A spot transaction is when the exporter and the importer agree to pay using today's exchange rate and settle within two business days. Another non-hedging technique to minimize FX exposure is to net foreign currency receipts with foreign currency expenditures. For example, the U.S. exporter who receives payment in pesos from a buyer in Mexico may have other uses for pesos, such as paying agent's commissions or purchasing supplies in pesos from a different Mexican trading partner. If the company's export and import transactions with Mexico are comparable in value, pesos are rarely converted into dollars, and FX risk is minimized. The risk is further reduced if those peso-denominated export and import transactions are conducted on a regular basis.

FX Forward Hedges

The most direct method of hedging FX risk is a forward contract, which enables the exporter to sell a set amount of foreign currency at a pre-agreed exchange rate with a delivery date from three days to one year into the future. For example, U.S. goods are sold to a German company for €1 million on 60-day terms and the forward rate for "60-day euro" is 0.80 euro to the dollar. The U.S. exporter can eliminate FX exposure by contracting to deliver €1 million to its bank in 60 days in exchange for payment of $1.25 million. Such a forward contract will ensure that the U.S. exporter can convert the €1 million into $1.25 million, regardless of what may happen to the dollar-euro exchange rates over the next 60 days. However, if the German buyer fails to pay on time, the U.S. exporter will still be obligated to deliver €1 million in 60 days. Accordingly, when using forward contracts to hedge FX risk, U.S. exporters are advised to pick forward delivery dates conservatively or to ask the trader for a "window forward" which allows for delivery between two dates versus a specific settlement date. If the foreign currency is collected sooner, the exporter can hold on to it until the delivery date or can "swap" the old FX contract for a new one with a new delivery date at a minimal cost. Note that there are no fees or charges for forward contracts since the FX trader makes a "spread" by buying at one price and selling to someone else at a higher price.

FX Options Hedges

If an SME has an exceptionally large transaction that has been quoted in foreign currency and/or there exists a significant time period between quote and acceptance of the offer, an FX option may be worth considering. Under an FX option, the exporter or the option holder acquires the right, but not the obligation, to deliver an agreed amount of foreign currency to the FX trader in exchange for dollars at a specified rate on or before the expiration date of the option. As opposed to a forward contract, an FX option has an explicit fee, a premium, which is similar in nature to the premium paid for insurance. If the value of the foreign currency goes down, the exporter is protected from loss. On the other hand, if the value of the foreign currency goes up significantly, the exporter simply lets it expire and sells the foreign currency on the spot market for more dollars than originally expected; although the premium would be forfeited. While FX options hedges provide a high degree of flexibility, they can be significantly more costly than FX forward contracts.

GEOPHYSICAL, ENVIRONMENTAL, SUSTAINABILITY

Operating globally creates an array of geophysical exposures that can vary dramatically depending upon where you are, the seasons, weather, catastrophic occurrences and the local infrastructures ability to deal with all those circumstances and keep business and people safe.

Typically, *geophysical* is defined as the science devoted to the study of the physical properties and processes of geological phenomena, including fields such as meteorology, oceanography, and seismology. Weather will typically be indirectly involved in these fields of concern as it is impacted by their circumstances and events in both directions—being impacted and impacting. For example, the oceans are the major drivers of weather conditions worldwide. A volcano discharge can impact weather conditions for huge areas of its activity. Meteorological events can impact flooding, erosion, accessibility, functionability, and so on.

When viewing these fields in protecting your organizations assets, they are typically analyzed together with a comprehension of their mutual impacts.

Events such as but not limited to earthquakes, tsunamis, floods, hurricanes, typhoons, monsoons, El Nino, extremes in cold and hot temperatures, and high and low humidity are but a few of the yearly events that occur that can wreak devastation to both peoples, cities, and the businesses in those areas.

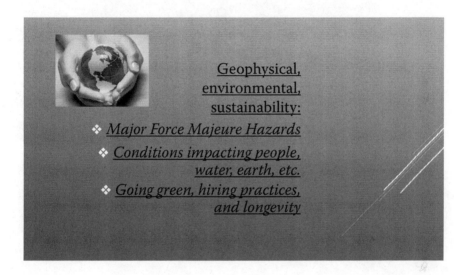

Geophysical, environmental, sustainability:
* *Major Force Majeure Hazards*
* *Conditions impacting people, water, earth, etc.*
* *Going green, hiring practices, and longevity*

These geophysical areas of concern are usual concerns involved in site selection and must become important considerations in making those ultimate choices. Additionally, there are typically seasonal variations of likelihood that will also come into the decision-making process. Most companies employ personnel who specialize in these areas particularly in certain industries like energy, transportation, and with the military.

Going Green

The *Green Initiative* has as its main objective the offsetting of greenhouse gases emitted by human activities that can range from complex industrial production processes to simply driving a car, with reforestation projects in riparian areas that need to be recovered.

Corporations with high ethics and socially responsible cultures will have green initiatives in their organizations and then built into their global supply chains. In the last 20 years, these "green initiatives" have expanded globally. The case is made as follows as offered by a number or organizations such as "Business Plans" (bplans.org):

> There will always be costs involved in going green. The key is the opportunity to make those expenditures pay-off in the long run. In operating your own business, determining your "return on investment" is always top of mind when making decisions. One big decision for your company is whether to implement green initiatives, and that includes everything from reducing waste, refuse discharge, energy consumption to wasting less paper. "When considering the decision to 'go green,' look at both the short and long term results of green initiatives and, chances are, you'll discover a number of benefits."
>
> When considering the decision to "go green," look at both the short and long term results of green initiatives and, chances are, you'll discover several benefits.
>
> Creating a favorable impact to your business is important. Those benefits go well beyond feeling good about helping the environment. They also directly impact your business, both in terms of reducing your operational

costs, as well as streamlining your processes by making them more efficient.

Green assessments are a good way of starting any green programs. Before you implement your new green plan, you'll also have the chance to assess how your company is currently performing and audit where all your money is being spent. That way, you can make the best adjustments possible when you enact your green plan.

Business Benefits

All companies want to drive risk and cost from their global supply chains. Other than decreasing your business's impact on the environment, *one of the biggest benefits of implementing green initiatives is cutting costs,* particularly in regards to energy consumption. In addition to cutting your utility costs, it's also quite possible to cut down on the costs of transportation, water, waste disposal, and paper.

As you enter the supply chain the goal is to extend your internal green initiatives to your suppliers, vendors, channel partners, contract manufacturers and customers.

Your biggest savings in these areas will depend on the kind of company you operate. Those with manufacturing plants might find the most savings come from altering their energy utilization, waste disposal plans or internal energy controls but this can be difficult to change if they handle multiple chemicals every day, which often require strict and limited disposal options.

On the other hand, a business like a restaurant may optimize their cost savings by sourcing ingredients locally, which can not only help the environment, but also maximize efficiency. After all, it's more efficient to get ingredients from a local market rather than placing orders and waiting for food deliveries.

While there are many economic benefits to implementing green initiatives, there are a few costs as well. For instance, if you decide to start using solar power to provide some of your company's energy, there will be an upfront cost to get an estimate for the solar panels, get them installed, and ensure they're working properly—and it's not cheap. In the long run, you'll probably save money on your energy bills, but it may not be a savings you see right away.

The Pros and Cons

Here's a quick look at some of the pros and cons, from an economic standpoint, of going green:

Pros

- Buying local can be cheaper than importing, plus you are helping the environment by reducing the fuel needed to bring something from far away to your company.
- You may be able to get grants and other incentives for taking your company green, which can put money back in your pocket.
- Going paperless can save lots of money on the printing out of documents.

Cons

- Alternative fuel sources can be expensive. While wind power, for example, is better for the environment than fuel provided by coal, it's simply not cost-effective for most businesses.
- If you own a small business, you may not be able to negotiate the favorable deals on green energy that bigger companies can facilitate.
- Going paperless means everything is saved on your company's computers. If they are damaged or stolen, it could cost you a lot of money to reconstruct those records, and you could be out even more money if the lack of documents leads to less reimbursement from the insurance company.

All these "cons" can easily be managed successfully to mitigate their negative impacts on your organization and the overall green initiatives.

In the end, sometimes a greater economic cost can be worth it, if it's going to win you long-term benefits or the goodwill of customers. *Remember, green initiatives are not always about the bottom line, but about helping your company do the right thing.*

Business Plans for Going Green

We have developed a specific strategy for companies building green into their global supply chains:

1. Obtain senior management's commitment to build green into the global supply chain. It will take resources and funding. Create a P&L with a ROI. Senior management will also dictate to all business owners and fiefdom managers to build green initiatives into their annual business and strategic plans with potential goals.
2. Create a green leadership with a committee structure.
3. Assess where you are at. External consultants who provide this expertise are available to provide technical support.
4. Create Green SOPs and Protocols.
5. Train personnel on what they need to do and their role in any green initiatives.
6. Develop an expectations list that gets worked into all agreements with vendors, suppliers, contract manufacturers, carriers, service providers and channel partners. Create very specific guidelines on what you want these companies to do as respects to going green. Larger relationships in the Tier One and Two categories can move forward to their own vendors and suppliers the same expectations.
7. Create a "green audit" function that reports into senior management how the company is doing both specifically by vertical and overall.

"Going green" is a big trend right now, and it's not going anywhere. Draw up a social responsibility statement that you can disseminate to your employees, post on your website, and use in your marketing. "Marketing your business as a green business can also establish you as a 'business that cares' in the local community."

With your marketing plans, in particular, you can stress your dedication to green initiatives, and that in itself can potentially attract new customers. The same marketing can also establish you as a "business that cares" in the local community.

This sort of recognition is priceless in terms of public relations. The Green Business Bureau reports that more and more customers are looking specifically for environmentally conscious companies to do business with. When you develop a reputation for doing the right thing in terms of the environment, then you will naturally gain status with potential clients.

Going green demonstrates you care about more than just your bottom line, since as we've already established, it can cost more to go green than it can to stick with traditional business approaches. Let's look at some examples of environmentally conscious companies whose green practices have really put them on the map.

Some Corporate Examples of Going Green

Blue Tiger International

- Panasonic: Though you probably know Panasonic as a manufacturer of TVs and cameras, which are business-to-consumer products, it's also a big business-to-business company as well. That's where its green practices are really paying dividends. As a maker of lithium ion batteries used for electric cards and in-seat airline entertainment systems, Panasonic has gained a big following because of its green practices. It makes sustainable products that other companies can feel good about using.
- Chipotle: The category of upscale quick-service restaurants has been growing like wildfire since the recession. People want a nicer meal than they can get at McDonald's, but they don't want to spend too much money. Chipotle has benefited from this trend, but it's also booming because it has been a leader in environmental concerns. The chain only uses meat that is free of hormones and antibiotics, and it has called on other restaurants to do the same, though it costs a lot more.

- Starbucks: The world's largest coffee chain has long been vocal about its support for recycling, reusing, and supporting sustainability. One of its biggest projects has been encouraging people to employ reusable cups. Paper coffee cups create a huge amount of waste each year; even the ones that are recyclable aren't always tossed in the right can. Starbucks has long offered reusable heavy-duty coffee mugs, but it also recently introduced lower-key plastic cups designed to look like the iconic original Starbucks cup (for those who really like to advertise that they went to the coffee shop that morning). Although Starbucks is a chain, this is one reason why people are eager to announce their allegiance to it. Starbucks has also installed low-flow water fixtures, and uses low-energy light bulbs as additional ways to help the earth.
- Adidas: The sneaker and clothing label undertook a major initiative a few years ago to decrease its worldwide energy use by 15 percent by next year. That has helped boost its image both in the U.S. and abroad, and the company has hired experts in every country where it operates to help figure out how best to wean itself off energy. Adidas has even undertaken a project in Brazil that encourages people to donate their old athletic shoes, which are made into sustainable energy sources.
- Blue Tiger International: The premier global supply chain and risk management consulting firm engaged green initiatives just over four years ago, to align itself with many of their clients "green" programs and saw an immediate financial benefit in its global efforts in this regard. Employees and managers became engaged and many initiatives were extended into their personal lives expanding the entire green initiative.

Personnel Considerations

Not all benefits of your green initiatives are easy to quantify. In general, some surveys have reported that employees are generally happier with their job, and the company as a whole, when the company is doing as much as possible to be "green." This is most likely because green initiatives typically motivate employees to work as a team toward a common purpose. *As you establish your business as a green company, people will start to recognize you as such, and it can also help with recruiting new employees.*

Prove You Are Eco-Friendly

Leaders across the globe have made LEED the most widely used green building rating system in the world with 1.85 million square feet of construction space certifying every day. LEED certification provides independent verification of a building or neighborhood's green features, allowing for the design, construction, operations and maintenance of resource-efficient, high-performing, healthy, cost-effective buildings. LEED is the triple bottom line in action, benefiting people, planet and profit.

While there are several benefits to implementing green initiatives, don't let it be all talk. After you create a plan to implement your green initiatives, follow through. Get ISO 14001 certified as well as LEED certified. In doing so, you may also increase your chances of getting recognized for your efforts and even win awards, once again extending your brand's notoriety.

Going green is entirely up to you, but consider this: If your competitors are implementing green initiatives, then that's one way they've differentiated themselves from you in a way that reflects poorly on your company. Not to mention, there seems to be more regulation requirements each day. *Don't fall behind the times—start implementing a green plan that makes sense for your company, and start reaping the many benefits as soon as possible.*

The ISO 14001 Environment Management System (EMS) standard is an internationally recognized environmental management standard which was first published in 1996. It is a systematic framework to manage the immediate and long term environmental impacts of an organization's products, services and processes.

CORPORATE REPUTATION BRANDING AND MARKETING

When any occurrence happens to an organization overseas they are at risk of exposure to damage to reputation, branding, marketing, and even intellectual property rights (IPR) concerns.

There are insurance mitigation and risk transfer products and services available.

> A trusted reputation is the cornerstone of long-term business success. This has been recognized since the earliest days of commerce, but has never been more true than today, in the multimedia environment of the digital age.
>
> **Alliaz and RIMS**

A business's value and its future success are now directly linked to its reputation, not only in the eyes of the media but also as viewed by other stakeholders such as customers, nongovernmental organizations (NGOs), shareholders and regulators, not to mention the company's employees themselves. Despite the best preventative plans and procedures, an unintentional error or infringement can quickly escalate into a major incident, drawing the full spotlight of the media—with potentially disastrous results for an unprepared company unless a robust and prompt response is professionally deployed.

The protection and defense of a company's reputation has therefore become a major challenge for businesses worldwide, especially those built around consumer brands or subject to the media spotlight. Yet, while much time and effort is invested in protecting the physical assets of companies, often far less attention is given to protecting the company's reputation— which some regard as the most precious asset in the long term.

Any listed corporation runs the risk to almost 80%–90% that they will face a major crisis in any five-year business cycle.

To meet this challenge, a number of insurance companies provide various levels of protection, such as but not limited to Allianz Global Corporate & Specialty (AGCS), which has devised a unique insurance solution, in conjunction with a leading media analysis consultancy and a select panel of international communications consultancies.

Reputational Risk Exposures

Several business elements can leave your company exposed to the threat of reputational risk:

- Certain property and liability related exposures
- Marketing and sales effort blunders
- Health and safety incidents
- Operational crises and events (e.g., pollution)
- Product recalls and quality control errors
- Business and service interruptions
- Financial losses and irregularities
- Negative associations with third parties
- Management and governance topics
- Governance, legal, and regulatory investigations
- Circumstances and allegations over business practices
- Ethical violations and challenges

IPR (INTELLECTUAL PROPERTY RIGHTS)

IPR includes areas of

- Enforcement programs focus on criminal, civil, customs, and border enforcement areas.
- Patent programs focus on administration, budgeting, examination procedures and industrial procedures.
- Trade secret programs focus on protection, enforcement, and discussion on developing awareness of trade secret protection.
- Trademark programs focus on administration, budgeting, examination procedures, recruitment, training and treaty protocol.
- Copyright programs focus on exclusive rights, fair use, liability, cutting-edge issues in emerging technologies, and piracy.

UNITED STATES PATENT
AND TRADEMARK OFFICE
GLOBAL INTELLECTUAL PROPERTY ACADEMY

Training becomes an integral part of any company's defensive actions to mitigate risk. One such organization is the Global Intellectual Property Academy (GIPA), which provides training on a variety of intellectual property topics. The topics primarily focus on enforcement, patents, trade secrets, trademarks, and copyrights as well as trade-related aspects of intellectual property.

Many internationalists involved with IPR management will concede that China is a major concern for all companies in the West.

MICHAEL JORDAN WINS TRADEMARK CASE IN CHINA

THE RULING COULD BE A LANDMARK CASE IN TRADEMARK LAW IN CHINA.

Nyima Pratten with contributions from Aria Hughes
December 8, 2016

BEIJING—China's Supreme People's Court today ruled in favor of former basketball superstar Michael Jordan in a trademark case against Qiaodan Sports, a popular Chinese sportswear company.

The court overturned a previous ruling, meaning that the Chinese brand will be forced to give up its trademark registration on the Mandarin character version of Jordan's name, Qiaodan. But the court upheld a ruling allowing the firm to use the Romanized version of Qiaodan.

Jordan took his case to China's highest court last April after unsuccessfully pursuing the case in China's lower courts. In 2012, the athlete initially requested the State Administration for Industry and Commerce to suspend the sportswear company's use of multiple trademarks, including Qiaodan, the Chinese transliteration of his surname, the number 23, and logo, which bears a resemblance to the silhouette of a basketball player.

Qiaodan Sports, which was founded in 1984, released a statement on its web site today acknowledging the ruling and declaring its intention to respect the court's decision and fulfill the intellectual property protection of the brand.

"I am happy that the Supreme People's Court has recognized the right to protect my name through its ruling in the trademark cases. Chinese consumers deserve to know that Qiaodan Sports and its products have no connection to me. Nothing is more important than protecting your own name, and today's decision shows the importance of that principle," Jordan said.

"Over the past three decades, I have built my reputation and name into a globally recognized brand. From my earliest playing days in the NBA, through my trip to China last fall, millions of Chinese fans and consumers have always known me by my Chinese name, 'Qiaodan.' Today's decision ensures that my Chinese fans and all Chinese consumers know that Qiaodan Sports and its products have no connection to me," he added.

"I respect the Chinese legal system and look forward to the Shanghai Court's ruling on the separate naming rights case," Jordan said.

The positive outcome for Jordan could herald a shift in judgments on intellectual property rights in China. International companies such as Under Armour and Apple have fallen foul of lax trademark laws in China this year alone.

"It's an interesting case because China gives trademarks to whoever files for that trademark first, so on the face of things Jordan wouldn't necessarily expect to have finally won this suit before China's supreme court. But, I think this is also a case of the Chinese government becoming increasingly serious about protection of consumer rights," said Benjamin Cavender, principal at China Market Research Group.

"This was a clear case of a company misleading consumers about the origins of the brand and I think allowing Jordan to take back the usage rights to the Chinese character version of his name supports the idea that they do not want to see consumers getting taken advantage of by companies that make false claims," said Cavender.

Jordan, who is popular in China, had argued that the Chinese sportswear company had put his legal right to use his name in the country in jeopardy.

"In the end, I think companies need to be very aggressive about registering their trademarks in China or another firm may take advantage by getting there first," said Cavender.

Counterfeit textile and apparel products made in China have been particularly burdensome to U.S. textile and apparel companies and have been reported to affect U.S. textile sales in China, in the United States, and in third world markets. Since joining the World Trade Organization (WTO) in December 2001, China has strengthened its legal framework and amended its IPR and related laws and regulations to comply with the WTO Agreement on Traded-Related Aspect of Intellectual Property Rights (TRIPS). Despite stronger statutory protection, China continues to be a haven for counterfeiters and pirates.

Early trademark registration is essential in China. While the United States confers trademark rights to the first party to use a trademark in commerce, China has established a "first-to-file" system that grants trademark rights to the party that first applies to register the trademark. Registration and enforcement are handled by the Trademark Office of the State Administration of Industry and Commerce (SAIC). For optimum trademark protection, it is also advisable to register trademarks in other locales within "Greater China" (Hong Kong, Macau, Taiwan, and Singapore) and in nations bordering China.

In China, the National Copyright Administration (NCA) is responsible for copyright administration and enforcement. The NCA is also responsible for nationwide copyright issues, including investigating infringement cases, administering foreign-related copyright issues, developing foreign-related arbitration rules and supervising administrative authorities.

Though administrative remedies are available, the NCA generally encourages complainants to use the court system due to lack of personnel.

Unlike the patent and trademark protection, copyrighted works do not require registration for protection. Protection is granted to individuals from countries belonging to the copyright international conventions or bilateral agreements of which China is a member. However, copyright owners may wish to voluntarily register with the NCA to establish evidence of ownership, should enforcement actions become necessary.

State Administration for Industry and Commerce (SAIC)
Trademark Office
8 Sanlihe East Road
Xicheng District
Beijing, 100820
Tel: 86-10-6803-2233
Fax: 86-10-6801-0463
Website: http://www.saic.gov.cn (Chinese language only)
National Copyright Administration of China (NCAC)
85 Dongsi Nan Dajie
Beijing, China 100703
Tel: 86-10-6512-7869 or 6527-6930
Fax: 86-10-6512-7875

Contacting the U.S. Embassy for Resources in China. The U.S. Embassy in Beijing and the U.S. Foreign Commercial Service (FCS) offices in China can provide in-country information about IPR enforcement resources. Companies can go directly to the U.S. Commercial Service at DOC.gov.

To competently perform rectifying security service, two critical incident response elements are necessary: information and organization.

Robert E. Davis

4

Supply Chain and Logistics

The supply chain has a huge logistics component that interfaces with every aspect of the business model. Purchasing and sales are controlled by utilization of the correct INCO Terms, freight purchasing, and inclusive of trade compliance management.

E-commerce is growing at a rate of over 20% annually and will continue to expand into global markets and become a dominant means of reaching consumers.

INCO TERMS

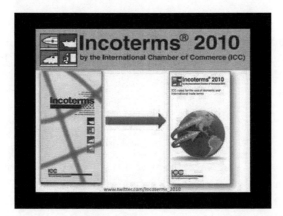

INCO Terms are part of an international contract of purchase and/or sale between two or more parties and determine a point in time and trade where the responsibility and liability transfers from the seller to the buyer. I hold true that they can be considered the most important term in the international transaction.

INCO Terms are often misunderstood by customer service, operations, finance, and logistics personnel. This fact makes *INCO Terms training* a very important step in understanding risk and spend issues in international business.

What we need to know about INCO Terms, as advised by the International Chamber of Commerce (iccwbo.org):

Basic History

INCO Terms were created in 1936 with the purpose of providing a set of international rules for the interpretation of the most commonly used trade terms in foreign trade. Since then, ICC expert lawyers and trade practitioners have updated them six times to keep pace with the development of international trade.

Pre–Inco Terms Rules

INCO Terms was first conceived by the International Chamber of Commerce (ICC) in 1921, and brought to fruition with the first INCO Terms rules in 1936. This set in motion a long and vibrant history of INCO Terms publications that continues today with INCO Terms 2010, which went into effect on January 2011. A Trade Terms Committee with the assistance of the ICC National Committees developed the first six rules in 1923: FOB, FAS, FOT, FOR, Free Delivered CIF, and C&F, which were the precursor of what would later be known as the INCO Terms rules.

Why Revise the INCO Terms?

As commercial practices, types of goods and transports, and international laws evolve, the INCO Terms rules need to be regularly updated by experienced international experts.

Some Significant Revisions

1980—FCA was introduced in order to provide a rule that dealt with the frequent case where the reception point in maritime trade was no longer the ship's rail (the traditional FOB point) but rather a point on land, prior to loading on board a vessel, where goods were stored in a container for subsequent transport by sea or by different means of transport in combination.

1990—The clauses dealing with the seller's obligation to provide proof of delivery permitted a replacement of paper documentation by EDI messages provided the parties had agreed to communicate electronically.

2000—(1) The placing of the export clearance under FAS on the seller (previously on the buyer); (2) the specification of the seller's obligation to load the goods on the buyer's collecting vehicle and the buyer's obligation to receive the seller's arriving vehicle unloaded under FCA.

How Are the INCO Terms Revised?

Revision of the INCO Terms rules is initially entrusted to a small global Drafting Group. The group is formed by experts from various nationalities chosen for their extraordinary contribution to international commercial law and to the International Chamber of Commerce along the years.

- Revised drafts are then circulated broadly and internationally through ICC National Committees, with the resulting comments and suggestions channeled back to the Drafting Group.
- The final draft, once approved by the ICC Commission on Commercial Law and Practice, is submitted for adoption by the ICC Executive Board.
- The broad international consultation aims to ensure that official ICC products possess an authority as representing the true consensus viewpoint of the world business community.

Rules for Any Mode or Modes of Transport

- EXW, Ex Works—"Ex Works" means that the seller delivers when it places the goods at the disposal of the buyer at the seller's premises or at another named place (i.e., works, factory, warehouse, etc.). The seller does not need to load the goods on any collecting vehicle, nor does it need to clear the goods for export, where such clearance is applicable.
- FCA, Free Carrier—"Free Carrier" means that the seller delivers the goods to the carrier or another person nominated by the buyer at the seller's premises or another named place. The parties are well advised to specify as clearly as possible the point within the named place of delivery, as the risk passes to the buyer at that point.

- CPT, Carriage Paid To—"Carriage Paid To" means that the seller delivers the goods to the carrier or another person nominated by the seller at an agreed place (if any such place is agreed between parties) and that the seller must contract for and pay the costs of carriage necessary to bring the goods to the named place of destination.
- CIP, Carriage and Insurance Paid To—"Carriage and Insurance Paid To" means that the seller delivers the goods to the carrier or another person nominated by the seller at an agreed place (if any such place is agreed between parties) and that the seller must contract for and pay the costs of carriage necessary to bring the goods to the named place of destination.

  The seller also contracts for insurance cover against the buyer's risk of loss of or damage to the goods during the carriage. The buyer should note that under CIP the seller is required to obtain insurance only on minimum cover. Should the buyer wish to have more insurance protection, it will need either to agree as much expressly with the seller or to make its own extra insurance arrangements.
- DAT, Delivered at Terminal—"Delivered at Terminal" means that the seller delivers when the goods, once unloaded from the arriving means of transport, are placed at the disposal of the buyer at a named terminal at the named port or place of destination. "Terminal" includes a place, whether covered or not, such as a quay, warehouse, container yard or road, rail or air cargo terminal. The seller bears all risks involved in bringing the goods to and unloading them at the terminal at the named port or place of destination.
- DAP, Delivered at Place—"Delivered at Place" means that the seller delivers when the goods are placed at the disposal of the buyer on the arriving means of transport ready for unloading at the named place of destination. The seller bears all risks involved in bringing the goods to the named place.
- DDP, Delivered Duty Paid—"Delivered Duty Paid" means that the seller delivers the goods when the goods are placed at the disposal of the buyer, cleared for import on the arriving means of transport ready for unloading at the named place of destination. The seller bears all the costs and risks involved in bringing the goods to the place of destination and has an obligation to clear the goods not only for export but also for import, to pay any duty for both export and import and to carry out all customs formalities.

Rules for Sea and Inland Waterway Transport

- FAS, Free Alongside Ship—"Free Alongside Ship" means that the seller delivers when the goods are placed alongside the vessel (e.g., on a quay or a barge) nominated by the buyer at the named port of shipment. The risk of loss of or damage to the goods passes when the goods are alongside the ship, and the buyer bears all costs from that moment onwards.
- FOB, Free On Board—"Free On Board" means that the seller delivers the goods on board the vessel nominated by the buyer at the named port of shipment or procures the goods already so delivered. The risk of loss of or damage to the goods passes when the goods are on board the vessel, and the buyer bears all costs from that moment onwards.
- CFR, Cost and Freight—"Cost and Freight" means that the seller delivers the goods on board the vessel or procures the goods already so delivered. The risk of loss of or damage to the goods passes when the goods are on board the vessel. The seller must contract for and pay the costs and freight necessary to bring the goods to the named port of destination.
- CIF, Cost, Insurance and Freight—"Cost, Insurance and Freight" means that the seller delivers the goods on board the vessel or procures the goods already so delivered. The risk of loss of or damage to the goods passes when the goods are on board the vessel. The seller must contract for and pay the costs and freight necessary to bring the goods to the named port of destination.

  The seller also contracts for insurance cover against the buyer's risk of loss of or damage to the goods during the carriage. The buyer should note that under CIF the seller is required to obtain insurance only on minimum cover. Should the buyer wish to have more insurance protection, it will need either to agree as much expressly with the seller or to make its own extra insurance arrangements.

Incoterms® 2010 Quick Reference Chart

Services	Rules for any mode or modes of transport							Rules for sea and inland waterway transport			
	EXW Ex works	FCA Free carrier	CPT Carriage paid to	CIP Carriage and insurance paid to	DAT Delivered at terminal	DAP Delivered at place	DDP Delivered duty paid	FAS Free alongside ship	FOB Free on board	CFR Cost and freight	CIF Cost, insurance and freight
	Who pays	Who pays	Who pays	Who pays	Who pays	Who pays	Who pays	Who pays	Who pays	Who pays	Who pays
Export packing	Seller	Seller	Seller	Seller	Seller	Seller	Seller	Seller	Seller	Seller	Seller
Marking and labeling	Seller	Seller	Seller	Seller	Seller	Seller	Seller	Seller	Seller	Seller	Seller
Block and brace	1	1	1	1	1	1	1	1	1	1	1
Export clearance (license, EEI/AES)	Buyer	Seller	Seller	Seller	Seller	Seller	Seller	Seller	Seller	Seller	Seller
Freight forwarder documentation fees	Buyer	Buyer	Seller	Seller	Seller	Seller	Seller	Buyer	Buyer	Seller	Seller
Inland freight to main carrier	Buyer	2	Seller	Seller	Seller	Seller	Seller	Seller	Seller	Seller	Seller
Origin terminal charges	Buyer	Buyer	Seller	Seller	Seller	Seller	Seller	Buyer	Seller	Seller	Seller
Vessel loading charges	Buyer	Buyer	Seller	Seller	Seller	Seller	Seller	Buyer	Seller	Seller	Seller
Ocean freight/air freight	Buyer	Buyer	Seller	Seller	Seller	Seller	Seller	Buyer	Buyer	Seller	Seller
Nominate export forwarder	Buyer	Buyer	Seller	Seller	Seller	Seller	Seller	Buyer	Buyer	Seller	Seller
Marine insurance	3	3	3	Seller	3	3	3	3	3	3	Seller
Unload main carrier charges	Buyer	Buyer	4	4	Seller	Seller	Seller	Buyer	Buyer	4	4
Destination terminal charges	Buyer	Buyer	4	4	4	Seller	Seller	Buyer	Buyer	4	4
Nominate on-carrier	Buyer	Buyer	5	5	5	5	Seller	Buyer	Buyer	Buyer	Buyer
Security information requirements	Buyer	Buyer	Buyer	Buyer	Buyer	Buyer	Seller	Buyer	Buyer	Buyer	Buyer
Customs broker clearance fees	Buyer	Buyer	Buyer	Buyer	Buyer	Buyer	Seller	Buyer	Buyer	Buyer	Buyer
Duty, customs fees, taxes	Buyer	Buyer	Buyer	Buyer	Buyer	Buyer	Seller	Buyer	Buyer	Buyer	Buyer
Delivery to buyer destination	Buyer	Buyer	5	5	5	5	Seller	Buyer	Buyer	Buyer	Buyer
Delivering carrier unloading	Buyer	Buyer	Buyer	Buyer	Buyer	Buyer	Buyer	Buyer	Buyer	Buyer	Buyer

Notes: 1—Incoterms® 2010 do not deal with the parties' obligations for stowage within a container and therefore, where relevant, the parties should deal with this in the sales contract. 2—FCA Seller's Facility: Buyer pays inland freight; other FCA qualifiers, Seller arranges and loads pre-carriage carrier and pays inland freight to the "F" delivery place. 3—Incoterms® 2010 does not obligate the buyer nor must the seller to insure the goods, therefore this issue be addressed elsewhere in the sales contract. 4—Charges paid by buyer or seller depending on contract of carriage. 5—Charges paid by seller if through Bill of Lading or door-to-door rate to buyer's destination.

* Incoterms® is a registered trademark of the international chamber of commerce. This document is not intended as legal advice but is being provided for reference purposes only. Users should seek specific guidance from Incoterms® 2010 available through the international chamber of commerce at www.iccbooks.com.

The proper choice of INCO Terms reduces risk and spend in the global supply chain. The ICC, located in Paris, with offices and affiliations worldwide, is a great resource for companies operating in international trade. The ICC has numerous products and services that can help importers and exporters navigate the pitfalls of international supply chains.

Alongside INCO Terms are related issues that also need to be navigated:

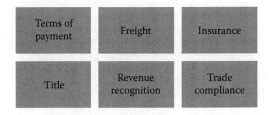

Terms of payment	Freight	Insurance
Title	Revenue recognition	Trade compliance

A full comprehension of the relationship between the INCO Term choice and these six concerns have always have to be considered when making logistics choices.

SOURCING AND PURCHASING

Americans, appetite for inexpensive consumer goods had created a huge demand for global sourcing. Over the past 30 years this has grown to a huge complex of countries, products, and resources coming into the United Sates from foreign markets. Although all products are "touched," consumer items represent the greatest commodity.

> **Landed cost**: The total cost of a landed shipment including purchase price, freight, insurance, and other costs up to the port of destination. In some instances, it may also include the customs duties and other taxes levied on the shipment.

One of the most important aspects of making the decision to source globally is the impact on "landed cost." Many companies only view the acquisition cost or unit purchase price in the decision-making process. They lose sight of all the additional costs in the import process, such as freight, duty, and taxes, all of which can add significant expense to the purchase price. Ultimately adding in all the landed cost considerations could impact the decision-making process on where to source products: domestically, internationally, and, if overseas, where?

The goal of most international businesses is to be competitive in the scope of their global trade activities. Service providers and carriers who support the management and partner with their client's global supply chains can impact their clients' landed costs.

Establishing landed costs for the products that a company handles can be difficult and convoluted. All businesses that import or export need to understand what the total cost of goods is for what they are buying or selling. In order to accurately calculate the landed cost, all factors beyond the obvious primary price must be considered. Calculating landed cost is critical in understanding what a product actually costs and therefore what it can be sold for. This impacts margin considerations, which are one of the most important aspects of managing a business in a competitive market place. Thinking globally, reducing costs are the mantra of growth, profits, and survival.

Landed cost is the total cost of a product once it has arrived at the buyer's door. This list of components that are needed to determine landed costs include the original price of the item (converted to U.S. dollars), all customs brokerage and handling charges, complete freight and shipping costs, customs duties, tariffs, taxes, insurance, packaging costs, and surcharges. Not all of these components are present in every shipment, but all that are must be considered part of the landed cost.

- **Purchase price of goods** – variable depending on unit price and quantity (converted to USD)
- **Buying Agents** – variable depending on level of service
- **Consolidation** – securing LCL shipments into larger shipments and coordinating freight from several suppliers
- **Transportation** – variable, depending upon choice of mode, carrier, freight rate negotiation and sur charges
- **Duty** – variable percentage of the value Customs put on your goods, typically origin and HTS# factored
- **Tax** (Goods and Services Tax or Value Added Tax) – $ variable percentage of (The Customs value of cost of goods + freight + insurance + Customs duty)
- **Insurance Charges, typically referred to as cargo insurance**
- **Customs Clearance, ISF, etc.**
- **Storage** and deconsolidation
- **Inland Freight** – from inbound gateway to final destination
- **Demurrage** – if applicable when potential delays occur

The calculation and model for landed cost must be customized to the variables in every supply chain. As a generic model, for imports outlined above, which list can be utilized, recognizing that specific nuances in each supply chain might modify how this list would appear.

The choice of INCO Term will be a major factor in how costs, responsibilities, and risks are distributed between the seller and the buyer. It is critical that both parties when agreeing to the use of an INCO Term that they understand the risks and cost they are assuming in the transaction.

Importers into the United States by ocean freight typically buy FOB outbound gateway. In China this might be written as FOB Shanghai. This means that the buyer will assume all risks and costs once the goods are placed onboard the ocean-going vessel in the port of export from overseas. The key words being "risks and costs." The risks are pretty straightforward. They are principally physical loss or damage from an external cause during transit. Sinking, fire, stranding, water damage are a few of the risks covered.

Marine insurance, when thoroughly written offer "all risk," "warehouse to warehouse" coverage for the buyer at specific terms and a rate of premium to be agreed. Marine insurance can be considered a necessary evil, but certainly is prized when loss or damage occurs. However, it adds cost to the transaction.

Marine insurance is another line item in the list outlined earlier that impact landed costs. The buyer must take a few steps to impact landed costs:

- Utilize comprehensive freight forwarders, customhouse brokers, and professional service providers that have expertise and can lend value in the global supply chain.
- Pay attention to the choice of INCO Term. Many choices give you control over various aspects of the supply chain where you can impact cost.
- Review each line item in the landed cost model to determine where costs can be reduced. An example would be the HTS (Harmonized Tariff Schedule) number. Is it correct? Is there a more correct option that would lower duties and taxes? Another example is freight costs. Can a more competitive freight option be offered with less expensive rates?
- Mode of transportation will impact landed costs. Many times, air freight is utilized when ocean freight could be a less expensive option. This means better demand planning and coordination between purchasing/sales/sourcing and the logistics department handling the transportation choices. Included in this area is control over the suppliers with setting more realistic expectations, tighter control over order status and communications, contractual obligations, and penalties for nonperformance.
- Reducing the opportunity for demurrage costs, which can be severe and expensive. This typically happens when a tight reign over the logistics process and all sorts of contingencies are managed proactively.
- Inland freight expenses can be included in the ocean freight, where there is an opportunity to leverage the larger ocean freight spend to obtain a better inland freight cost.
- Utilization of technology and reducing "paper" in the transaction can reduce ISF (Importer Security Filing), Customs clearance, and handling charges when automation replaces repetitive human handling of import and export documentation.
- When freight does not have to be consolidated or deconsolidated and can be shipped in units direct from suppler to point of end use, will also reduce costs.
- Negotiating away with surcharges such as PSS (peak season surcharge), GRI (general rate increase), and BAF (bunker adjustment factor) will also favorably impact landed costs.

- By leveraging your spend with a minimum number of service providers and carriers will place a focus on a smaller group of partners that will maximize the opportunity to obtain a better deal. You may not want to place your eggs all in one basket, but a new theory is, if you do, then watch that basket carefully or at least reduce the number of baskets you work with.
- Develop a partnership mentality with all your service providers and carriers. Favor tenured relationships and work as a team in your supply chain. Loyalty and a working mind-set will have true rewards in lieu of short-term benefits.

Another huge area that is impacting landed costs are the utilization of numerous programs such as but not limited to NAFTA and other free trade agreements, foreign trade zones, and bonded warehouses, which can substantially lower and impact the cost of buying, selling, and shipping goods globally.

Just understand that studying landed cost and all the variables, and then applying some sound cost reduction principles can make your supply chain operate significantly more competitive.

LOGISTICS

Foreign Trade Zones (FTZs)

An excellent opportunity exists for companies competing in global trade to leverage their business model through reviewing their supply chain process options. One such option is the utilization of foreign trade zones, not only here in the United States but also available in most key trading centers of the world.

The primary reasons for considering FTZs in your global supply chain are

- Ease of moving freight to and from the borders between trading countries
- Reduction or elimination of duties, taxes, and other import/export costs
- Financial incentives on a local level
- Lowering the landed costs in your import/export business model

There are other advantages that may be unique to geographic location and industry verticals. The automotive industry, which is dominated by foreign competition, has been one of the major industry verticals to capitalize on FTZs here in the United States, as well as many countries abroad.

The basic FTZ model allows a company to manufacture or assemble finished products in a country abroad utilizing local labor for the specific purpose of reducing landed cost. For example, a German car manufacturer sells a car in the United States for $50,000. Duties and taxes can add another $1,500 to the landed cost. Through the utilization of an FTZ strategically placed here in the United States, that German car manufacturer could import parts from Germany and utilize U.S. labor to work in its U.S. factory. Upon entry into the U.S. FTZ, duties and taxes on the parts are deferred. Upon assembly completion, the car leaves the FTZ for ultimate sale and that is when the deferred portion of the tax and duties are paid. If labor costs make up 50% of the $50,000 value, only $25,000 is applicable to duty and tax. This model reduces the landed cost by approximately $750 per vehicle. Compare this against 200,000 units and the savings could amount to over $150,000,000 annually.

There are numerous other benefits to FTZs that would need to be considered in any business model assessment. In the preceding FTZ model, the utilization is assembly and manufacturing. More recent options allow high volume importers to have their goods pass through FTZs as they transit from the gateway through to their warehouses and distribution facilities. This step allows a "weekly manifest clearance," which reduces entry fees and merchandise processing fees (MPFs) creating a significant financial savings impacting landed cost.

Bonded Warehouses

Bonded warehouses is a supply chain option which allows importers and exporters to temporarily hold freight where the import is deferred along with duties, taxes and other import costs, until such time the goods enter the country or are exported from that country.

For example, let's take a Cleveland-based electronics distributor importing consumer music products from Asia, totaling over 200m annually with an average duty rate of 4.5%. Approximately 20% of the products are then re-exported to Canada, the Caribbean and Latin America.

Under their current supply chain model, they utilize CBP's drawback program to obtain up to 99% of the duties and taxes for those exports, totaling 1.8m annually. While drawback is a great program, it can be arduous and costly to manage and takes time to receive the refund of duties.

As an alternative, the distributor can apply to CBP to make their warehousing facility a bonded location. This will defer the duties and taxes to goods entering the warehouse to the point in time they are extracted from the facility. Additionally, the 20% of the goods that are re-exported come in and leave the USA in bond and no duties or taxes are obligated to be paid providing significant savings in supply chain costs.

Bonded warehouses provide additional benefits, but the operations permitted in a bonded warehouse are limited so sorting, weighing and repacking. If the goods enter the warehouse as a widget, they must leave as a widget.

Free Trade Agreements

Free trade agreements (FTAs) offer numerous advantages to both importers and exporters. Currently the United States participates in over thirteen agreements with numerous ones pending. The most well-known FTA is the North American Free Trade Agreement (NAFTA), which underwent considerable scrutiny in the 2016 presidential debates. When the three participating countries—United States, Canada, and Mexico—trade with one another, there is a serious reduction of duties and taxes on qualified goods and merchandise. The most advantageous benefit of FTAs are the free movement of goods between participating countries where duties and taxes are reduced or eliminated.

"Near sourcing" is the recent phenomenon in global trade where trade is coming back to our NAFTA partners or here in the United States. FTAs provide a more level playing field, particularly against lower Asian-based sourcing models.

Lower freight costs, reduced lead times, and elimination of duties and taxes can very easily make manufacturing in Mexico or in a U.S.-based FTZ a much more competitive option, thereby leveraging critical logistics business model options.

Logistics Bidding

Logistics managers and all those involved in running global supply chains periodically put their freight purchasing out to bid. This bidding process, usually accomplished on an annual up to every two to three years, keeps incumbents sharp and allows new players to show what they can do.

In the majority of these RFPs (request for proposals), *price drives the process*. I have managed over 300 RFPs and have developed a formula based on an alternative concept that looks at the process from a different angle and can produce better results.

The key ingredient in this process is to remove price from the equation until the very end of the RFP process. Carriers, freight forwarders, custom-house brokers, 3PLs (third-party logistics), and others would much prefer to be judged on their capabilities first and price second. This process does not minimize the importance of price, as we all know how critical that element is in running cost-effective supply chains. This process just removes that consideration to a later point in the overall RFP process, which can ultimately provide better results to the importer, exporter, or domestic shipper. This process ensures that the service providers can perform and meet the customer's expectations before price enters the equation.

The ten steps of the bidding process are

1. Engage senior management in the process, as their support is critical to any changes with major suppliers and vendors.
2. Do your homework and know what qualified transportation providers exist that could be potentially included in the RFP.
3. Create a committee of internal stakeholders with vested interests and/or impacted by supply chain issues.
4. Identify and prioritize your supply chain needs and create a list of these key factors.
5. Reach out to your initial RFP participants list. This might be from three to five or as many as thirty, to determine their readiness to respond to your RFP.
6. Following the initial interview and/or meeting, create a "response inquiry form" or "scorecard" for them to complete.
   Sample control areas may include
   a. Technology (PO Management System)
   b. EDI Interface
   c. Tracking and Tracing
   d. Experience of Customer Service and Operations Team
   e. Foreign Office and Agency Structure
   f. Trade Compliance Officers
   g. Risk and Insurance Issues

    h. Consolidation Capabilities
    i. Drayage Costs
    j. Domestic Distribution
    k. Demurrage and Ancillary Charges
    l. Transition Management
    m. Free Time Allowances
    n. Value Add Services
    o. Quarterly Business Reviews (QBRs)

This partial listing creates two needed control points: one identifying needs that are both generic and specific to your supply chain, and the second beginning the setup of a "scorecard" to assist in the evaluation stage of the RFP process.

Freight score card (Sample) Rank (1–5)	Alto Shipping	XYZ Freight Forwarding	Delivery International	From A to B Logistics	China Transportation Inc.
Customer service	4	5	3	3	5
Technology	3	4	3	5	5
Pricing strategy	5	4	4	5	5
Consolidation services	5	4	5	4	4
Transit time	3	3	4	3	4
Trade compliance management	4	4	4	3	5
Total	24	24	23	23	28*

* From a metrics perspective, China Transportation offers a more comprehensive response to the RFP analysis

7. Have the RFP participants respond to the list above and outline how they differentiate themselves in all those areas important to you. The scorecards created can utilize an "operations analysis" format allowing metrics to enter the formula that is necessary to obtain a clearer and more comprehensive perspective.

8. Run "dog and pony" shows with all RFP participants. This usually results in moving the participant list to a smaller group, maybe two to three. Now price enters into the equation.

Benchmarking is an important responsibility of logistics and supply chain managers. When benchmarking is done with diligence, you will know what the range of pricing should come in at.

At this point, you will be certain that the final list of providers has all the capabilities, skill sets, and resources to meet your needs list. Hopefully, there will be some "value adds" that will also provide real benefit and enhancement. This is when you are now having the finalists compete with one another over price. Keep in mind that price by itself is not fixed and has other variables that will carry weight, such as but not limited to

a. Transit times
b. Minimum volume commitments
c. Origin and destination ports
d. Surcharges and ancillary costs
e. What services are included in the overall base and adjusted pricing schedules
f. Payment terms
g. Consolidation and deconsolidation services
h. Chassis and drayage requirements
i. Technology interface

These are but a few of the variables that need to be clearly identified and when done responsibly will allow for a true apples-to-apples comparison between the finalists.

9. Bring the committee back together, review the pricing, make comparisons to the scorecards, raise a debate, then make the best choice balancing cost, risk, and service capabilities.
10. Create a transition strategy with the favored party and execute, allowing for flexibility, tweaking. and rethinking as the change or repositioning takes place.

Many experienced logistics and supply chain managers will utilize their own sensibilities in the decision-making process and this is okay as another factor in the overall RFP process exercise. When sensibilities, relationships, and metrics are all brought into the RFP process it will allow for the best opportunity to get the most favored results.

An additional consideration should include trade compliance management as a key factor in determining the final selection. When you are successful at negotiating the best price—if the goods cannot make it through customs successfully or you are faced with government agency scrutiny—the benefit of that great price will be significantly diminished.

Freight

When freight is managed as a commodity, there is little opportunity for long-term, more successful, and profitable relationships in the purchasing of global transportation services between shippers of cargo, service providers, and carriers.

When we have "sustainable relationships" we capitalize on the following:

- Better working relationships between shippers, service providers and carriers. We all want to work in an atmosphere in global trade where we would describe our relationships in the global supply chain as excellent. This allows for less stress and overall better results.
- Longer tenured relationships. Changing of service providers and carriers frequently is disruptive and costly and never a preferred option. Everyone engaged in the supply chain does better in longer-term relationships.
- Reduction of risk and spend in the global supply chain. When the relationships work well we always see a direct relationship to the reduction of costs and risks as goods move through the supply chain cycle both domestically and internationally.
- Consistency in pricing and service agreements. If we always have spikes and steep changes in our business models, no one will be happy in your company, and managing operational issues will be very difficult all the time. The preference always is to have a smooth, more rhythmic path in the business model to follow so changes are not large or small but even out on a more consistent basis.
- Less angst in day-to-day business dealings. Angst causes stress. Stress causes anger. Anger causes bad decisions. Bad decisions usually produce bad results. Eliminate angst and have more success.
- Ability to work through problems and bringing quicker resolve to issues at hand. Global supply chain managers face challenges every day. Even in the best managed supply chains, problems will occur daily. They need to be resolved quickly. Good working relationships open the door to quick, swift, and comprehensive resolution.
- Access to better security and trade compliance initiatives. Every international supply chain requires due diligence, reasonable care and supervision and control to meet various government security and trade compliance regulatory requirements. Better working relationships foster a more secure and compliant environment to ship freight in.
- Better access to and utilization of technology resources. Technology will always enhance business relationships with all the benefits of expediency, efficiency, exactness, and information flow.

- Creating a partnership approach. I cannot emphasize enough the importance of establishing a mind-set between all the parties to approach matters on a partnership basis. This is the best course of action to achieve trust and confidence between shippers, service providers, and carriers. Trust and confidence become hallmarks and allows all parties to both compromise and benefit from all the actions that impact one another in the day-to-day movement of freight throughout the world.

The following key factors create a path to better relationships and sustainability.

Transparency—Share all the information necessary to get the job done right. Eliminate a mind-set of clandestine behavior, working through "secret passage ways or working in the shadows" mentality. Put up all the data. Shippers should outline clear expectations. Service providers and carriers should outline clear capabilities. A no-nonsense, direct, no-BS approach works best.

Valuing favored incumbents—Always be loyal to companies that have serviced you well. Loyalty is what you expect from your customers, so give it to your vendors and suppliers, when well deserved. If you need to conduct an RFP and bring in competition, always give some advantage to a favored incumbent.

Be open and honest, consistently—The value of being open falls in line with being transparent, but also adds on elements of frankness, truthfulness and honesty. People trust those who are honest, period. When you are more honest, you can get more done as people better respect you and are more open to participate and go the extra yard to get better results.

Be creative—The challenges of global trade can be daunting. Every approach will require a potentially different and maybe even a new revolutionary approach. Creativity is a necessary element of being able to compete successfully, as creativity opens the door for problem resolution, progressive options, aggressive tactics and, at times, advanced/rebellious/extreme/mutinous behaviors.

Make sure "insurance" is addressed—Claims are inevitable if you ship goods internationally. If you want to see a relationship go south quickly, have an unresolved claim. Liability for loss and damage in global trade is an area of major concern. All parties in the supply chain—shipper, service provider, and carrier—need to know where their risk begins and ends, and if there is a claim, where indemnification will originate. When this is left unclear, it creates frustration between the parties and eventually a loss of confidence, which leads to a breakdown in any opportunity for sustainability between the parties. Address insurance concerns proactively, comprehensively and with transparency, and you will mitigate future relationship issues.

Quality relationships drive sustainability, which is always a preferred option in global trade.

Reducing International Supply Chain Costs without Beating Up Your Carrier or Service Provider

Every supply chain executives' primary responsibility is to find ways to reduce risk and cost in their global supply chain. Typically, negotiations take place on an annual basis between principal shippers and the carriers and service providers that move their freight. These negotiations can be intense and sometimes even a slugfest, where freight rates are reduced and, depending upon your perspective, either not enough and way too much!

Shippers have other options and courses of action to reduce supply chain costs without impacting freight rates. In my consulting practice, this is often the challenge we face in meeting customer expectations.

The first task in most companies is to assess to what extent a company's demand planning systems are in synch with logistics. Too often they are not and, as a result, supply chain risks and costs increase. There will be too many LCL (less-than-container load) orders and not a dominant mix of FCL (full-container-load) shipments, which based on a cubic measurement, is a less expensive option, maybe as much as 20% to 30%.

Demand planning also includes understanding inventory needs and placing replenishment orders on a timely and lean basis.

Many times, airfreight can be as much as 18 times more expensive than ocean freight. But airfreight has to be utilized sometimes because product needs to be moved more expeditiously then ocean freight allows. Too often this is not a strategic planning event but a negative consequence of poor planning or lack of coordination between the various fiefdoms and verticals in any organization responsible for inventory, replenishment, purchasing, demand planning, supply chain, and/or logistics.

The best run supply chains have a tight and intense collaborative process between all stakeholders in the supply chain to make sure they understand how every decision made has a potential impact on how well freight will move from supplier to destination or from manufacturer to customer.

Technology that allows an interface between all the internal stakeholders, service providers, carriers, and suppliers is an integral component of any well-run global supply chain. For inbound logistics, these systems, often referred to as "PO management systems," can become an invaluable tool in the arsenal to create very defined efficiencies in supply chain operations.

Technology can become an extension of a corporation's operating platforms or a "value-add" available from quality service providers, 3PLs, and carriers. The technology creates timely information transfer, transparency, lean practices, and accountability between all the vested parties involved in the international transaction.

Every global supply chain will have disruptions occur each year; some very unexpected, others more predictable. These disruptions can add both risk and expense to any import and export operation. In managing these exposures proactively, global supply chain executives can create contingency plans in advance producing the strategies and action steps that will mitigate these risks and costs.

Another strategy in reducing logistics costs that has proven successful is by reducing the number of service providers and carriers. Some experts on international transportation caution companies in putting all their eggs in one basket. I have found while that concern is real, it can be managed. If you reduce the number of providers and carriers to better leverage spend and place more eggs in the basket, then you better watch and manage that basket. Over the last five to seven years as more companies have pressed hard to run leaner supply chain operations, we have moved them into a reduction of carrier and service providers. The benefits outweigh the potential consequences. For very large companies with diverse and expansive supply chains, we may move 90% of their spend into one solution to leverage spend and the balance with another option to have some other player involved and engaged as a contingency option.

Another option available to shippers whose freight originates in Southern Asia is what is referred to as the sea–air combination. Freight is shipped to various Middle Eastern cities, such as Dubai, and then transferred to the airfreight mode that moves it to Europe, and North and South America. Cost savings on freight of as much as 45% are available with arrival time reduction moved from 28 days to as little as 14 days. This allows larger bulk moves to occur from Asia to the West with costs significantly less than airfreight direct, but at transit times almost cut in half. The sea–air option both reduces cost and risk to the global supply chain while creating a value add of efficiency and convenience well worth taking a look at by those who operate global supply chains.

When a Major Carrier Goes Bankrupt: Managing the Aftermath and Future Loss Preventive Measures

The recent events surrounding the bankruptcy of South Korea's Hanjin Shipping has resonated with serious negative overtones impacting global supply chains in almost every industry and worldwide: vessels and cargoes are being seized, crew members are facing arrest and prosecution, senior executives are being pursued by government authorities, and freight are being held from meeting delivery and destination requirements.

In my consulting practice, we faced numerous and intense concerns raise by purchasing, import, traffic, and supply chain executives who were dealing with major delays and potentially more serious cargo issues in their import and export operations. Our recommendations provide a blueprint for what steps a supply chain professional can do when this scenario arises. Hanjin was not the first and it will not be the last serious bankruptcy in the world of international business.

Have a plan, as follows:

Assessing the damage is the first step to mitigation. Evaluate where your shipments are and which ones may cause negative impacts. Prioritize which shipments require immediate attention and which ones are not of looming concern.

Communicate the issues internally to all the stakeholders. Even though it may be embarrassing that you are facing this concern, a direct, nononsense approach to your colleagues and vested interests, including customers ,will always prove to be a more successful "take the high road" tactic with numerous benefits. This allow others with vested interests to take necessary action as early as possible.

Mitigate your circumstances. Once your assessment is done, create a strategy and action plan that can mitigate your overall issues. Moving freight with other carriers, pulling freight where possible, and air freighting small balances to fulfill immediate needs are but a few of mitigation techniques.

Read the documentation. Reviewing the back of an ocean bill of lading to determine your rights and the carrier's liabilities, something you would do "on a cold and lonely night, while sitting on the john" becomes a necessary evil and component of the overall risk management evaluation and assessment process. Bills of lading, INCO Terms in the sale or purchase, purchase orders (POs), commercial invoices, carrier contracts, and forwarding and brokerage agreements will all impact responsibility, liability, and your eventual course of action.

Speak with an attorney. At an early point, if you have an internal counsel they should be advised of the situation. The nature of this maritime event will call for access to maritime and admiralty expertise, often obtained from a few of the specialty law firms engaged in these international and global trade arenas.

Loss Prevention

Many supply chain executives proactively mitigated their situation with Hanjin, way before the actual bankruptcy event on August 31, 2016. They followed sound supply chain principals of due diligence, reasonable care, and proactive engagement, as follows:

Manage your carrier contracts. Many supply chain executives secure a competitive and comprehensive freight contract with carriers and service providers. But is does not end there. You have responsibilities to stay abreast of industry events, circumstances with critical supply chain partners, and supply chain information flows. Although many were caught by surprise on August 31, others anticipated the potential of the event and began moving freight to other carriers late in the spring. Reading the daily reports and monthly columns in a magazine like the *American Shipper* is a critical component of any prudent supply chain's executive information flow.

Also, *understand at a granular level the responsibilities and liabilities* of both parties in all the bills of lading, contracts, and agreements you have signed. Be proactive and not just reactive once a potential problem has arisen. Keep in mind that short-term delays are not the only problem. Seizures can create significantly extended delays, and the more time freight sits idling, it is exposed to greater threats of loss and damage from water, handling, theft, and pilferage.

Diversify your supply chain carrier options. Many import and export executives have found that diversifying your carrier options and spreading the freight, therefore the risk over several variable contracts may offer a great risk management strategy.

Create a contingent strategy. Executives who proactively assess potential threats or conduct a SWOT (strengths, weaknesses, opportunities, and threats) analysis will be in a better position when disruption occurs. This affords a futuristic profile of potential supply chain disruptions and then allows management to create contingent strategies so if they occur you already have a plan of action that will fold out and seriously mitigate the impact of any potential supply chain problems.

The Hanjin bankruptcy was considered one of the largest in all of global trade with current and futuristic negative consequences to supply chains all over the world. Rumors tell of other carriers with similar financial woes.

Those supply chains with aggressive mitigation strategies will have the best chance to survive these type events with the least amount of disruption. Those supply chains that proactively create risk management programs that prevent these disruptions from gaining any traction before they even occur are often in the best positions to provide resolution way before any negative event.

It becomes a choice; put your head in the sand and deal with what comes your way or manage risk and maximize the best opportunity to protect your supply chain for growth, profit, and to successfully run domestic, import, and export operations!

GLOBAL E-COMMERCE

In 2017, the growth of e-commerce during the past ten years has been nothing less than phenomenal. E-commerce now dominates consumer sales here in the United States and is working its way into most countries on all six continents.

E-commerce in the United States has both replaced and supplemented retail sales distribution outlets, which have been the main place where consumers find and buy everything they need. E-commerce has always been in the 5% to 10% range of sales for most companies, but it has now grown in some industry verticals to more than 50% of overall sales volume, and is still growing. Any company not thinking about e-commerce as a factor in overall sales both at the consumer and commercial levels will be left behind.

The following recommendations are based upon my experiences in helping companies enter into or further develop e-commerce markets globally.

E-commerce is expanding globally and becoming an integral part of every company's global strategy.

1. Determine the viability of your product sales country by country before committing to any larger initiative. Test marketing and local resources can assist you in this evaluation stage. International e-Commerce sales are very different than U.S. domestic e-commerce sales.
2. Determine whether your website can be accessed on a local basis. In many countries, the population has none or limited access to external Internet resources. Additionally, in many countries, the best access may be through Internet trading platforms such as Amazon, Alibaba, Newegg, and Overstock.
3. You need to investigate an array of issues when selling into a new market overseas:
    a. Competitive products and their approach to sales in that country
    b. Legal issues regarding your products sale in that country
    c. Any intellectual property rights (IPR) issues of concern
    d. Import documentation requirements
    e. Other government agency requirements, such as their equivalent to our Department of Agriculture; Food and Drug Administration; Federal Communications Commission; Bureau of Alcohol, Tobacco, Firearms, and Explosives; and so on
    f. Packing, marking, and labeling requirements
    g. Review of denied party listing
    h. Website entry (your own or third party)
4. In the United States, we have a mature and competitively based infrastructure for domestic distribution of products to consumers in home deliveries. Although this system in the United States works well, it is a huge component of the overall costing model, and e-commerce sellers are always looking for less expensive and more

timely options. Internationally, this has become more of a challenge, as many countries do not have a mature domestic infrastructure for sales and deliveries to consumers and their homes. The importance of resolving this issue is cost. E-commerce sales only work when the cost of shipping from origin to destination is significantly minimized. Amazon has made it very clear its potential use of drones as a delivery mode. Testing began in 2015 and continues into 2017. Some companies in North America are looking at driverless vehicles, and in 2016, Budweiser successfully tested commercial driverless vehicles on routes in Colorado.

Amazon drone in testing mode.

Budweiser driverless test vehicle in Colorado.

5. Globally those companies who have been successful in e-commerce sales in an array of foreign countries have mastered the cost of

logistics and distribution. This is best obtained following this outline of action steps:

a. Partner with service providers who have defined expertise in e-commerce sales and distribution.

b. Consolidate shipments in the United Sates and ship overseas in larger bulk orders. This will reduce the cost of the international leg.

c. Obtain all the necessary information proactively on packing, marking, labeling, and documentation requirements.

d. Make sure the websites you are utilizing contain all the necessary shipping information and costs relative to the buyers' need to be made aware of.

e. Arrange for competitively priced customs clearance along with the "last mile" delivery requirements. This is much easier said than can be accomplished. Customs clearance costs and home deliveries are typically an expensive component of the overall sale or purchase. E-commerce companies have had to be very creative to resolve these costing and business process concerns for low cost consumer items typically handled individually.

f. Those companies like Amazon and Alibaba in countries such as China have been successful in developing low cost and expedient processes to handle this area successfully for their e-commerce clients.

g. Structure systems for return shipping need to be planned, as they will potentially be cumbersome and add cost to your e-commerce global supply chain.

h. When starting e-commerce capabilities, do beta testing in every foreign market before committing to a final deployment of resources and capabilities. This helps to

　i. Work out the bugs in advance

　ii. Reduce initial costs if the process does not work

　iii. Create a better foundation before diving in fully

i. Make sure payment options are addressed in advance and tested before offering the product for sale.

j. Trade compliance concerns for all export and import regulations still apply in e-commerce sales, as it does in all commercial transactions. Areas such as but not limited to the following all need to be addressed:

i. Denied parties search
ii. HTSUS (Harmonized Tariff Schedule of the United States) and Schedule B numbers
iii. Documentation
iv. Record keeping
v. Origin determination
vi. Export license requirements

k. Protect the electronic "collecting order information." When you are ready to sell internationally, make sure that essential customer information does not fall through the cracks. Use these tips to create clear, customer-friendly payment descriptions:

i. Label your fields as clearly as possible and provide alternatives to help customers who do not speak English (or for whom it is not the primary language). For example, "First" could be displayed as "First Name/Given Name" and "Last" as "Last/Family Name/Surname."
ii. Add a third or even fourth line to the address field to accommodate longer international addresses.
iii. Add a field for "Country."
iv. Insert a "Country Code" field above or to the left of the "Telephone Number" field.
v. Ask for "State/Territory/Province" rather than just "State."

    vi. Request "ZIP/Postal Code" rather than just "ZIP Code." Also, if your system uses the "ZIP Code" entry to automatically fill in the "City" and "State" fields, you might want to offer separate fields for "ZIP Code" and "Postal Code." Many other countries use five-digit postal codes, and a postal code keyed into the "ZIP Code" field could gum up the customer's address.

l. Act with due diligence in avoiding exposure to fraud. Best practices include:

    i. Accepting online payment, even with established credit cards, exposes the seller to some risk. According to Cybersource's 2010 11th Annual Online Fraud Report (cybersource.com), U.S. merchants continue to reject three times as many international orders (7.7%) as domestic orders (2.4%). Merchants reject orders they have reason to believe may be fraudulent. But there is some good news: The same survey notes that actual international e-commerce fraud rates for U.S. merchants fell from a 2008 average of 4.0% of total online orders to 2.0% in 2009. The drop can be attributed in part to firms that use various methods to safeguard against unauthorized use of credit cards.

    ii. Although the trends in online fraud are encouraging, U.S. firms need to continue to be vigilant. This is true especially in countries that used to be considered "safe" for e-commerce retailers. The U.S. Commercial Service has a long history of reports from U.S. exporters about online fraud coming from China and Nigeria, but now fraudulent activity is occurring in places where it was once rare. The U.S. Commercial Service is now receiving complaints about fraudulent activity in Singapore and the Scandinavian countries, among other previously low-risk countries.

    iii. The key is to address fraud concerns proactively with due diligence and reasonable care standards. This will reduce fraud opportunity and maximize the best outturns.

TRADE COMPLIANCE

Trade compliance management is typically associated with import and export activity. Trade compliance is typically defined as the process by which companies that ship goods or operate internationally work to strategize to comply with all laws and regulations of the countries operating in or goods being shipped to and from. For example, the U.S. Customs Service (CBP.gov) is the entity responsible for checking all incoming cargo for compliance with U.S. import rules and regulations. The goal of an importing country's legal checkpoint is to freely accept legally qualified goods while enforcing rules consistently.

Shipping companies that transit products internationally have both moral and practical responsibilities when exporting to a particular country. It is the duty of exporting companies to comply with foreign country trade regulations to promote U.S. goodwill and to avoid unnecessary expenses. International shippers should be trade compliant solely because it is the responsible and ethical practice to follow.

Additional benefits of compliance are that it can "save you money, prevent negative publicity, and improve your overall business efficiency." Trade compliance can also be utilized to leverage opportunities associated with Foreign Trade Zones, Free Trade agreements and Bonded Warehouses.

Buying Internationally: Import Supply Chain

The United States imports over $200 billion a month, which represents over 70% of the global supply chain. The inbound supply chain may consist of purchasing components, raw materials, and finished goods as well as returned merchandise and receiving samples. Many importers focus on the landed cost of a product, typically the duties and costs to clear shipment and deliver, without taking into account other factors that present risk in the inbound supply chain such as partnering with a customs broker who will help the importer be compliant, making certain goods are properly marked with the country of origin, avoiding copyright infringement, and so on. Understanding the U.S. import regulations and working with a knowledgeable customs broker can reduce the risks of importing.

Duties and Fees

The amount of duty to be paid on an import shipment is determined by a number of factors including the country of origin, the harmonized tariff number, the circumstances of import, and the use of the goods. Most duty is paid ad valorem, based on the value of the goods. However, in some

AMERICAN SHIPPER

TRADE COMPLIANCE MANAGEMENT: NOT JUST A NECESSARY EVIL BUT A TOOL TO LEVERAGE THE GLOBAL SUPPLY CHAIN

Thomas A. Cook

The events of 9/11 significantly integrated "Trade Compliance Management" to the forefront of every global supply chain's operation and ultimately a necessary component of successful importing and exporting.

Now, some 15 years later, the functionality of global trade include trade compliance in every aspect of how goods and services move in international business.

Almost every company, service provider, and carrier engaged in global supply chain operations has at least one dedicated person serving in the responsibilities of trade compliance or it is one of the many "hats" one wears in logistics and transportation management.

Many supply chain professionals view trade compliance as an intrusion of government regulation and oversight and to an extent that could be a truism. Many see it is a necessary evil related to managing the impact of terrorism and keeping our country secure and safe.

Irrespective of your view, it is a reality of expense, time, and resources that we all must manage in our global supply chain operations, purchasing and export global reach.

Having said all that, many corporations have embraced trade compliance as a corporate silo, that managed successfully, can reduce risk and cost, as well as improve effective operations and performance.

Key edicts of trade compliance are

- Due diligence
- Reasonable care
- Supervision and control
- Engagement

Government agencies such as, but not limited to, Customs Border and Protection, Bureau of Industry and Security, and the Departments of State and Treasury are all very proactively engaged in regulations, operating guidelines, and legal controls on how companies manage their import and export operations.

They require companies to follow these guidelines as principal importers and exporters along with the companies providing forwarding, brokerage, and related transportation services to follow the four edicts outlined above as general guidelines, followed by a vast amount of regulatory minutia that needs to be incorporated into their global business operations.

Of the 50,000-plus companies here in the United States involved in global trade, a small number have embraced trade compliance as a tool to gain competitive advantage.

Examples of trade compliance areas that can provide operational or financial benefits:

- Access to government programs such as C-TPAT and FAST that move freight more quickly through the borders
- Less opportunity for fines, penalties, and the hassles involved in delays and seizures
- Correct utilization of the Harmonized Tariff Codes to lower duties
- Access to foreign trade zones
- Utilization of bonded warehouses
- Leveraging of free trade agreements
- Utilization of technology

There are numerous methods on how companies can change their mind-set about trade compliance and utilize it both as a necessary point of control, but more importantly as a method to reduce both risk and spend and thereby providing certain advantages.

Trade compliance managers, and supply chain and logistics professionals need to maintain a regular flow of information, intelligence, and regulatory updates to be in the best position to maintain operational excellence in their global supply chains.

Successful trade compliance managers can contribute to:

- Keeping companies out of regulatory cost and entanglements
- Reduce risk in the global supply chain
- Provide competitive options in how goods and services move internationally
- Impact bottom line on profits and margins

Successful trade compliance managers need to be contemporary in the information flow necessary to maintain the challenges they face in handling the multitude of compliance and regulatory concerns not here in the United States, but in all the countries they import from or export to.

Periodicals and information sources such as the *American Shipper* (www.AmericanShipper.com) offer a very reliable and contemporary flow of data that can be very useful in leveraging trade compliance opportunities.

Accessing key important government websites (www.cbp.gov; www.bis.doc.gov) is another option.

Continuing education and training are also critical elements of any trade compliance program and the process of learning contemporary options in importing and exporting. The American Management Association (www.amanet.org) and the National Institute for World Trade (www.niwt.org) are two excellent options for certificated public and in-house instruction, coaching, and educational capabilities specializing in international business and supply chain.

In August 2016, *American Shipper* hosted an Executive Summit in NYC, "The Data Driving Next Generation Logistics," which provided a remarkable interface with many trade professional offering timely intelligence on utilizing technology in your global supply chain, for which trade compliance is a big part of.

> Conferences and seminars offer excellent intense information flows that can be of immediate and of long-term value along with the networking and professional colleague interface that always prove beneficial.

instances there may be compound duties paid, such as with shoes. There is a tariff rate paid on the value of the import shipment and an additional charge per pair of shoes. In addition to duties there are merchandise processing fees, which are assessed by Customs as a document fee, and harbor maintenance fees, which are assessed on ocean shipments. These duties and fees are the more obvious part of landed cost and somewhat easier to nail down provided the importer can properly classify their product to obtain the correct duty rate. Tariff classification can be a bit tricky though and what may seem obvious may not be as clear as first thought in reviewing the 99 chapters of the Harmonized Tariff Schedule of the United States (HTSUS).

Harmonized Tariff Classification

Importers are responsible to provide Customs with the correct harmonized tariff classification for each item entered on the import declaration. This is done through the guidelines established in the HTSUS. Importers are also responsible to understand the principles of classification so they can oversee the advice offered by their customs brokers.

Many importers rely on their internal experts to take a look at the HTSUS and make a determination as to the correct classification. This is usually done by an online search resulting in jumping directly to the classification, choosing a number closest to the product and following through with the applicable tariff rate.

While this makes sense in using internal experts who have the best understanding of the properties of a product, those internal experts may not understand there are specific rules to follow in classification. The General Rules of Interpretation (GRIs), Section Notes and Chapter Notes are the map legend for the HTSUS.

Arriving to the classification that makes the most common sense is actually a noncompliant practice and represents a failure to meet reasonable care. For example, an importer has a shipment of relief maps, which is a flat map that has raised surfaces. A quick look at the alphabetical index will easily identify maps in Chapter 49 under Printed Maps. However, a closer look at the Chapter 49 chapter notes will identify that relief maps are specifically excluded from Chapter 49 (Printed Books, Newspapers, Pictures and other Products of the Printing Industry; Manuscripts, Typescripts and Plans) and should be classified in Chapter 90 (Optical, Photographic, Cinematographic, Measuring, Checking, Precision, Medical or Surgical Instruments and Apparatus, Clocks and Watches). While the duty rate is free for either tariff classification, the tariff classification is still incorrect. Failure to properly supervise the classification process can result in false information being tendered to customs. This false information is legally viewed as a false statement.

Country of Origin Marking

Importers are responsible to ensure that all merchandise is properly marked with the country of origin upon entry into the United States. Import documentation must also indicate the proper country of origin on all shipments, as a separate invoice requirement.

Many importers are not aware of the specific requirements for marking goods imported into the United States. Imported goods must be marked to indicate the country of origin to the ultimate purchaser of the goods. For most articles, with the exception of textile apparel products, the country of origin is the country of growth, manufacture, or production.

Unless the product is exempt, permanent marking is required on every imported article. In cases where the item itself cannot be individually marked, customs may accept the marking on the outer carton.

For those instances in which Customs believes imported merchandise does not comply with the legal requirements, Customs may issue a redelivery notice, requiring the importer to redeliver all of the imported items, previously released, back to Customs and may do so up to thirty days from the date of Customs release. As another option, Customs may release the goods to the importer and require the importer to properly mark the goods and submit a sample of the item to Customs to prove the marking was completed.

Trade Compliance

The Bureau of Customs and Border Protection (CBP) operates under 19CFR (Code of Federal Regulations). In addition to Customs regulations, importers are required to follow the regulations of any other government agency that may be involved in the import clearance process. For example, an importer of retail household items may find itself responsible for Food and Drug Administration (FDA) requirements in addition to CBP regulations for the appliances that may be sold in its stores.

Many importers use a customs broker to assist with the customs clearance process. While an importer is permitted to clear their own goods into the United States, the customs broker provides a level of expertise in communicating with the CBP electronically as well as in their understanding of tariff classification, valuation, and country of origin determination, and other factors involved in the customs process. The customs broker facilitates the import process and a knowledgeable and qualified broker can be an importer's best asset in navigating the import clearance process.

Customs requires importers and their service providers to exercise reasonable care in the clearance process. Failure to do so may result in fines, penalties, and other consequences including shipment delays.

Reasonable Care Standard

Under the reasonable care standard an importer

- Should seek guidance from customs for proper compliance using the formal rulings program.
- Should consult with "qualified experts" like a customs broker or attorney, or a consultant specializing in customs law.
- If using a broker, must provide such broker with full and complete information sufficient enough for the broker to properly make an entry (import declaration) or for the broker to provide advice as how to make entry.
- When appropriate, obtain analyses from accredited labs to determine technical qualities of an imported product.
- Use in-house employees like counsel, a customs administrator, or if valuation is an issue, a corporate controller, who has experience and knowledge of customs laws, regulations, and procedures.
- Must follow any binding ruling requested and received from customs.
- If importing any textile or apparel product, ensure that the products are accompanied by documentation, packaging, and labeling that are accurate as to its origin.

- Cannot classify own identical merchandise or value own identical transactions in different ways.
- Must notify Customs when receiving different treatment by Customs for the same goods in different transactions or at different ports.
- Must examine entries (import declarations prepared by the broker to determine accuracy in classification and valuation.

Failure to exercise reasonable care may result in:

- Two times the loss of duties for negligence
- Four times the loss of duties for gross negligence
- 20% of the entered value of the shipment for nonrevenue loss
- 40% of the entered value of the shipment for nonrevenue loss

The concept of reasonable care means the importer must be able to evidence to Customs how they have implemented reasonable care into the clearance process. This may be through documented and verifiable procedures on the import process, training presentations including training rosters, recordkeeping checklists, and a review of entry files. The importer should seek guidance from Customs for proper compliance using the formal rulings program and should consult with "qualified experts" like a customs broker or attorney, or a consultant specializing in customs law.

Typical questions that an importer may have regarding an import shipment may range from classification of one or multiple items; how to treat specific circumstances of import such as an item returned after having been repaired or an item being temporarily imported into the U.S.; whether an import meets the preference criteria of a specific trade agreement or is eligible for special tariff treatment; and how to value a product correctly. An importer will be meeting their reasonable care responsibility by contacting Customs or a qualified expert to assist with researching these questions and applying the information as part of the entry process.

Customs publishes informed compliance manuals that cover a number of different aspects of the customs clearance process as well as how to classify specific commodities. Topics of these publications include valuation, classification of aircraft parts, tariff classification, country of origin marking, and children's wearing apparel.

If using a broker, the importer must provide such broker with full and complete information sufficient enough for the broker to properly make an entry (import declaration) or for the broker to provide advice as how to make entry. Importers are not required to use a customs broker. If a customs broker is used, the importer must provide sufficient information to the broker so the broker can properly advise the importer. It should be noted this also helps the broker fulfill their requirement to meet reasonable care as well. The importer should disclose full information to the broker as what the broker does not know may prevent the broker from providing a complete picture to the importer and this may be detrimental to the importer. For example, an importer advises the broker that the product being imported was previously imported to the United States and subsequently returned for repair to the foreign supplier. Under import regulations, the importer need only pay duty on the value of the repair made to the product and not on the full value of the import. If the importer fails to notify the broker of this and the broker does not know these circumstances, the importer will be paying additional duties to Customs unnecessarily.

Similarly, if an importer advises the broker that the product being imported was previously imported to the United States and subsequently returned for repair to the foreign supplier but the foreign supplier was unable to repair the item and replaced it for free with a new product. If the broker is not made aware the item being imported is actually a replacement, the importer may end up with a false declaration stating the goods are returned after repair and subject to reduced duty when in fact the item is subject to duty based on the full value of the new imported item.

When appropriate, obtain analyses from accredited labs to determine technical qualities of an imported product. If an importer is not sure of the actual make-up of a product, the importer has an option of obtain an analysis from their internal experts or outside experts to correctly determine the technical qualities of the product. This is especially important for tariff classification, whether or not the duty rate for the imported item is free. In addition to collecting revenue through duties and fees, Customs is also collating statistical data for Census. Failure to provide Customs with the correct tariff classification and other statistical information is a lack of reasonable care and may result in a penalty.

An importer should use in-house employees like counsel, a customs administrator, or, if valuation is an issue, a corporate controller, who has experience and knowledge of customs laws, regulations and procedures. In order for in-house employees to be knowledgeable about customs regulations and procedures they need training and access to resources to expand their knowledge, keep current and network with fellow importers. This can be done through webinars, on-site or off-site training, membership in local and national associations focusing on compliance, and attending government-sponsored seminars.

The importer must follow any binding ruling requested and received from Customs. There is a process for obtaining official advice from Customs called the binding ruling process. If an importer requests such advice and receives a binding ruling from CBP, they are obligated to follow this advice even if the importer believes the advice to be incorrect. While a binding ruling is an option for an importer, the first step for advice is usually better off being the customs broker or a customs attorney.

If importing any textile or apparel product, ensure that the products are accompanied by documentation, packaging, and labeling that are accurate as to its origin. Textiles and wearing apparel have very specific requirements as to the packaging and labeling of these commodities. A textile declaration that details the weight, fabric weave, and many other details may also be required to accompany the customs entry. Country of origin for textile items also carries its own rules. Take for example, a shirt that is cut to shape in Denmark but sewn in Dominican Republic. The country of origin may appear to be Dominican Republic, but the country of origin for shirts is determined by where the article is cut to shape.

It should be noted that while this reasonable care requirement is targeted for textiles and wearing apparel, it is an import requirement that all imported items must declare the correct country of origin on the product itself (with a few exceptions) and the documentation presented to customs must be in accordance with Customs regulations as we will discuss further on.

The importer cannot classify own identical merchandise or value own identical transactions in different ways and must notify Customs when receiving different treatment by Customs for the same goods in different transactions or at different ports. Importers must be consistent in the declarations they make to Customs. A leather wallet imported into the port of San Francisco must be classified and valued in an identical manner to the same wallet being imported at the port of Newark. Customs also requires importers to notify Customs if they are receiving different treatment by Customs in different ports. If the leather wallets are being pulled for examination each time they are imported in San Francisco but cleared paperless each time in Newark, importers are required to advise Customs. This is swift water to navigate as the importer does run the risk that Customs management may approach Newark for its lack of diligence rather than question San Francisco for being overly diligent.

Importers must examine entries (import declarations prepared by the broker to determine accuracy in classification and valuation). While an importer may be providing the broker with the information to make entry, the importer is still required to make certain the broker is properly clearing the import. Many importers will just accept the broker's invoice, glance at the back-up paperwork and hand the bill off to accounts payable for payment. This is a lack of reasonable care. The importer must implement a process for reviewing the entry paperwork whether through reviewing ACE (*Automated Commercial Environment*) reports or examining the entry paperwork and ideally, the information being submitted to Customs should be approved by the importer prior to entry submission and then verified again following entry.

The concept of reasonable care means the importer must be able to evidence to Customs how they have implemented reasonable care into the clearance process. In addition to the above referenced steps, importers can also exercise reasonable care through documented and verifiable procedures on the import process, training presentations including training rosters, recordkeeping checklists, and a review of entry files. Proactive management of the importer's relationship with the customs broker or customs brokers is another key to exercising reasonable care.

Customhouse Brokers

Customhouse brokers are licensed by customs to clear goods into the United States. Brokers are governed by Customs regulations and may collect duty and taxes on behalf of Customs.

In choosing a custom broker it is important to find a broker that is a good match for the importer's size and needs. Friendly competitors, carriers, international trade organizations, and even Customs in the local inbound gateway can all be sources used to assist in making the right selection.

Custom brokers are required to have a valid customs power of attorney on file from the importer in order to conduct customs business on behalf of the importer. The power of attorney legally authorizes the customhouse broker to act on behalf of the importer, which legally binds the importer to its obligations to Customs.

Extreme care needs be exercised in this selection process. Unfortunately, many brokers operate at a level below the reasonable care and compliance standard that is legally required of them. This lack of reasonable care and compliance equates to fines and penalties for the importer and broker.

As previously mentioned, a customs broker does not have to be used in clearing an importer's goods. Customs brokers are not only familiar with Customs and other government regulatory agencies, but they also have tremendous experience in logistics and coordinating the movement of goods once they have been cleared by working with freight forwarders, warehouses, and trucking companies. Importers who partner with a knowledgeable and compliant customs broker will eliminate some of the risk involved in the import process.

Just as reasonable care is mandated for importers, customs brokers are required to follow Customs regulations and to exercise reasonable care in managing their business, their employees, and their relationship with their importer clients.

Under the Reasonable Care Standard, a broker:

- Must exercise due diligence to ascertain the correctness of information that is imparted to a client
- Shall not knowingly import false information to a client to any Customs business
- Shall not withhold information from a client who is entitled to that information
- Shall establish internal procedures to limit advice being given by qualified licensed individuals
- Shall obtain and receive directly from the importer complete and accurate information sufficient to make entry or to provide proper advice

The penalty for a broker not meeting reasonable care is up to $30,000 per violation.

A broker must exercise due diligence to ascertain the correctness of information that is imparted to a client, and obtain and receive directly from the importer complete and accurate information sufficient to make entry or to provide proper advice. Customs brokers are required to have a valid power of attorney in place with their importer client. Most brokers require the importer to complete a questionnaire and broker letter of instruction as part of the entry process. Truly diligent brokers will go out of their way to ensure reasonable care by visiting their clients to gain a better understanding of their business.

Customs brokers must understand the use of a product, the circumstance of import and make certain they receive accurate information from the importer. An importer may not know they should be sharing certain information with the customs broker that may change the advice being offered. For example, an importer advises they have an import from their sister company overseas. If the broker does not request additional information from the importer, such as if the relationship between the companies affecting the pricing, the importer may unknowingly declare the import under transaction value (the price paid or payable), which may not be an acceptable method of valuation if the price paid or payable by the importer is 90% below market value.

A customs broker shall not knowingly import false information to a client to any Customs business nor withhold information from a client who is entitled to that information. Customs brokers are considered experts and are required to provide truthful information as to the status of a clearance and correctness of information in the entry process.

Customs brokers should establish internal procedures to limit advice being given by qualified licensed individuals. Customs brokers are required to have procedures in place as to how client information is dispersed and who is advising an importer client on proper marking and/or valuation. The circumstances surrounding specific commodities may designate a unique situation requiring a different set of marking, as we read with the wearing apparel example above. If an employee without much experience in the import process mistakenly advises a customer that marking is not required on a table because they are familiar only with the business of a client who imports hairnets, which are exempt from marking, that employee may create a penalty situation for the importer and a reasonable care violation for the customs brokerage office.

In selecting a customhouse brokerage service the following steps should be taken into consideration:

- Confirm the brokerage operation has qualified customs brokerage personnel with at least five years of operational experience in handling customs entries.
- Verify the number of license holders in the company and how they supervise the operations staff. A brokerage office consisting of ten employees with one to two licensed brokers supervising activity is certainly preferable over a brokerage office of one hundred employees with one to two licensed brokers supervising activity.
- Confirm the operations staff receives training on a regular basis. Ask to see training records.
- Verify the operations staff has experience in valuation concepts, harmonized tariff classification, and country of origin determinations. Ask to speak with the operations staff and pose an assist question and see how well it is answered.
- Ask questions regarding compliance knowledge and value added services to importer clients including in-house training and webinars.

- Confirm how the broker will share clearance information including entry status and reports with clients.
- Ask for references and contact the references to discuss their experience with the broker.

Internal Supervision and Control

The importer of record is responsible for operating their inbound supply chain in compliance with U.S. import regulations. Written procedures encompassing compliance help mitigate the risk of being noncompliant with CBP regulations. Internal supervision and control represents a measure to control the correctness of information being provided to Customs and any other government agency (OGA). These procedures should include monitoring all communications made on behalf of the importer to CBP or any other government agency by the broker on behalf of the importer.

It has been a common practice for the importer to outsource the day-to-day responsibilities of importing to their broker and allow the broker to handle the entire import process. Many importers continue to rely heavily on their broker, which is a noncompliant practice. For example, the foreign vendor e-mails the import notification and importer security filing directly to the broker; the broker handles the clearance and advises the importer when the goods have cleared and are being delivered. The broker follows that up with an invoice. There are many decisions that need to be made prior to the entry, which requires feedback and instruction from the importer. This practice is not compliant on the part of the importer and the customs broker.

Importers who demonstrate supervision and control over the import process have established an import notification process to validate the shipment information, to match up purchase orders against the shipping documentation, and to ensure invoices are accurate. Brokerage providers do not typically have access to this depth of information and therefore cannot substantiate the validity of the overseas vendor or accompanying entry documentation.

If piece count is off due to a change made between the supplier and importer, the broker would not be a party to those communications and may submit entry declarations on behalf of the importer that are inaccurate. Failure to implement such a process could result in entry corrections and amendments being made after the fact which is allowed but is not a compliant practice if it is done as common practice.

Supply Chain Security

Supply chain security has become an integral part of global supply chains. CBP implemented the Customs-Trade Partnership against Terrorism (C-TPAT) in 2002 as a voluntary program open to importers, carriers, consolidators, brokers, and highway carriers. The program has matured to now include exporters as well.

The threat of terrorism in the supply chain is a global effort. CBP has established mutual recognition agreements with over a dozen countries that also have their own national supply chain security program.

Participation in the C-TPAT program has many benefits that reduce risk in the supply chain including:

- Reduced compliance exams.
- Reduced number of inspections.
- Reduce waiting time for cargo to be examined.
- If cargo is selected for exam, it will receive priority and moved to the front of the exam line.
- Decreased transportation times.
- Assignment of CBP supply chain security specialist.
- Access to FAST (Free & Secure Trade) lanes at Mexico and Canada borders.
- Invitation to participate in C-TPAT training seminars offered by CBP.
- Incorporation of security practices into existing logistical management methods.
- Greater supply chain integrity.
- Reduced freight surcharges such as exam fees and demurrage.
- Meet C-TPAT customer requirements.
- Lower insurance costs.
- Reduce theft/loss of inventory.
- Mutual recognition allows freight exported from the United States to move faster through participating countries local customs more quickly.
- When another event occurs that closes the borders C-TPAT member shipments will be prioritized when the borders reopen.
- Mitigation of fines and penalties for participants.
- Five to eight times fewer exams than non-CTPAT importers.

Companies considering participation in the program must review the eligibility requirements and the security criteria of the program. This is best completed through a security assessment to determine where security gaps exist in the supply chain between what must be in place to participate in the program and what should be in place but is not mandatory. The individual security criteria has flexibility, as no single supply chain is identical. Additionally, the security criteria will differ depending on whether the company is entering the program as an importer, exporter, broker, and so on.

Supply chain security must include a review of the cargo from the point of origin overseas to the point of receipt in the United States. The foreign location and origin of shipments may also pose a geographical threat that must be taken into consideration as well. There is a minimum requirement of container and trailer security for ocean and cross border shipments, how air shipments are packaged and screened, advanced shipment notification, product identification, shipping controls, photo identification of drivers, visitors and contractors, employee access controls, company badges, hiring practices, container inspection, tracking containers and shipments, surveillance cameras, alarm systems, lighting, physical security maintenance, separation policies, integrity of documentation, seal controls, visitor logs, resolving discrepancies in receiving of cargo, seal verification, protection of information, and information technology controls, to name a few. Training employees on threat awareness to the supply chain will also be part of the threat assessment.

Supervision and control of where merchandise is sourced and background checks on overseas vendors will also be scrutinized. A detailed knowledge of the storage and handling of all imported cargo is the responsibility of the importer, even when delegating such services to outside service providers like freight forwarders and common carriers.

Invoice Requirements

The import invoice is the engine that drives the international shipment and clearance process. Incorrect statements of fact on an invoice can inadvertently lead to circumvention of governing authorities from properly exercising control and safety over imported goods.

Importers must understand there are actual requirements that must be contained on an import invoice in order to be presented to CBP. It is a common practice to judge a complete invoice by the amount of information that is contained on the document rather than the quality and actual information. Submission of incomplete and inaccurate information is considered to be non-compliant and may result in clearance delays and/or a penalty. Penalties for this type of violation can be assessed at the value of the merchandise plus estimated duties.

Customs expectation is for the importer to review the contents of the invoice to affirm the correctness of information on a transactional basis. Random postentry audits by the importer do not meet the regulatory requirement of supervision and control. Most brokers use the foreign shipper's invoice as the key point of reference for the entry declaration. The information contained in each invoice must be properly reviewed prior to submission to the brokerage provider and prior to the customs entry declaration being submitted. While this may be viewed as a delay in the import process, it is actually a compliant practice and is a requirement.

For some types of commodities, there may be additional invoice requirements required. For most imports, the importer should ensure the following information is contained on the import invoice:

- The name and address of the foreign shipper or manufacturer
- The name and address of the importer of record and consignee
- A full and accurate description of the imported merchandise
- Quantity of the merchandise being imported with net weights and measures included
- The unit price of the imported commodity
- Terms of sale associated with the international transaction
- Invoice date
- Invoice number and purchase order number
- A detailed breakdown of any and all prepaid freight and insurance charges associated with the transaction of sale
- All discounts offered and or taken
- Any commissions must be detailed on the invoice
- Invoice must be in the English language or have an attached translation
- Any royalties that exists must be indicated on the invoices
- A complete invoice value
- Country of origin of the imported merchandise
- A name of a responsible person as the preparation party of the invoice
- A statement of use is recommended to establish special entry procedure

Bonds

Importers are required to have a bond on file with CBP. The first bond condition is for the importer to pay duties, fees, and taxes on a timely basis. It is the importer's responsibility to establish and verify that all duties, fees, and taxes are being submitted in accordance with CBP regulations.

As a common practice, many importers use the services of the brokerage provider to layout the duty payment to customs on their behalf or pay the duty as part of the periodic monthly statement. The importer then reimburses the broker as part of their invoice or the importer pays the broker's invoice, including the duty, and the broker pays the duty on the next statement. It is important to note that the payment of duties, taxes, and fees to CBP is the obligation of the importer. Using a broker to pay duties on behalf of the importer does not relieve the importer of their responsibility to pay duties, taxes, and fees owed to CBP. Copies of the receipts of payment need be reviewed and retained by the importer to ensure the broker is paying the duties on time.

In the customs audit process an importer will be asked how they manage the duty payment process. It is an unacceptable answer to simply state, "my broker pays the duty for us." A system of accountability needs to be implemented to ensure that timely payment is being managed as part of supervision and control over the import process.

Copies of the final ACH statement copy will serve as proof of payment as will copies of checks with a receipted copy of the CBP 7501 Customs Entry summary or a copy of the ACE report reflecting payment was received. It should be noted that a stamped copy of the CBP7501 is not proof of payment and only represents entry submission.

Record Retention

Importers are responsible to establish a record retention system that maintains all records relative to an import transaction for five years from the date of entry of the merchandise into the commerce of the United States. Many importers do not keep satisfactory records in accordance with the customs regulations.

In its regulatory audits, Customs finds multiple errors associated with record keeping. Importers must be aware of all documents that they are responsible to maintain as outlined in the (a)1(a) listing of the customs regulations.

All records associated with the import transaction from the point of purchase inquiry throughout the customs clearance process up to the final disposition of the merchandise at the ultimate place of delivery needs to be retained. Once all of the required documents are identified every importer needs to create a standard operating procedure to ensure that these documents are properly collected on a transactional basis.

Third-party service providers, like brokers and freight forwarders, need to be a part of this process to ensure that all documents that are generated by their services are duly tendered to the importer. The importer is responsible to keep all of the aforementioned records. This obligation cannot be delegated to a third-party service provider.

Custom brokers have their own recordkeeping requirements, which are not necessarily the same requirements as the importer. Many brokers do not properly advise importers of the full obligation to maintain correct records. Importers who rely on their brokers to maintain their records also create risk in the event they change brokers and no longer have access to those records.

The importer is not only responsible to keep records but they must also be able to retrieve their records in a reasonable amount of time. Records that are maintained yet are not retrievable do not meet the customs regulatory standard of compliance.

Selling Internationally: The Export Supply Chain

In 2016, the United States exported over $2.2 trillion in goods. There is tremendous opportunity for export sales for many businesses. It is important to understand the risks involved with exporting. These risks may include compliance risks such as exporting to prohibited destinations or denied parties, exporting controlled items without prior government authorization, or financial risks such as making sure receivables are protected. Managing risk in the export supply chain requires diligence, recurrent training, and the support of senior management.

Export trade compliance is a very important topic for both executives and companies engaged in export trade. This chapter section focuses on the necessary information flow and actions necessary to be trade compliant in exports.

Government Agencies Responsible for Exports

The export supply chain is subject to various government agencies regulating the export process. Minimally, exports require reporting to the Bureau of Census, knowing and screening business partners through the Consolidated Screening List, reviewing purchase orders and documentation for boycott language, and understanding to which country the goods will ultimately be shipped. Prior government authorization may be required for specific commodities.

Exporters may find themselves working with all or a few of the following government agencies:

- Department of State, Defense Trade Controls
- Department of Commerce, Bureau of Industry and Security (BIS)
- Department of Commerce, Bureau of Census
- Department of Treasury, Office of Foreign Asset Controls (OFAC)
- Department of Homeland Security, Bureau of Customs and Border Protection

International Traffic in Arms Regulations

Exports falling under the International Traffic in Arms Regulations (ITAR) require registration with Defense Trade Controls and the prior approval of a license for exports, temporary exports, and temporary import of United States Munitions List (USML) items. If an activity is controlled under the ITAR it follows that most transactions require a license. This includes furnishing a defense service as well as providing proposals to sell significant military equipment.

Defense services include furnishing assistance to foreign persons, whether in the United States or abroad, in the design, development, engineering, manufacture, production, assembly, testing, repair, maintenance, modification, operation, destruction, processing or use of defense articles.

Violations of the ITAR can include policy of denial of export licenses, debarment, criminal fines up to $1 million, imprisonment as well as civil penalties up to just over $1 million per violation.

Export Administration Regulations

Most exporters are not subject to the tighter controls of the ITAR but will be subject to the Export Administration Regulations (EARs). The Export Administration Regulations are broad and cover exports from the United States, re-exports of U.S. products, U.S. persons overseas, foreign subsidiaries of a U.S. parent, foreign-made products of U.S. technology and/ or U.S. component parts, and the transfer of information to a foreign national. One of the key differences between the EARs and the ITAR is that most transactions under the EARs do not require an export license provided the commodity is not controlled.

Commerce Control List

If a product is not controlled under the ITAR, then the product is subject to the EARs. Subject to the EARs require the exporter to understand their export transaction, the parties to the transaction, the destination of the product, and how their product will be used. The EARs may define some products as being controlled for export. These items are identified under the Commerce Control List (CCL).

If an exporter determines that the product is subject to the Commerce Control List and falls under a specific Export Control Classification Number (ECCN), then they must take the next step in determining whether government approval in the form of a license is required prior to export. The first step is to review the Reasons for Control, which are indicated at the beginning of the Commerce Control List. Once the Reasons for Control have been determined, the Commerce Country Chart must be examined.

The Commerce Country Chart is a matrix bringing together the Reasons for Control for all commodities listed on the Commerce Control List against all countries. The exporter needs only to review the Reasons for Control for their particular commodity as well as the destination country to which they are shipping. If there is an "X" in the box, the shipment requires export authorization. If there is not an "X" in the box, the shipment does not require export authorization based on the commodity.

Should an exporter determine their product is not listed on the Commerce Control List, then that product will be designated as EAR99. EAR99 means the product is subject to the Commerce Control List but not specifically controlled for export based on the commodity. The majority of products exported from the U.S. are EAR99. However, a product being EAR99 does not mean the product is not subject to additional regulations governing exports. Exporters must be aware of the additional compliance responsibilities they have under the EARs as well as the Office of Foreign Asset Control Regulations and Foreign Trade Regulations, which also cover EAR99 items.

Electronic Export Information

The Department of Commerce, Bureau of Census requires the exporter to report information on their exports. This information is used to compile official trade statistics and is called the Electronic Export Information (EEI).

The EEI serves an additional purpose as it is also used as a compliance tool by other government agencies such as the Bureau of Industry and Security (BIS), the Bureau of Customs and Border Protection (CBP), and Defense Trade Controls (DTC).

An EEI is required when merchandise is shipped from one USPPI (U.S. Principal Party in Interest) to one consignee on the same flight/vessel to the same country on the same day and where the shipment is valued over $2500 per Schedule B or Harmonized Tariff Number or any dollar amount if a license is required.

The EEI may be filed by the exporter or the exporter may choose to have their freight forwarder file the EEI on their behalf. The transmission of information is done through the Automated Commercial Environment (ACE), which is the same platform used for processing import entries.

Information contained on the EEI must be true, accurate, and complete. Late EEI filings and/or incorrect information (false statements) may lead to penalties. Any EEI record filed later than ten calendar days after the due date will be considered failure to file. Failure to file could result in a penalty up to $10,000. Late filing penalties can be $1100 per day up to $10,000. Filing false/misleading information carries a penalty up to $10,000 per violation. In addition to these penalties, any property involved in a violation is subject to forfeiture.

If the USPPI chooses to delegate the filing of the EEI to a freight forwarder, the USPPI will be held liable for these penalties in addition to the freight forwarder. This is one of the most important reasons to purposefully manage freight forwarders and for exporters to take the time to train their personnel if the exporter is filing their own EEI.

U.S. Principal Party in Interest

The Foreign Trade Regulations defines the USPPI as the person or legal entity in the United States that receives the primary benefit, monetary or otherwise, from the export transaction. The USPPI is the party who is responsible for filing the EEI and for complying with export regulations. The USPPI is generally the U.S. selling party, manufacturer or order party. A foreign entity may only be the USPPI if they were in the United States when purchasing or obtaining the goods for export.

Although the INCO Terms note where risk and costs, responsibility, and liabilities shift from the seller to the buyer, it is important to keep in mind that the Foreign Trade Regulations apply to the USPPI, the FPPI (Foreign

Principal Party in Interest), and the authorized agent in the U.S. regardless of the INCO Term.

Schedule B Number/Harmonized Tariff Number

One of the key data elements required in the reporting of the EEI is the Schedule B number or Harmonized Tariff number. The Schedule B numbers are based on the same numbering system as the Harmonized Tariff Schedule issued by the U.S. International Trade Commission. The Harmonized Tariff Schedule identifies commodities by a ten-digit number. Globally, the first six-digits are shared but the last four-digits can be different.

Harmonized tariff schedule of the United States (2011)
Annotated for statistical reporting purposes

XI
60.2

Heading/ subheading	Stat. suf- fix	Article description	Unit of quantity	Rates of duty		2
				General	Special	
6001		Pile fabrics, including "long pile" fabrics and furry fabrics, knitted or crocheted:				
6001.10		"Long pile" fabrics:				
6001.10.20	00	Of man-made fibers (224)	m² .... kg	17.2%	Free (BH, CA CL, IL, JO, MA, MX, P, PE, SG) 3% (AU) 6.8% (CM)	79.5%
600.10.60	00	Other (224)	m² .... kg	9%	Free (BH, CA CL, E*, IL, JO, MA,MX, P, PE, SG) 3% (AU) 3.6% (CM)	40%
6001.21.00	00	Looped pile fabrics: Of cotton (224)	m² .... kg	9.8%	Free (BH, CA CL, IL, JO, MA, MX, P, PE, SG) 8% (AU) 3.9% (CM)	40%
6001.22.00	00	Of man-made fibers (224)	m² .... kg	17.2%	Free (BH, CA CL, IL, JO, MA, MX, P, PE, SG) 3% (AU) 6.8% (CM)	79.5%
6001.29.00	00	Of other textile materials (414)	kg	7%	Free (BH, CA CL, E*, IL, JO, MA, MX, P, PE, SG) 3% (AU) 2.8% (CM)	61.5%

The Schedule B numbers tend to be a bit broader in their description than the Harmonized Tariff numbers, which are very specific. For example, other cattle are broken down into two categories—"other" and "buffalo"—under the Schedule B numbers, but under similar Harmonized

Tariff numbers other cattle are broken down into several categories based primarily on weight.

Schedule B numbers may only be used for EEI reporting, whereas Harmonized Tariff numbers may be used for both EEI reporting and import entries. However, not all Harmonized Tariff numbers may be used for EEI reporting.

Valuation

In capturing statistical data through the EEI reporting, the value must be accurately reported. For EEI reporting purposes, the value is the selling price (or the cost if the goods are not sold) in U.S. dollars, plus inland or domestic freight, insurance, and other charges to the U.S. seaport, airport, or land border port of export. The cost of goods is the sum of expenses incurred in the USPPI's acquisition or production of the goods.

Many exporters and their authorized agents fail to report the FOB/ FCA value on the EEI, as they generally take the bottom line of the export invoice as the value of the shipment. For those exporters shipping samples or company material, values tend to be underreported and a minimum value declared that does not reflect the actual value.

The final area where value is incorrectly reported is the value of repair work performed in the United States. The actual cost of repair should be reported and if the repair was performed under warranty, then the value of what the repair cost would have been should be the value reported.

Record-Keeping Requirements

Export shipments are subject to a record-keeping requirement of five years from the date of export. Records to be retained include notes, correspondence, contracts, memoranda, invitations to bid, books of account, financial records, restrictive trade practice reports and boycott documents, and documents created in support of shipment including bills of lading, commercial invoices, packing lists, and EEI transaction copies. Exporters are well advised to retain their own documentation and not rely on their service providers.

Denied Party Screening

While a product may not be specifically controlled for export, there may be other factors that come into play that must be addressed. Who is receiving, handling, and buying the product? Where is the product transiting? What is the final destination country for the product?

The Bureau of Industry and Security (BIS) maintains an electronic tool called the Consolidated Screening List on its website. This list should be consulted for all export transactions for all parties to the transaction including service providers, carriers, vessels, customers, end-users, foreign freight forwarders, financial institutions, and distributors. The names of the companies as well as individuals should be screened.

Embargoed Country Screening

While the Export Administration Regulations contain a list of countries for which specific products may be controlled for export, the BIS also maintains a list of countries that are considered Terrorist Supporting Countries. These are Iran, North Korea, Sudan, and Syria.

The Department of Treasury, Office of Foreign Asset Controls (OFAC) administers and enforces economic trade sanctions. OFAC maintains a listing of Specially Designated Nationals, which can be found through the Consolidated Screening List. Additionally, OFAC also maintains a listing of countries with active sanctions programs. This listing is provided on the OFAC website.

Each of the sanction programs summarizes the reason for the sanction, the scope of the sanction, prohibitions under the sanction, the type of authorized activities and transactions permitted, if any, and if a General License exists or if a Specific License must be applied for through OFAC.

Due to the scope of some of the sanction programs, some transactions may be allowed without any prior authorization while other transactions may be permitted and other transactions may be prohibited.

It is important to learn how to utilize this information. The website http://2016.export.gov/ecr/eg_main_023148.asp enables you to obtain access to the screening lists.

Instructions for Downloading and Using the Delimited
Consolidated Screening List Files

How to Download the CSV and ASCII Files   The following instructions are provided for downloading both Consolidated Proscribed Party Screening List files in a delimited format. Right click on the "TSV Download (ASCII encoded)" link or the "CSV Download" link. On Macintosh computers, use "Control-click". From the dialogue box that appears, select "Save Target As" or "Save Link As" and save the file. The downloadable files name will be saved as csl-yyyy-mm-dd.csv or .tsv where yyyy is the year, mm is the month, and dd is the day when the files were updated.

What Is a Delimited Text File?   A delimited text file is formatted so that each line of text is a record, and each field is separated by a character. The TSV file available here uses a TAB character to separate fields. The CSV file available here uses a comma to separate fields. Each row contains one record of information and each record contains multiple fields of data. This is a popular format for transferring data from one application to another, because most database systems are able to import and export delimited data.

Importing into Popular Applications   Many popular databases, spreadsheets, and similar applications will import a delimited file and format it as a table. For specific information on how to import either file into a particular application, please consult that application's documentation.

If you would like to use the Consolidated Screening List in Microsoft Excel, choose "Open" from Excel's File menu and navigate to the folder that contains the downloaded delimited text file. Be sure to look under "All Files", as Excel will usually default to show only Excel files. When you open the CSV file, it should already be in the proper format. When you open the TSV file, Excel will automatically enter "Text Import Wizard" mode. Be sure to select "Delimited" as file type that best describes the data at the first prompt, and select "Tab" as the type of delimiter at the second prompt. Then click "Finish" and the ASCII file will open in Excel. You may save either delimited file as an Excel file for quick and easy access to it through Excel.

What Is the Advantage of Using This File Format? The delimited text file format will allow you to import data into programs that search and organize based on fields of information, which are outlined in the Data Specifications section. For example, you can sort by geographical location. This file also may facilitate incorporation of the data into your own export management system(s).

Data Specifications Each file contains 27 columns, one for each field. The first row consists of the field names. Please note that some of the field names (e.g., source, entity_number) are longer than the data length of those fields.

Changes to the Files On July 1, 2015, both the CSV and TSV files were updated to accommodate changes in how the data is organized. Several of the field names have been updated and some of the fields contain additional information. For example, the City, State/Province, Postal Code, and Country have been combined into one "addresses" field. If an entity has more than one Address, then they are all included in the one field separated by semicolons. This is true for "alternate names" as well. Because multiple addresses and alternate names have been combined, there are far fewer rows in the CSV/TSV files than previously.

Also, there are several new fields that provide information found on an entity's ID such as Nationality or Place of Birth.

The field names are as follows:

Column	Field Name	Description
A	Source	3-position code describing the source (agency or agency list) of the record (DPL= Denied Persons List, UVL= Unverified List, EL= Entity List, SDN= Specially Designated Nationals, DTC= AECA Debarred List, ISN= Nonproliferation Sanctions)
B	entity_number	A number used by OFAC to uniquely identify the names of the Specially Designated Nationals (SDNs) (For SDN only. Null if not SDN)

(Continued)

Column	Field Name	Description
C	Type	Specifically identifies if the Specially Designated National (SDN) is an individual or vessel
D	Programs	The program in which the Specially Designated National falls under, as designated by OFAC, or the Nonproliferation Sanction, as designated by the legal authority of the State Department's International Security and Nonproliferation (ISN).
E	Name	Name of the company, entity or person
F	Title	Title or position held by the Specially Designated National
G	Addresses	Addresses of the company, entity, or person. If the entity has more than one address, the addresses are separated by semi-colon.
H	federal_register_ notice	The official source of information about the parties on this list
I	start_date	The effective date of the company, entity or person being on the list as defined by the Federal Register Notice
J	end_date	The date the company, entity or person was lifted, waived or expired on or from the lists
K	standard_order	Whether or not (Y/N) the standard order applies to the Denied Party as defined by the Bureau of Industry and Security
L	license_requirement	The license requirement as determined by the Export Administration Regulations for the names on the Entity List (EL)
M	license_policy	The policy set forth in the Export Administration Regulations regarding denial of the name on the Entity List (EL)
N	call_sign	Call sign of the vessel listed on the Specially Designated Nationals list
O	vessel_type	Describes the type of vessel (ferry, bulk cargo, tug) listed on the Specially Designated Nationals List
P	gross_tonnage	The gross weight in tons not-registered for the vessel on the Specially Designated Nationals list
Q	gross_registered_ tonnage	The gross weight in tons registered for the vessel on the Specially Designated Nationals list
R	vessel_flag	Country flag of the vessel on the Specially Designated Nationals List
S	vessel_owner	Owner/operator of the vessel on the Specially Designated Nationals List
T	Remarks	Additional remarks or notes regarding the company, entity or person on the list

(Continued)

Column	Field Name	Description
U	source_list_url	Website of the specific agency list
V	alt_names	Alternate identity names separated by semicolon
W	Citizenships	Countries of citizenship separated by semicolon
X	dates_of_birth	Alternate dates of birth separated by semi-colon
Y	Nationalities	Alternate nationalities separated by semi-colon
Z	places_of_birth	Alternate places of birth separated by semi-colon
AA	source_information_url	Website of the source federal agency

Breakdown of the Consolidated Screening List

Department of Commerce, Bureau of Industry and Security

Denied Persons List—Individuals and entities that have been denied export privileges. Any dealings with a party on this list that would violate the terms of its denial order are prohibited.

Unverified List—End-users who BIS has been unable to verify in prior transactions. The presence of a party on this list in a transaction is a "red flag" that should be resolved before proceeding with the transaction.

Entity List—Parties whose presence in a transaction can trigger a license requirement supplemental to those elsewhere in the Export Administration Regulations (EAR). The list specifies the license requirements and policy that apply to each listed party.

Department of State, Bureau of International Security and Nonproliferation

Nonproliferation sanctions—Parties that have been sanctioned under various statutes. The Federal Register is the only official and complete listing of nonproliferation sanctions determinations.

Department of State, Directorate of Defense Trade Controls

AECA Debarred List—Entities and individuals prohibited from participating directly or indirectly in the export of defense articles, including technical data and defense services. Pursuant to the Arms Export Control Act (AECA) and the International Traffic in Arms Regulations (ITAR), the AECA Debarred List includes persons convicted in court of violating or conspiring to violate the AECA and subject to "statutory debarment" or persons established to have violated the AECA in an administrative proceeding and subject to "administrative debarment."

Department of the Treasury, Office of Foreign Assets Control

Specially Designated Nationals List—Parties who may be prohibited from export transactions based on OFAC's regulations. The EAR requires a license for exports or reexports to any party in any entry on this list that contains any of the suffixes SDGT, SDT, FTO, IRAQ2, or NPWMD.

Foreign Sanctions Evaders List—Foreign individuals and entities determined to have violated, attempted to violate, conspired to violate, or caused a violation of U.S. sanctions on Syria or Iran, as well as foreign persons who have facilitated deceptive transactions for or on behalf of persons subject to U.S. sanctions. Transactions by U.S. persons or within the United States involving foreign sanctions evaders (FSEs) are prohibited.

Sectoral Sanctions Identifications (SSI) List—Individuals operating in sectors of the Russian economy with whom U.S. persons are prohibited from transacting in, providing financing for, or dealing in debt with a maturity of longer than 90 days.

Palestinian Legislative Council (PLC) List—Individuals of the PLC who were elected on the party slate of Hamas, or any other foreign terrorist organization (FTO), specially designed terrorist (SDT), or Specially designated global terrorist (SDGT).

The List of Foreign Financial Institutions Subject to Part 561 (the Part 561 List)—The Part 561 List includes the names of foreign financial institutions that are subject to sanctions, certain prohibitions, or strict conditions before a U.S. company may do business with them.

Non-SDN Iranian Sanctions Act List (NS-ISA)—The ISA List includes persons determined to have made certain investments in Iran's energy sector or to have engaged in certain activities relating to Iran's refined petroleum sector. Their names do not appear on the Specially Designated Nationals or Blocked Persons (SDN) List, and their property and/or interests in property are not blocked, pursuant to this action.

Consularization and Legalization

Many countries require export documentation to be consularized and legalized. This process can add additional costs and time into the export process. In some instances, a visit to the local Chamber of Commerce is sufficient, but if documents need to be sent to a consulate office, there will be additional fees including messenger delivery fees and consularization charges, which can run between $125 and $500.

Exporters should have a discussion with the foreign customer to find out if the destination country has an import requirement regarding consularization. The answer can differ from country to country and may also differ depending on the commodity and value of the shipment. In the event a shipment is moved without proper documentation, there may be a customs hold at destination resulting in additional storage fees, potential customs penalties, and a frustrated customer.

Solid Wood Packing Material (SWPM) Certificates

The International Plant Protection Convention (IPPC) is an international plant health agreement that focuses on prevention of the introduction and spread of pests into wild plants and the protection of natural flora. The convention recognizes the introduction of pests can be spread through vessels, containers, aircraft, storage facilities, and soil.

This convention affects exporters, as the materials used for packing and transporting shipments must meet the IPPC specification as part of the import requirement in over 175 countries. These materials must be heat treated, fumigated, or special heated. Exporters must be certain the materials used to package their shipments meet the current standard. This is typically reflected by materials containing a certificate and/or marking indicating they meet the IPPC standard.

Preshipment Inspections

Depending on the commodity, value, and destination country, a preinspection of goods prior to export may be required. This may also be a requirement within a letter of a credit. There are a number of agencies that specialize in this inspection process, which can include verification of quantity, quality, price, customs classification, and import eligibility.

The surveying company will schedule a qualified inspector to certify the cargo is meeting the requirements of the foreign importer's purchase order. The preshipment inspection is usually paid for by the foreign customer. Additional time may need be built into the export process to accommodate the scheduling of the preshipment inspection.

Free Trade Affirmations

Special certificates may be requested by the foreign customer for countries with which the United States has free trade agreements. Some certificates of origin including those required by the North American Free Trade Agreement (NAFTA), and the FTAs with Israel and Jordan are prepared by the exporter.

In order to issue a valid FTA affirmation, the exporter must know that the goods are eligible and qualify for the FTA. This can be done by reviewing the preference criterion for the product and following the rules of origin relevant to the product. The rules of origin may be found in the General Notes section of the Harmonized Tariff Schedule or through the trade.gov website.

It is important to keep in mind that creation of an FTA affirmation requires the exporter to retain documentation validating the facts contained within the document. Failure to retain this back-up documentation or completing the documentation incorrectly can result in a fine and penalty.

Many companies make the mistake of assuming these FTA affirmations are an import requirement, but they are not. They are merely the method of complying with the free trade agreement in place to access duty-free status.

Getting Paid

An important function of export documentation is to ensure the exporter receives payment according to the agreed terms of sale and payment. One of the methods of receiving payment is a letter of credit.

In a letter of credit transaction, the exporter anticipates receiving funds once the goods are shipped. While this may be true in theory, in practice the exporter will only receive payment once the required documentation is received and approved by the confirming bank. This process can be difficult if errors are found, documents are incomplete, or documents are presented outside the agreed upon time frame.

The bank scrutinizes the documentation thoroughly, and the primary reason for this is the bank never sees the freight. Discrepancies in documentation create extra expense, payment delays, and aggravation. Using letters of credit can create risk if the bank presentation is not handled by a freight forwarder or company that is knowledgeable in letters of credit.

ATA CARNETS

Passport for goods

The ATA Carnet is an international customs document that permits the duty-free and tax-free temporary export and import of goods for up to one year. ATA is an acronym of the French and English words "Admission Temporaire/Temporary Admission." I highly recommend the ATA Carnets to reduce risk and spend in temporary shipments.

ATA Carnets cover:

- Commercial samples
- Professional equipment
- Goods for presentation or use at trade fairs, shows, exhibitions and the like

That means almost everything from the ordinary to the extraordinary, the usual and unusual: computers, repair tools, photographic and film equipment, musical instruments, industrial machinery, vehicles, jewelry, clothing, medical appliances and aircraft, race horses, old masters, prehistoric relics, ballet costumes, rock group sound systems and so forth. If you can name it and it is not consumable or perishable, then it can probably be covered by an ATA Carnet.

The ICC WCF World ATA Carnet Council (WATAC) is the body within ICC WCF that manages the International ATA Carnet Guarantee Chain, which comprises the organizations appointed by their Customs to operate the ATA System around the world. The ATA Carnet is enforced in 75 countries today.

SUMMARY OF LOGISTICS CONSIDERATIONS

Corporations engaged in global trade, importing, exporting, and distributing their products and services worldwide need to follow the following guidelines to minimize risk and enhance opportunity.

The ability to move goods in the international arena will make or break a sale or even maintain a client relationship. The ability to deliver various products on a timely and loss free basis is a critical component.

This "summary" created for global supply chain and risk managers addresses six steps to follow to help reduce risk and cost in the area of international shipping, freight, and logistics.

The Six Steps

The following six steps originate from the author's 35-years experience in moving freight all around the world and in assisting corporations with global logistics that are cost effective and reduce risk to themselves and their clients:

1. Chose the best INCO term
2. Insure the shipment
3. Chose the right freight forwarder and carrier
4. Track all shipments proactively
5. Understand the total "landed costs"
6. Be trade compliant!

Choose the Best INCO Term

The INCO Term, established by the International Commerce Commission, is followed by all countries belonging to the United Nations for goods that pass through international borders. There are 11 Options in the 2010 edition:

Incoterms

Incoterms for any Mode or Modes of Transport
    EXW—Ex works
    FCA—Free carrier
    CPT—Carriage paid to
    CIP—Carriage and insurance paid
    DAT—Delivered at terminal (new)
    DAP—Delivered at place (new)
    DDP—Delivered duty paid
Incoterms for Sea and Inland Waterway Transport Only
    FAS—Free alongside ship
    FOB—Free on board
    CFR—Cost and freight
    CIF—Cost, insurance, and freight

The INCO Term is a term of sale between a seller and a buyer that picks a point in time in the transaction where risk and cost is transferred from one party to the other. It does not address other contractual concerns, such as payment method, title, and details of marine insurance.

What it really does is advise an exporter till what time and place in a transaction is it responsible for cost and risk, and conversely where the importer picks up responsibility. Depending upon the INCO Term utilized, the risks and costs could be dramatically impactful for either the seller or the buyer. One should learn at a very detailed level all they can about INCO Terms and more specifically how to best leverage the term to reduce risk and cost in their transactions.

The author is available to bring in-house classes on INCO Terms to the readers and always available to assist with any questions (tomcook@bluetigerintl.com).

Insure the Shipment

The typical importer and exporter never worries about loss or damage until it occurs. And at that point everyone from the forwarder to the carrier is blamed for the occurrence. Freight will always get lost or damaged at some point in time, when you ship frequently and all over the world.

It is very important to make sure that you first identify through the purchase or sales contract who has risk of loss or damage. What INCO Term is being utilized? How is payment being made?

Once the risk is understood, then marine cargo insurance should be acquired on an "all risk," "warehouse to warehouse" basis with a reputable international cargo insurance underwriting company.

Additionally, some loss control elements need to be considered to mirror the insurance policy that considers

- That the freight is packed, marked, and labeled well.
- A responsible forwarder and carrier is utilized.
- Freight needs to pass through the system quickly. Delays at border pints open the door for loss and damage.
- Freight needs to clear customs, thoroughly and legally, following all import regulations, and timely. All this will mitigate the potential for loss and damage.

Chose the Right Freight Forwarder and Carrier

As an extension of your shipping personnel, the forwarder and carrier take responsibility to move your freight through the global system. They need to do this

- Timely
- Safely
- Cost effectively

Choosing the right company that is qualified becomes some very important criteria to make sure the shipment, the freight, and the logistics moves your package to your customer's satisfaction.

My company, Blue Tiger International, has developed some very key relationships with an array of freight forwarders and carriers and can assist you in making sure you have all the necessary information to make the best choices. Helpful freight trade associations include the National Customs Brokers and Forwarders Association of America (NCBFAA), Airforwarders Association (AfA), and Transportation Intermediaries Association (TIA).

Track All Shipments Proactively

Making sure the shipments arrive on time and in workable condition is the guarantee of customer satisfaction, long-term relationships, less headaches, and greater margins. This can be a service your freight forwarder or carrier provides, but it needs to be clearly identified in that vein and it must be done proactively through every step of an international shipment.

Depending upon distances involved, countries of export and import, and choices of mode and carrier, some freight can travel 12,000 miles, through four to five carrier handoffs, via several customs authorities and in several modes of transit.

All these convolutions can create exposure to loss, damage, or delay. All three concerns should be avoided. They lead to loss of revenue, customer dissatisfaction, and lots of stress within your organization.

To mitigate these concerns, you need to structure a proactive system to track and trace all your international shipments through all the convolutions, hand-offs, and modes of transit. Many track and trace systems can be electronic and advise you through web portals, e-mails, and other electronic means on all your shipping activity.

The benefits of being proactive in lieu of a reactionary mind-set will pay off in spades over the course of time and client relationships.

Understand the Total "Landed Costs"

Landed costs are the total of all the accumulated expenses attached to a shipment moving internationally. Many of these costs are outlined as follows:

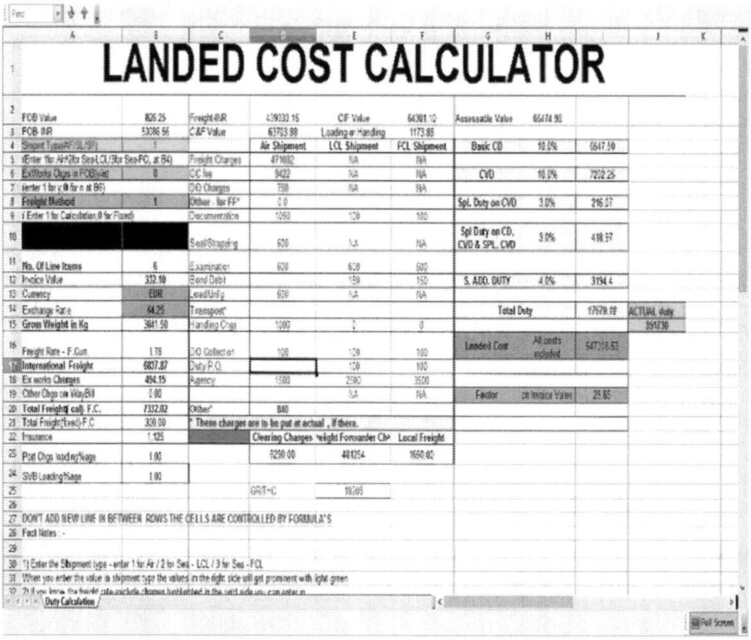

- International freight
- Duties, taxes, and fees
- License charges
- Handling charges
- Domestic freight
- Clearance and handling charges
- ISF fees
- Carrier surcharges
- Demurrage
- Storage and warehousing

Sometimes the landed costs can exceed the value of the actual shipment. In order to protect margins and profits, it is critical to make sure that you completely understand what the landed costs are for your shipment, then you can make sure these costs are covered in the eventual client invoicing that will follow.

Remember no one likes surprises; particularly those that have an additional price tag attached to them.

Be Trade Compliant!

It is imperative that both importers and exporters operate their global supply chains trade compliantly. Following procedures and operational practice involves

- Due diligence
- Reasonable care
- Supervision and control
- Engagement

This includes

- Understanding the regulations
- Building internal standard operating procedures (SOPs) to comply with the regulations
- Training personnel on how to interpret and practice the SOPs and in a regulatory manner
- Engaging in government programs that provide evidence of managing secure and compliant global supply chains, such as C-TPAT

C-TPAT is a voluntary program of security created for importers into the United States managed by the CBP, now open to include exporters from the United States.

Areas also included in trade compliance have to do with documentation, classification (HTSUS/Schedule B numbers), valuation, record Keeping, export license requirements, and denied party listing to name a few of the operational concerns.

The penalties for noncompliance are fines, penalties, and potential loss of import or export privileges. More serious areas can include criminal prosecutions.

Summary

Importing and exporting successfully means paying attention to detail. These six areas outlined earlier are a good foundation for creating a detailed and comprehensive approach to managing global supply chain responsibilities.

Those companies that are diligent about how they manage freight, logistics, and distribution of parts and equipment will create the best opportunity to

- Protect margins and grow profits
- Increase customer satisfaction
- Decrease stress and problem areas in global markets
- Improve their reputation, which converts to client retention and expansion

Business people need to understand the psychology of risk more than the mathematics of risk.

Paul Gibbons
The Science of Successful Organizational Change: How Leaders Set Strategy, Change Behavior, and Create an Agile Culture

5

International Insurance and Global Risk Management

Insurance is an important element of any global risk management strategy, which is discussed in this chapter with a focus on marine insurance and cargo loss control, directly impacting risk transfer and mitigation in the goods imported and exported worldwide.

MARINE INSURANCE

A form of property risk is that of goods that are shipped from one country to another or even within that country (domestic transportation or inland marine). Marine insurance is one of the oldest forms of insurance in the world and many historians point to the risks established with early cargo shipments on sailing vessels that began the process of insuring these transportation risks, which led to the modernization of insurance in general, to what we have today as a multibillion-dollar industry in six continents.

Cargo insurance covers freight moving in global supply chains, typically designed for goods moving from one country to another. Specifically, it provides coverage for goods in transit or temporarily in storage. It covers for "physical loss or damage from an external cause, during its period of transit."

Cargo insurance is one of the primary exposures that operators in global supply chains have. It is often misunderstood, not well explained and a limited amount of insurance professionals with subject matter expertise.

Most cargo insurance professionals would tell you that many importers and exporters don't even insure for these exposures, mainly because they are unaware of the risks—until a loss occurs. Every company no matter where they ship to and from or even irrespective of what they sell or buy will encounter some sort of loss or damage to their cargo at some point in time. The more sensitive, fragile, special needs or high end the freight, the more likely exposure exists for loss and damage to the cargo as it moves through the global supply chain. This concern makes obtaining marine cargo insurance a very important purchase for companies that ship special needs cargoes.

Cargo insurance requires expertise on the side of brokerage and underwriting. The policies are tailored to meet the individual needs of global supply chains, which makes obtaining that expertise an important step in customizing the coverage to meet the risks of moving freight internationally.

Some key considerations in obtaining marine cargo insurance:

- Only work with brokers and underwriters who have specialized capabilities in marine cargo insurance. Roanoke International with offices worldwide is an example of a broker that specializes in cargo insurance. The office in Chicago, Illinois, is a flagship office sales run by Glenn Patton, vice president, gpatton@roanoketrade.com, 310-729-2301. He is one of the few experts in the field of marine cargo insurance and is always readily available to assist companies in the risks of global trade and providing various risk transfer options. Obtaining access to expertise is a best practice to minimize risk and exposure in global trade.
- Cargo insurance policies are boilerplate only as a starting point. As all supply chains have similarities, they also have differences. From a risk perspective, those differences could be very consequential in how insurance coverage's are designed. Cargo insurance can be a great management tool to reduce risk, but the policy must be
  - Tailored
  - Customized
  - Manuscripted
  to meet the specific risks in that unique supply chain.

- Cargo insurance needs to have provisions that fall in line with the risks involved in how freight moves from various origins to multiple destinations. Some key provisions in cargo insurance policies are
  - Geographic areas covered
  - Named insured
  - Modes of transit covered
  - Limits of liability
  - Valuation
  - Underwriting terms
  - Special terms
  - War, SRCC (strikes, riots, and civil commotion) coverage
  - Terrorism
  - Effective dates
  - Storage/warehousing
  - Consolidation and deconsolidation
  - Domestic transit
  - Interruptions in transit
  - Exclusions
  - Cancelation

Geographic Areas Covered

When analysis of risks is completed and the geographic scope of where your company operates in, typically identified by the countries of origin and destination, along with any geographic areas of trans-shipment should all be outlined in great detail, assuring you are afforded the coverage globally, as you need. Some policies are broader than others and utilize the phrase "covering shipments worldwide."

Named Insured

In many corporations there are separate operating units that may be identified by similar or separate EIN numbers. You should make sure that the parent, along with all operating units are named under this section.

Modes of Transit Covered

Ocean and airfreight make up the majority of international shipments. Freight moving by rail and truck such as within Canada, Mexico and the

United States will also create certain risks that need addressing. It is prudent to make sure that all the modes utilized in your global supply chain are covered. This might include hand carried, messenger, express mail, parcel post, sailing vessels, barges, and pack animals. In some remote areas of the world, eighteenth century transit (e.g., caravans, sailing vessels, camel, horseback, etc.) still prevails.

Limits of Liability

Cargo policies typically provide limits of liability measured against the various modes of transit utilized. Purchasing and sales personnel need to be consulted to determine insured values in order to make sure the necessary limits are achieved.

Limits need to be updated timely as supply chains grow and values are increased. I have witnessed too many times over the past 35 years claims that exceed arranged limits because no one updated the policy underwriting limits of liability.

Additionally you need to make sure that when freight accumulates, under both controlled and uncontrolled circumstances, that coverage is afforded under the various terms of the policy. Some policies have accumulation clauses to address these risks.

Valuation

The most typical method for insuring international fright is the CIF +10% formula. The INCO Term CIF includes the invoice value, freight, and insurance, plus 10% for good measure.

But marine underwriters provide options to their assured that allow them to choose before risks are transferred to underwriters to manage valuation under the policy with a formula that meets their needs. If an exporter wanted to insure for sales price (inclusive of profit) that would be an option. The FOB (Free on Board; INCO Term) price is an option. Basically the assured has an option to arrange the valuation at a number they can negotiate with the underwriter, as long as it is before the risk occurs.

It would be typical that the corporate risk manager, along with the chief financial officer and other senior management, looking at risk tolerance levels, along with expected claim recovery amounts to set guidelines to follow for valuation standard operating procedures (SOPs).

Underwriting Terms

The standard cargo policy should be written as follows. "All risks" is typically the broadest coverage available and provides protection from physical loss or damage from an external cause during transit. Special attention needs to be paid here, as some underwriters offer reduced terms, for example, free of particular average (FPA) or certain named perils only. You need to make sure the terms are the broadest available and are sync with the risks you have in your global supply chain.

Special Terms

Special needs cargoes require underwriting terms to meet the special risks caused in these types of supply chains. Food products, perishables, pharmaceuticals, high value electronics, machinery, chemicals, and hazardous materials are but a few categories of special needs supply chains.

For example, Kelly Global is a Cincinnati-based importer of temperature-sensitive and frozen food products from New Zealand into various warehouse locations in the United States and Canada. Most freight is shipped by 20' and 40' Ocean Reefer Containers. Its cargo insurance policy contains specialized wording that restricts coverage, called the "24 Hour Reefer Breakdown Clause." The basis of this policy limitation is science and practicality. If the reefer units break down for a period of time, there should be a certain number of hours that the integrity of the closed and sealed container should still protect the freight from exposure to ambient temperatures. The policy wording advises the assured that in order for them to put in a claim for loss or damage, say from spoilage, the reefer unit would have to have been broken down (not running) for at least 24 hours.

Shippers of perishables often place temperature recorders in containers so they can demonstrate problems from this recording capability, making claims handling and payment much easier to manage. The burden of proof for marine claims always lies with the insured.

War and SRCC Coverage

For decades now, marine underwriters have placed endorsements onto cargo policies and typically receive additional premiums to cover the risks of war, and strikes, riots, and civil commotions (SRCC). These risks are typically exclusions under the "all risk" provisions and are a separate risk and exposure, and handled as a separate indemnification by the underwriter. Because of all the strife around the world, it is always recommended as part of a comprehensive marine cargo insurance program.

Terrorism

The events of 9/11 brought on another more defined risk referred to as terrorism coverage, which extends more clearly what might be "defined as terrorism, versus war" and extends the policy, sometimes for additional premiums the certainty of this coverage. By covering war, SRCC, and terrorism, a more comprehensive black and white coverage is afforded.

Effective Dates

Cargo policies typically have anniversary dates and not expiration dates like other forms of property and liability insurance policies. This means the policy is automatically renewed at the anniversary date and remains in force unless canceled by the assured or the underwriter, following policy cancelation guidelines.

Storage/Warehousing

Some insureds will extend the cargo policy intentionally to cover merchandise while it is in inventory and being warehoused or stored. Marine cargo insurance underwriters are very willing typically to extend marine policies for goods held in storage through agreement and endorsement. In some instances insureds can obtain broader coverage and less expensive premiums for warehousing coverage than in traditional property insurance markets. Your insurance broker will be able to assist you in determining the best place to insure these storage exposures, when they exist.

Consolidation and Deconsolidation

A majority of international freight moves in ocean containers. Many times there is a need to consolidate at origin points and/or deconsolidate from these containers at destination points.

Ocean freight containers.

It is important to know when your supply chain calls for these types of consolidations, which typically will occur at outbound or inbound gateway ports. This would call for a possible extension of coverage to provide indemnification in case a loss occurs at these points during the consolidation/deconsolidation process.

Domestic Transit

The primary intent of marine cargo insurance programs is to cover the risks of loss and damage for goods crossing international borders. Marine cargo insurance companies have always been willing to extend their coverages to include domestic transit. The cargo portion of the policy covers "warehouse to warehouse." This includes the domestic portion of an international transit. Covering domestic freight is intended to provide insurance on freight that moves domestically and never leaves the country.

Interruptions in Transit

There will be circumstances in every supply chain when freight is stopped and does not move along the intended transit. These interruptions, which are unintentional, need to be covered during that period of time when the freight is not moving. Typical policies provide certain levels of protection for freight stopped temporarily, but they are likely to only include a few days or weeks. When "interruption in transit" wording is included in the insuring terms and conditions, it will extend coverage for a longer term or even indefinitely, depending on what was negotiated.

Exclusions

Some cargo insurance policies will not have specific named perils that are not covered. But tradition and case law advises us that though the policies provide "all risk" coverage there are exclusions by specific wording or implied:

- Loss of market
- Delay
- Business interruption or consequential damages
- War SRCC
- Inadequate packing

Loss of Market

If a loss occurs and as result of the loss you lose a contract, a customer, or a market, that is not covered.

Delay

If a transit conveyance gets delayed and as a result there is a financial consequence, the marine cargo policy will not respond.

Business Interruption or Consequential Damages

If a physical loss or damage occurs that causes a business interruption or consequential claim, it is not covered.

War SRCC

War SRCC is excluded from typical cargo policies and added on as an endorsement or as an extension of the primary coverages.

Inadequate Packing

Some cargo insurance policies will state that the goods must be packed contemplating the intended journey, or "adequately packed." Whether the

AMERICAN SHIPPER MAGAZINE, MAY 2016

CARGO AND LIABILITY INSURANCE: THE NECESSARY EVILS!

Thomas A. Cook

Like lawyers, insurance is a real problem, until you need it!

And that is not the way it should be. Lawyers are integral component of the global supply chain and their value is not only when you need them but in assisting you to grow and manage your business.

Those of us who have been involved in global supply chains know that loss and damage to cargo in transit is always going to happen … it is just a matter of when and to what extent.

Typically, few executives focus on cargo insurance or liability exposures until a loss occurs. And that is when it is too late!

Insurance can also be a tool to:

- Understand risk and exposure in the supply chain
- Mitigate the opportunities for loss and damage

- Transfer the risk to a third party
- Determine acceptable levels of risk tolerance

Importers and exporters can go direct to insurance companies, like the Travelers, Zurich, Hartford, AIG or Lloyds of London, or they are more likely to approach underwriters through specialized cargo insurance brokers such as Roanoke, AON, Marsh and Gallagher.

Roanoke, which is one of the leading and more specialized cargo insurance brokers, arranges marine cargo insurance policies through their own company based in London or through other third party carriers.

Companies like Roanoke will work with both shippers, forwarders and carriers in assessing their risks and providing customized and tailored terms and conditions to the benefit of their clients' exposures for goods or services in transit.

Tied into the assessment is the opportunity for mitigation. This is also referred to as Cargo Loss Control, which is defined as steps or actions in packaging, marking, labeling, materials handling, routing or stowage or any measure which will favorably impact cargo outturn.

Loss Control actions can prove to be a very wise spend in that many extoll for every dollar spent the return comes back ten-fold.

I recently worked with a company in Chicago that imported chemicals in 55 gallon drums in 40 foot ocean containers originating in Shanghai, China. In almost every shipment, particularly through the winter months almost 5–8% of the drums had damage. In the investigation from our staff cargo loss control professional, it was determined that the break bulk stow in the container, which maximized space utilization, combined with the ordinary motions of the vessel in heavy seas was the culprit.

The recommendation from the cargo loss control consultant was to unitize the loads on pallets which would provide greater stability to the load and prevent shifting from occurring. The consequence of the palletizing was that each shipment contained 2% less load, and there was the cost to the pallets and the pallet certification process.

On the other hand, the importer utilized pallets in the domestic distribution and could unload the containers mechanically which reduced the unloading time.

Additionally, the underwriter offered a 15% premium discount on the cargo insurance when the freight was shipped unitized on pallets in lieu of bulk in containers, where losses had occurred.

After 18 months and 37 shipments, loss frequency was reduced by over 80%. The loss control process clearly outweighed the loss of 2% of freight space on each shipment.

Importers and exporters also need to hold their forwarder, brokers, service providers and carriers liable for the freight in their *care, custody and control*. This transfer of risk is typically accomplished through a "contract" that goes above and beyond the liabilities set forth in "bills of lading."

In addition to expectation to recover loss and damage, most financial exposures as a result of an error or omission would be recoverable. The shipper would require the service provider or carrier to provide a third party legal liability policy along with a professional liability policy (E&O).

These are all best evidenced by certificates of insurance outlining the underwriter, terms and conditions. The underwriter should be assessed by reputation, experience and their overall Best Rating.

Most companies will have a risk tolerance. This is often referred to as a claim deductible or retention level. This is a "dollar amount" for when a claim occurs the loss will be shared between you and the insurance company at that agreed amount. It makes for a more cost effective approach to the purchasing of insurance.

Typically, the more risk the principal is willing to tolerate, the lower the insurance premiums and more liberal underwriting terms and conditions, that would be offered.

Keep in mind that marine insurance is written on "manuscript policy forms." This allows negotiation on terms and conditions and offers more room for customization and tailoring to specific supply chain requirements.

Managing global supply chain risks can be daunting. But taking the time to understand the exposures and applying some solid foundation risk policies can go a long way to reducing the opportunity for loss and damage and when it does occur, know that you have the necessary protections available.

policy states it or not, it is implied through court precedence that the insured must properly protect the freight from loss or damage by packing it properly for the intended transit. Most policies do not state this, it is implied. Nor do the policies advise what is "adequate packing." Nor are there any excellent references to go by to determine what adequate packing guidelines is. This becomes a very stereotypical issue between insured and underwriters when cargo claims are denied under this implication. The U.S. military along with marine surveyors and cargo loss control consultants are the only true sources to go to for guidance on packing goods for international shipping.

Cancellation

Most cargo policies have a 30-day cancellation clause. This can be negotiated to 60 or 90 days if your supply chain needs require. You need to make sure you have sufficient time to replace coverage in case it is canceled by the underwriters.

Commercial Insurances Overview

For companies operating in global markets and answering the following questions: Are you considering selling your product overseas? Do any of your employees travel overseas? Do you have manufacturing or recycling operations outside of the United States? If you answered "yes" to any of these questions, a foreign package policy is coverage you should be discussing with your broker. Following are several of the components that can make up a foreign package policy with a brief description of each:

1. Foreign Voluntary Workers' Compensation or Employers Liability: Extends workers' compensation benefits to employees when traveling outside of the U.S. This portion of the policy can also include

coverage for medical assistance programs and expenses for repatriation (the transportation of a sick or injured employee back to the U.S.).

2. Foreign Commercial Property, Including Business Income: Typically provides incidental coverage for property that you might take with you on an overseas trip such as laptop computers, trade show property or samples of your product. If you have a manufacturing location in another country, a more extensive, and sometimes separate, policy should be purchased in conjunction with the foreign package policy. It'll provide coverage on an "admitted" basis (i.e., the insurance company has operations and issues/services policies within the foreign country of your operations in accordance with local laws/regulations).

3. Foreign Commercial General Liability: Provides liability coverage for occurrences and lawsuits brought against a manufacturer outside of the U.S. and Canada (i.e., foreign jurisdictions). It's important to note that a U.S.-based liability policy will typically only provide coverage for lawsuits brought in the U.S. or Canada.

4. Foreign Business Auto: Can provide both liability and physical damage coverage for hired and non-owned vehicles that are operated in other countries. Please note that this coverage is meant to be over and above the local insurance that you must purchase from the rental company of a foreign country.

5. Kidnap, Ransom and Extortion: Depending on where your foreign travels might take your company's top executives or key employees, this coverage should be considered in the event that one of these important individuals, or their family members, is kidnapped.

Property Insurance

International commercial property programs need to offer a scope of comprehensive coverages in the following areas:

Business personal property—Provides coverage for moveable assets owned by the insured, such as furniture, inventory, and stocks.

Commercial property coverage—Protects buildings, inventory, and their contents from fire, lightning, vandalism and other covered losses.

Loss of business income protection—This coverage will help your organization compensate for the loss of money your business would have earned if you are forced to temporarily close your doors due to a covered loss.

Computer and data coverage—Protection for your organization's computer hardware, data processing systems, and software if damaged or destroyed by a covered loss.

Earthquake and flood coverage—Protection against property damage as a result of earthquake and/or flood.

Equipment breakdown coverage (heating, ventilation, and air-conditioning equipment)—Coverage for loss due to accidents involving the operation of pressure, mechanical, and electrical equipment. Covers loss of the boiler and equipment itself, damage to other property, and business interruption losses.

Liability Insurance

International commercial liability programs need to offer a scope of comprehensive coverages in the following areas:

Third-party bodily injury and third-party property damage—Coverage for suits arising out of the operations or premises of an organization.

Personal and advertising injury—Coverage for law suits arising out of slander, libel, wrongful eviction, malicious prosecution.

Products and completed operations—Coverage to protect against liability for loss or damage as the result of a defect in a product manufactured or installed.

Damage to rented premises—Coverage to a landlord/property owner in the event of destruction to the actual leased space.

Medical expenses—Coverage for medical bills as a result of third-party bodily injury that occurs on the insured's premises.

Crime and Fiduciary Liability Insurance

Lost funds—One of the most typical acts of fraud experience by organizations of all types and sizes is stealing of funds. This might occur by stealing customer payments, check or funds transfer fraud, misuse of company credit cards, or other types of forgery.

Replacement cost valuation for loss of inventory or property—Stolen inventory may include items stolen from a warehouse to sell via back channels or theft of other employee property including computers, office supplies, or even component parts. The insurance company will reimburse you for the replacement cost valuation for this loss of property.

Damages for lost income or other plan benefits as a result to changes made in benefit packages, including any personal liability awards.

The cost for defending a claim in a fiduciary case.

Cyber Liability Insurance Coverage

Data breaches are on the rise with a 62% increase year-on-year according to the Symantec "Internet Security Threat Report 2014." If your organization has not considered cyber security liability insurance, you should not wait any longer.

The average cost of a data breach is $201 per compromised record and hackers are no longer just targeting large, for-profit organizations. Every type of enterprise, including nonprofits, regardless of size is at risk, with 30% of incidents affecting organizations with fewer than 250 employees according to the Symantec "Internet Security Threat Report 2014."

Breaches do not just occur from hackers, but stolen laptops or viruses can also result in data breaches that have enormous financial and reputational consequences for an organization. Although your organization is probably not at fault if data is lost, customers or donors will fear continued interaction with your organization as a result of this breach. Therefore, investing in public relations and other tools to support your organization's reputation will be a critical part of your crisis response strategy.

Cybersecurity insurance coverage protects organizations of all sizes, including nonprofits, across a variety of costs including regulatory compliance, data recovery, and reputational support. A comprehensive policy will also support multinational organizations, which may have to address different regulatory challenges by country. It can be offered as a standalone policy as part of a suite of management liability protections.

International Directors and Officers Liability Insurance

It is critical for employers to address the risks associated with the decisions employees, board members, and officers make on behalf of the organization. Directors and officers liability insurance is designed specifically to provide your directors, officers, and board members with protection against employment practices liability and personal liability claims that could be brought against them as a result of their work.

A comprehensive directors and officers policy will ensure financial stability in the event of a lawsuit around issues such as errors in judgment, negligent supervision, conflicts of interest, or unauthorized payments.

With a directors and officers policy, both your international organization and staff are financially protected from any decisions employees make on behalf of the company. A comprehensive policy can act as a valuable recruitment tool for business executives, many of whom will not be eligible to serve on a board without proof of directors and officers insurance.

Excellent Resources for International Insurances

Clements Insurance Specialists on International 1-202-872-0060 or 800-872-0067 or email request@clements.com
Bradley & Parker 1-800-445-3393, Bradley-parker.com
Assurance, 888.429.0999, assuranceagency.com

When you mitigate risk, you maximize opportunity.

Thomas A. Cook

6

Structuring a Global Supply Chain Risk Management Best Practice Strategy

Now with all this information transfer and knowledge gain from the previous five chapters the goal of this chapter is to integrate and synthesize all the data and provide a comprehensive summary outlining a best practice strategy in global supply chain risk management. This summary and best practice approach outlines ten critical steps that can easily be understood and followed by management both at senior and mid levels.

The concepts outlined previously creates a "thought process and strategy" to achieve the desired results of

- Risk assessment
- Risk acceptance
- Risk transfer
- Risk mitigation

down to acceptable levels as determined by a predictive, proactive, contemporary, and well thought-out plan to manage risk in the global supply chain.

THE TEN STEP MASTER PLAN

1. Determine a point person
2. Obtain senior management support and authorization
3. Create a committee of stakeholders
4. Perform an assessment
5. Come up with a plan of attack
6. Develop resources
7. Outreach to all fiefdoms
8. Create SOPs (standard operating procedures)
9. Start internal training programs
10. Ascertain audit capability

Step 1: Determine a Point Person

One person needs to take ownership of this responsibility. The person would typically be in the risk management or supply chain verticals of the organization, but not absolutely. At the end of the day, it is where there is "will and capability." The individual needs knowledge in both risk and global supply chain management, and must integrate both disciplines into the overall strategy.

As outlined in all the preceding chapters, insurance, supply chain, importing, exporting, INCO terms, contract management, Foreign Corrupt Practices Act, currency, sourcing, purchasing, export sales, and political risks are a few of over 40 areas and skill sets that must be organized and managed successfully.

The individual must be able to additionally have skill sets in

- Leadership
- Communications
- Project management
- Collaborative process
- Ability to reach across company silos and fiefdoms
- Negotiation traits
- Comprehension on a multinational, multicultural basis
- Organizational prowess

The choice of this point person will determine the success of the entire enterprise risk management in the global supply chain initiative.

The technical knowledge combined with leadership and project management skill sets is a rare combination but necessary considering the scope of this type of responsibility and the comprehensive tasks involved in getting to job done the right way.

Step 2: Obtain Senior Management Support and Authorization

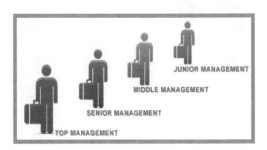

It is both critical and imperative that senior management sanctions any huge project on an "enterprise" scale. Most projects in risk management and global supply chain require the following:

- Buy-in from various divisions/fiefdoms/profit centers, crossing a multitude of company verticals
- Have additional investment costs
- Require structural and internal changes
- Various levels of authority required
- Vision from a cultural and strategic perspective
- Financial considerations

It is for those requirements that senior management participate in the overall process, particularly obtaining their blessing and authorities to make any initiative happen successfully. Senior management support will provide an edge that will create the best opportunity for success.

Additionally, risk management projects need to understand management's taste for risk so tolerance levels can be determined. This will generally require collaboration with the chief financial officer (CFO), who controls the financial implications. Most risk managers report to the CFO or the vice president of finance so they will be involved typically in some supervisory way, but irrespective it is critical that they are involved in the decision-making process, as any risk issue will generally have a financial impact in and around the business model and certainly in the supply chain.

Step 3: Create a Committee of Stakeholders

When the project creates a collaborative approach among all the key stakeholders you are directly and vibrantly obtaining the best opportunity to succeed in your risk management strategies.

People are typically resistant to change and any perceived additional work may cause various levels of pushback. When you engage those who would be impacted by any developed risk management strategies at the beginning, they are more than likely to cooperate and collaborate. This will be important as you are opening the door for their advice, feedback, opinions, and recommendations, all of which could prove to be very valuable input! Additionally, the impact of risk for various stakeholders gives them the right and authority to provide very defined input as to how that risk is perceived and managed.

We cannot be so arrogant as not to consider how the actual stakeholders need to be involved in the risk management decision-making process, therefore, making the entire process more legitimate and also one that provides customized solutions to the various aspects of the supply chain.

The committee of stakeholders should provide a diverse set of corporate interests, when called for, such as, but not limited to

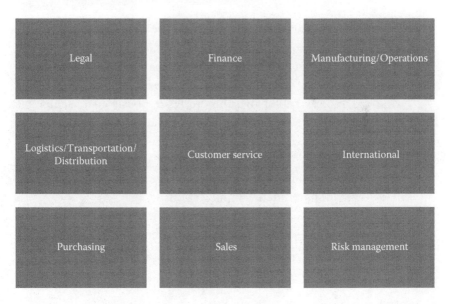

The collaboration and engagement with all the various verticals/silos/fiefdoms/divisions will set the stage for success when implementation and actions start to evolve.

Great ideas and strategies are not successful until implemented. This step helps the implementation process have the best opportunity for success.

Step 4: Perform an Assessment

Any risk management initiative requires a starting point and structure on how best to proceed forward.

The assessment stage creates the information flow into management, which affords the following information flows:

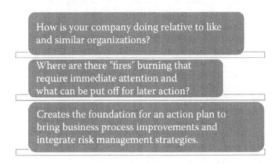

How is your company doing relative to like and similar organizations?

Where are there "fires" burning that require immediate attention and what can be put off for later action?

Creates the foundation for an action plan to bring business process improvements and integrate risk management strategies.

Additional assessment considerations include:

- These three necessary pieces of information flow creates a path forward.
- It is also an area consultants can help with, as their experience and client outreach can provide quality benchmarking.
- The benchmarking will allow a "range" to be established of where you will need to be as a company. This creates responsible and achievable goals and expectations. That range will then allow you an opportunity to create a business strategy on how you will get where you need to be.
- The assessment is also a line of accountability to senior management as it provides an evidentiary trail to the why and how decisions were made that will have financial implications.
- Additionally, the assessment can be utilized to evaluate the success of any risk management initiative, as it has benchmarks as necessary reference points.

Assessment begins the process of achieving success in any risk manage-ment strategy.

Step 5: Come Up with a Plan of Attack

The assessment stage, as outlined in the preceding section, creates the foundation for a strategy to bring resolution. This "plan of attack" becomes the actions necessary to achieve the desired results.

The plan has several components:

- Responsible parties
- Actions
- Time frames
- Results summary
- Required revisions, actions, and/or next steps

The plan can be best be outlined and managed from an Excel type of spreadsheet as

Action	Time frame	Responsible person	Results summary	Next steps

The action plan becomes a process "in motion," as it will develop and be tweaked as the project moves forward so the following ideals of the plan must be in place:

- The plan shows an ability to be flexible in its approach.
- It is reviewed timely.
- It creates reasonable compromise between all stakeholders.
- The project leader utilizes the Excel spreadsheet to hold the team accountable and responsible.
- It becomes a tool for senior management accountability.
- Allows all interested stakeholders to the document for transparency.

Step 6: Develop Resources

This sixth step is critical, as information gain leverages one's ability to make better decisions. Better decisions will lead to less volatility in the global supply chain, reduction of risk, and typically spend control and profit gain.

Step 7: Outreach to All Fiefdoms

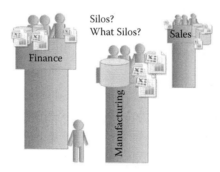

The strategy, followed by an action plan, will work best when there is total and transparent outreach to all the various fiefdoms, silos, and divisions in your organization.

As depicted earlier, every company has various divisions: legal, finance, sales, marketing, operations, purchasing, and so on. Typically, they all have something to gain or lose in any risk management initiative. Their participation as a business unit is a necessary component of the plan working successfully.

This is not an easy task to align all these various silos in your organization. More often than not, they have different agendas, priorities, and levels of being busy, all leading to potential conflict, not to mention the conflicting personalities of individuals.

Your outreach must contain:

- Total transparency
- Timely information flow
- Show of appreciation for their engagement and participation
- Patience with their involvement and support
- Respectful of the issues they face that might be different from yours
- Recognize that it may stretch across very different operating units, countries, cultures, and so forth
- Allow extra time for responses and input

Outreach creates another level of work, but when accomplished responsibly it will evidence numerous advantages toward a favorable outcome.

Step 8: Create SOPs

The hallmark ultimately is validated and confirmed through the application of creating standard operating procedures, (SOPs) business protocols, and processes.

EFFECTIVE SOPs

MAKE YOUR STANDARD OPERATING PROCEDURES HELP YOUR BUSINESS BECOME MORE PRODUCTIVE

SOPs need to be

- Comprehensive
- Engaging

- Easily comprehended
- Enterprise oriented
- Easily accessible
- Shared with all required personnel and external companies, such as but not limited to service providers, vendors, and contract manufacturers

SOPs are necessary because they

- Document compliance and adherence
- Provide a standard for all company personnel to follow
- Create a well-documented approach for company personnel to follow to comply
- Often contain regulatory requirements and documents to government authorities due diligence and reasonable care standards

SOPs should be reviewed and updated periodically to maintain a contemporary basis. Additionally, they should often be challenged and benchmarked, both internally and externally.

Step 9: Start Internal Training Programs

The basic SOPs in place are best transferred to the management teams and employees through training programs. Training programs need to be:

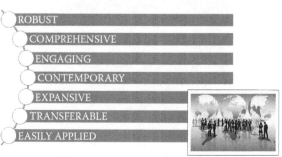

ROBUST
COMPREHENSIVE
ENGAGING
CONTEMPORARY
EXPANSIVE
TRANSFERABLE
EASILY APPLIED

Following these seven characteristics will create the best opportunity to succeed in moving the company forward on any risk management initiative.

The utilization of external consultants can also prove very valuable in this regard as they having relationships, experience, and overall knowledge can apply all of that to the creation of your SOPs quickly, easily and comprehensively. You then obtain the benefit of their prior SOP creations done for other interests, which you can now leverage.

SOP development should also be a collaborative process between business units, as they may need to be customized for the nuances of that specific silo.

Step 10: Ascertain Audit Capability

At the end of the day the true test of a company's adherence to SOPs, business processes, and protocol changes is to "audit." The audit verifies compliance and adherence and is the very best method!

Some corporations have internal audit units; others utilize external third parties. Both are good options as long as there is an expertise in the subject matter (in this case risk management) among the audit members.

Auditing is both an art and a science, but it ends up documenting reactively as to where a company stands in any area of its operations that can be inspected, measured, and scrutinized. Audits can be utilized to evaluate business process, personnel performance, and irregularities that can cause harm. Audits also can be utilized to benchmark, leading to the necessary changes and tweaks to SOPs and business processes for the purpose of rectification and enhancement. Audits become an affirmation of

The audit verifies compliance and adherence and is the very best method!

conformity and best practice. What company would not want that as part of its global supply chain risk management strategy?

An example of what an audit initiative would look for in a structured compliance program follows:

General Elements of an Effective Corporate Compliance Program

An effective corporate compliance program as defined by the Department of Commerce (doc.gov) is one that ultimately yields intended results: education, detection, and deterrence.

In structuring your corporate compliance program, you may want to consider the following general elements typically found in successful compliance programs.

- *Full support of upper management.* It is crucial that all of the elements of your company's corporate compliance program receive the full support of upper management. The corporate compliance program must be enforced at all levels within the company. If upper level management does not take efforts to combat corruption seriously, then neither will employees.

- *Establish and adhere to a written corporate code of conduct.* Corporate directors, officers, employees, and agents put themselves at risk of incurring criminal or civil liability when they do not adhere to the FCPA or similar anticorruption laws of other countries. A corporate code of conduct generally consists of a clearly written set of legal and ethical guidelines for employees to follow. A comprehensive and clearly articulated code of conduct—as well as clear policies and procedures relative to seeking guidance and making disclosures—may reduce the likelihood of actionable misconduct by your employees.

  It is important that a company's code of conduct be distributed to everyone in the company and, if necessary, translated into the languages of the countries abroad where your company operates.

  Finally, developing a code of conduct should not be the final act. The code must be effectively implemented and enforced at all times.

- *Establish an organizational compliance structure.* A compliance program may be run by one person or a team of compliance or ethics officers, depending on the size of your business.

  Implementation and responsibility for a corporate compliance program by high-level management employees are vital for accountability. Corporate compliance officers and committees can play key roles in drafting codes of conduct and educating and training employees on compliance procedures. Committee compliance members may include senior vice presidents for marketing and sales, auditing, operations, human resources, and other key offices.

  Past experience has shown that empowering compliance officers with access to senior members of management and with the capacity to influence overall company policy on integrity issues can be of utmost importance.

- *Provide anticorruption training and education seminars.* The overall success of a compliance program depends on promoting legal and ethics training at every level of the company. Regular ethics and compliance training programs should be held for all company employees, including board members and senior management officials. Compliance programs should educate employees at all levels of the company about the FCPA and, when necessary, other countries' anticorruption laws. More specific legal and ethical training may be necessary for employees in high-risk areas.

  A company should also take reasonable measures to communicate its values and procedures in an open environment to encourage participation and feedback. Employees should be informed as to whom they should contact to report violations or ask questions. Training materials that are both interactive and cost effective can help build employee support for a compliance program.

  Most important, compliance issues should not be limited to training classes and the compliance team: compliance should be stressed as an integral part of the company's way of doing business.

- *Undertake due diligence.* Conducting prompt and thorough due diligence reviews is vital for ensuring that a compliance program is efficient and effective. Due diligence reviews are also key for preventing potential harm to the company's reputation. Self-monitoring, monitoring of suppliers, and reports to the board of directors are all good tools for ensuring that a compliance program is being followed. Moreover, from vetting new hires, agents, or business partners to assessing risks in international business dealings (e.g., mergers, acquisitions, or joint ventures), due diligence reviews can uncover questionable conduct and limit liability.

- *Auditing and internal accounting controls.* Auditing and monitoring of systems of internal accounting controls contribute toward building an effective compliance program by the early detection of inaccuracies and misconduct (e.g., bribery, fraud, or other corporate malfeasance). Financial disclosure and reporting should be an integral part of a company's internal accounting controls.

 Companies should have a clear and concise accounting policy that prohibits off-the-books accounts or inadequately identified transactions. Companies should monitor their accounts for inaccuracies and for ambiguous or deceptive bookkeeping entries that may disguise illegal bribery payments made by or on behalf of a company. The FCPA requires compliance with various accounting and record-keeping provisions.

- *Compliance mechanisms.* Enforcement of a company's code of conduct is critical. Compliance officers should be accessible so that employees will feel comfortable discussing any of their compliance questions or concerns. Creating reporting mechanisms with adequate policies on confidentiality and nonretaliation as well as other safeguards related to reporting is extremely important. Whistleblowing protections, suggestion boxes, or helplines facilitate detection and reporting of questionable conduct.

 "I think I may have made a mistake." An effective and non-threatening environment that encourages reporting and questions is important to assist employees and agents (especially those in the field) when confronted with questionable situations. Companies should provide guidance to assist employees and agents on how to cope with and resolve difficult situations. Such counseling not only protects the person in the field, it also protects the company.

- *Discipline.* A company should ensure that all employees understand that failure to comply with its compliance policy and procedures will result in disciplinary action, ranging from minor sanctions to more severe punishment, including termination of employment. In instances of non-compliance, a company should take the necessary preventive steps to ensure that the questionable conduct does not recur in the future.

The measures listed above are general elements for developing an anticorruption corporate compliance program. Note that compliance programs' emphasis on specific elements will vary from one company to another depending on the particular risks engendered by the company's business (e.g., antitrust, healthcare fraud, or environmental issues).

You should seek the advice of legal counsel to learn more about what kind of corporate compliance program is most appropriate for your business.

RESOURCES

Developing resources is a critical and value-driven process for anyone engaged in risk management and global supply chain. An often-successful method for developing resources is to belong to industry associations, for which there are countless dozens. Outlined next are a few that I have had various levels of success in, both in global supply chain and risk management. As resources, they all offer access to information, training, and skill set development and often can be reached to help resolve problems or point you in the right direction.

The American Association of Exporters and Importers (AAEI)
Phone: (202) 857-8009
Fax: (202) 857-7843
Address: 1717 K St. NW, Suite 1120, Washington, DC 20006

For more than 90 years the AAEI has been the stepping stone of American business in support of fair and open trade between nations. They are one of the leading global trade organization experts that advocate on behalf of U.S. companies on trade policy issues. They also educate international trade compliance professionals through their ten standing committees and provide information concerning government regulations. Their main mission is to achieve definite benefits for their members by developing efficiency, economy, and professionalism, and monitoring export-related issues such as U.S. economic sanctions, export controls, intellectual property rights protection, and elimination of foreign barriers to U.S. exports.

They are devoted to representing their members and the importance of American exporters and importers before U.S. government. AAEI's membership is one of the largest and most diverse memberships that provide it with a high level of credibility among policy makers. Members include manufacturers, distributors, and retailers of a broad spectrum of products, and companies and organizations serving international trade. As a primary representative of the entire U.S. international trade community, they are effectively able to make the statement that trade restrictions and protectionism interfere with the world's largest consumer market and exporter, the United States.

Airforwarders Association (AfA)
Phone: (202) 591-2456
Email: info@airforwarders.org
Address: 529 14th St. NW, Suite 750, Washington, DC 20045

The AfA is a representative of the air forwarding industry, as an ambassador of indirect air carriers, cargo airlines, and related businesses located throughout the global transportation community. The AfA speaks for member companies devoted to transporting cargo in the timeliest and most cost efficient manner throughout the supply chain. Memberships range from small businesses to large companies, and business models from both domestic and worldwide freight forwarding operations. A wide variety of goods is shipped via air cargo, from organs for medical transplants to mail, to manufactured goods. Whatever it may be, the AfA will ensure timely and secure delivery of goods, which is necessary to remain competitive in the global market.

Transportation Intermediaries Association (TIA)
Phone: (703) 299-5700
Address: 1625 Prince Street, Suite 200, Alexandria, VA 22314

The Transportation Intermediaries Association (TIA) is the head organization for third-party logistics professionals doing business in the United States. The TIA provides resources, education, information, advocacy, and connections to establish, maintain, and expand ethical, profitable, and growing businesses in service to their customers. The TIA is as synergistic organization that honors the individual development of its members while speaking with a single voice to shippers, carriers, government officials and international organizations.

Foreign Trade Association (FTA)
Phone: (888) 223-6459
Fax: (310) 220-4474
Email: info@foreigntradeassociation.com
Address: 6216 E. Pacific Coast Hwy, #407, Long Beach, CA 90803

The Foreign Trade Association (FTA) was among the first organizations furthering the expansion of international trade in Southern California since 1919. It is a private, nonprofit trade association that represents over 200 members of the international trade community and one of the region's most admired trade associations. It constitutes as an instructive resource and networking mean for its members, and watches and campaigns legislative issues on a state and federal level. Members are represented by major exporters, importers, manufacturers, customs brokers, freight forwarders, international bankers, attorneys, and other prominent service industries. The FTA conducts meetings, educational courses, seminars, and conferences to develop and promote international trade.

National Institute of World Trade (NIWT)
Phone: (516) 993-4144
Fax: (631) 909-3308
Email: info@niwt.org
Address: 19 Benjamin Avenue, Suite 112, East Moriches, NY, 11940

Through the use of workshops and classes the National Institute of World Trade (NIWT) is educating, informing, and training professionals on the growing and changing topic of world trade. High-quality training and presentations come from its well-equipped team of experienced international trade experts. Entering an age of challenge in the global arena, the employees of the NIWT are there to help educate the future enthusiasts of world trade and guarantee the raising knowledge and professionalism in any company. NIWT has very defined expertise in both global supply chain and risk management spanning over 35 years, with experience, passion, and comprehensive talent leading the charge.

New York District Export Council (NYDEC)
Phone: (212) 809-2675
Address: 290 Broadway, Suite 1312 • New York, NY 10007

The New York branch of the National District Export Council (NYDEC) is a private, nonprofit organization that assists New York companies interested in entering or expanding into international markets. NYDEC helps New York companies by providing support, advice, and assistance to local and national governments. New York exports strengthen individual companies, spark New York economic growth, and make jobs.

United States Council for International Business (USCIB)
Phone: (212) 575-0327
Address: 1212 6th Ave. New York, NY 10036

The United States Council for International Business (USCIB) is an independent business that advocates in favor of open markets and sensible regulations. The USCIB's three function areas are policy advocacy, dispute resolution, and ATA Carnet administration. The organization promotes business interests to U.S. policy makers and to international groups like the United Nations. Dispute resolutions are accomplished by the business's affiliation with the International Chamber of Commerce (ICC) and its dispute resolution services.

U.S. Customs assigned them the task of handling the administration of international customs documents known as ATA Carnets. Policy positions are developed by the members who are some of the 300 multinational companies, law firms, and business associations that USCIB represents.

United States Chamber of Commerce (USCC)
Phone: (202) 659-6000
Address: 1615 H St. NW, Washington, DC 20062-2000
The world's largest American lobbyist group representing over 3 million businesses of all sizes, sectors, and regions, the U.S. Chamber of Commerce focuses on national issues at the federal government level, and works closely with a number of other young organizations in the nation about the value and role of business in our society. They focus on strengthening the competitiveness of the U.S. economy on ten key challenges: tax and entitlement reform, energy, health care, international trade and investment, a competitive workforce, capital markets, reliable and secure infrastructure, legal reform, innovation, and regulatory reform.

Global Purchasing Group
Phone: (212) 414-4001
Fax: (212) 414-3156
Email: Info@globalpurchasinggroup.com
Address: 1133 Broadway Suite 1128, New York, NY 10010
Since working at the age of 14 at her uncle's manufacturing company in the fashion district in New York City, Mercedes Gonzalez has had a love for industry. Using that passion she graduated from New York University and worked for one of the largest buying offices at the time, Frederick Atkins. She worked with many other private labels overseas and soon grew a love for international trade. In the last 19 years Gonzalez has worked with some of the most important buying offices in the country and has helped to open or restructure hundreds of stores in the United States and abroad.

Gonzalez started the Global Purchasing Group in 1990 and has been teaching other businesses around the world how to succeed in the global fashion industry. She teaches numerous classes and holds countless seminars in hopes that business owners can utilize her findings and experience to better expand their global reach.

Institute of Supply Management (ISM)
Phone: (480) 752-6276
Fax: (480) 752-7890
E-mail: membersvcs@instituteforsupplymanagement.org
Address: 2055 E. Centennial Circle, Tempe, AZ 85284-1802

The oldest and largest supply management association in the world, founded in 1915, the Institute of Supply Management (ISM) is a U.S.-based not-for-profit educational association that serves professionals and organizations with an interest in supply management and purchasing. ISM works on identifying, acquiring, and managing the products and resources needed to run a business or other organization; these include physical goods as well as information and services. The ISM has trained over 60,000 professionals in more than 30 countries through class education, certification, leadership development, and research. ISM offers two qualifications, the Certified Professional in Supply Management (CPSM) and the Certified Professional in Supplier Diversity (CPSDTM).

Council of Supply Chain Management Professionals (CSCMP)
Phone: (630) 574-0985
Fax: (630) 574-0989
Address: 333 East Butterfield Rd., Suite 140, Lombard, IL 60148

The leading global non-profit association for supply chain management professionals, the Council of Supply Chain Management Professionals (CSCMP) provides leadership in the development, design, and improvement in occupations that deal with logistics and management of supply chains. Its intent is to help its 9,000 members receive networking, research, and educational opportunities to further their companies. The business creates an environment that lets professionals communicate in order to develop and improve their supply chain management skills, and create awareness of the significance of supply chain to a business and to the economy.

Risk and Insurance Management Society (RIMS)
Phone: (212) 286-92925
Address: Bryant Park, 13th floor, New York, NY 10018

A not-for-profit organization helping to educate, engage, and advocate for the global risk community, the RIMS represents more than 3,500 industrial, service, nonprofit, charitable and governmental entities, and serves more than 11,000 risk management professionals around the world. The organization hopes to keep a continuous and compliant organizational network, gear risk professionals to achieve their goals in an evolving environment, increase engagement with members and the broadening risk management community, and expand risk management influence worldwide.

Green light, STOP—if you want to see where you are taking the most risk, look where you are making the most money.

Paul Gibbons
The Science of Successful Organizational Change: How Leaders Set Strategy, Change Behavior, and Create an Agile Culture

Being able to be repeated controllably is one key element in risk management.

Toba Beta
Master of Stupidity

Some risks that are thought to be unknown, are not unknown. With some foresight and critical thought, some risks that at first glance may seem unforeseen, can in fact be foreseen. Armed with the right set of tools, procedures, knowledge and insight, light can be shed on variables that lead to risk, allowing us to manage them.

Daniel Wagner

Opportunity and risk come in pairs.

Bangambiki Habyarimana
The Great Pearl of Wisdom

CREDITS

All these parties made various contributions to the book, through editing support, material, sources of information, and content. Their support is very much appreciated and acknowledged.

Kelly Raia
Dragonfly Global
NY District Export Council
Department of Commerce/U.S. Export Assistance Center
American Management Association
American Shipper magazine
Institute of Supply Management (ISM)
U.S. Naval Post Graduate School
Department of Commerce
Department of Justice
Securities and Exchange Commission
Clements Insurance Specialists
Bradley & Parker
Assurance
Allianz
Global Intellectual Property Academy
National Institute for World Trade
Stony Brook University
Blue Tiger International
FCPAméricas LLC
RIMS
Departments of Commerce, State, Treasury
Department of Homeland Security

Never take both hands off the pump. As an entrepreneur, you need to be on constant lookout for opportunity, and that will involve risk. But you minimize those risks by keeping one hand on the pump that is producing for you.

Kenneth E. Behring
Road to Purpose: One Man's Journey Bringing Hope to Millions and Finding Purpose Along the Way

Appendix A: Glossary of Business Terms

Audit committee: In large, complex enterprises, and recently as a matter of joint-stock company law, the board of directors often creates an audit committee to ensure the financial integrity of an enterprise. An audit committee investigates an enterprise's financial records and ensures that its financial operations are conducted on a transparent and accurate basis. The committee provides members of the board of directors with information about the financial and business operations of the enterprise. This information enables the board of directors to supervise implementation of the enterprise's financial and business plan and to ensure the efficiency of its internal control and risk management systems—two key components of any business ethics program.

Board of directors: The board of directors of an enterprise is the primary body responsible for representing the shareholders and safeguarding their interests. The board creates special committees—such as audit, executive compensation, and ethics committees—to fulfill this function. Increasingly, corporations will also appoint a social responsibility committee. These committees issue reports to the board, which uses the reports to make decisions concerning the development, implementation, and modification of the ethics compliance program. The board of directors makes the final decisions concerning any policy, program, or initiative that an enterprise may make.

Bribery: Bribery is a form of corruption. In the case of political corruption, bribery is the direct or indirect provision of illegal compensation to—or any other action in favor of—any employee of a government body. In return, the government employee acts in a manner advantageous to the company or refrains from acting to the company's disadvantage. Enterprises use bribery to obtain or retain business, receive patronage, or obtain an unwarranted advantage over other businesses.

Business ethics: Business ethics are an integral part of responsible business conduct. They describe an organization's commitment to a set of commonly understood core values and principles, which provide a basis for business decisions and conduct. Typically, business ethics presume that decisions will conform to standards articulated in law and regulations; internal policy and procedures; a set of core values determined by owners and managers, including honesty, integrity, respect, and fairness; and commercial principles such as profitability, customer satisfaction, product quality, health, safety, and efficiency. Business ethics issues range from practical, immediate ones, such as an enterprise's duty to be honest with its employees and customers, to broader social and philosophical questions, such as a company's responsibility to contribute to the welfare of the community and to preserve the environment.

Channel stuffing: Channel stuffing is the act of inducing customers or suppliers to increase purchases or decrease supplies or services that would be purchased or supplied in the ordinary course of business, solely to present a more favorable performance or financial picture to partners.

Code of ethics: A code of ethics is a blueprint for developing a culture of values in an organization. A code consists of a clearly stated and written set of guidelines that managers, employees, and agents of an organization must follow. A code of ethics is a reference tool that provides guidance to both employees and managers on how to implement and practice business ethics in the workplace. A code should embody both business standards (such as customer satisfaction, a high quality of products, safety, and employee rights) and values (such as mutual trust, respect, and honesty).

Conflict of interest: A conflict of interest occurs when the private interests of an individual who works for an enterprise interfere, or appear to interfere, in any way with the interests of the enterprise as a whole. A conflict arises when an employee, officer, or director of an enterprise performs an action that will interfere with that individual's ability to perform his or her official duties.

Core values: Core values are values shared by the leadership, the employees, and the stakeholders of a business that make the business special and determine its organizational culture.

Corporate governance: Corporate governance refers to the system that a corporation establishes to structure relations among managers, directors, and shareholders, and between the enterprise and civil society. Such governance measures are necessary when government charters provide limited liability to shareholders, which separates ownership of the enterprise from responsibility for day-to-day operations. Corporate governance practices are built on the ethical premise that the leaders of an enterprise have an obligation to be fair, transparent, accountable, and responsible in their conduct toward shareholders and civil society.

Corruption: Corruption is any choice or action made or taken that intentionally violates the reasonable expectations of enterprise stakeholders for the profit or gain of one responsible to some degree for meeting those expectations. Public sector corruption is easy to recognize when a politician or bureaucrat accepts large sums of cash to steer a government contract to a particular enterprise. However, corruption also exists when an owner or manager consciously chooses to fail to meet reasonable stakeholder expectations for personal gain. The damage done to the reputation of the enterprise and the social capital of its community may be as severe as in public sector corruption.

Declaration of integrity: A declaration of integrity is a public agreement among business enterprises in an industry or a locality that they will abide by an agreed-on set of norms, values, and standards with a view to improving the business climate of the industry or community. This term differs from an *integrity pact* in that the government is not necessarily involved and the agreement has broader application than with government procurement. Such a declaration, however, does not have the immediate risk of loss of an ability to bid on a contract that characterizes an integrity pact. A declaration of integrity might be particularly valuable when a community foundation intends to fund a community-driven development project.

Discipline: A discipline is a body of theory and practice that requires both reflection and action to be put into practice. The discipline of responsible business conduct is a study that will last a lifetime. This discipline requires an understanding that an enterprise is a system and part of yet wider systems. It recognizes that there are bodies of experience embedded in traditions, laws and regulations, industry best practices, and emerging global standards that practitioners will spend precious time acquiring and sharing. Ultimately, the practitioner of such a discipline generates new knowledge to further the discipline itself.

Economic progress: According to Peter Drucker, economic progress is "a steady rise in the ability of an economy to invest more capital for each job and thereby to produce jobs that yield better living as well as a better quality of work and life." (From Peter F. Drucker, "The Delusion of 'Profits': A Company That Loses Money Is Socially Irresponsible," *Opinion Journal,* available at *www.opinionjournal.com/extra/?id+110003570.*)

Employee survey: An employee survey is a mechanism that an enterprise may use to secure feedback from employees and to evaluate the effectiveness and impact of the enterprise's ethics program. Such a survey sets forth questions concerning the enterprise's organizational culture, the way the enterprise's ethics program works in practice, and the measurable expected program outcomes, such as observed misconduct, willingness to seek advice and report misconduct, issue awareness, and employee satisfaction and commitment to the enterprise. Owners and managers use the survey data along with other data to determine whether they have set and communicated the proper standards and procedures and have fostered reasonable stakeholder expectations.

Enron and WorldCom: Business scandals and failures are not new, but it is a sign of how closely connected the global economies are that these two companies in the United States have become symbolic of much that is wrong with businesspeople. Researchers calculate that the loss of confidence following the collapse of Enron and WorldCom will cost the U.S. economy $37 billion to $42 billion in reduced gross domestic product. Enron, in particular, went from being the seventh largest company in the United States to bankruptcy in a matter of months as confidence in its leadership faded.

Ethics committee: In large, complex enterprises, an ethics committee is often created and assigned overall responsibility for the ethics and compliance program. The ethics committee helps develop and implement the ethics program and the code of ethics of an enterprise. The committee ensures that ethical, regulatory, and policy standards have been established within the enterprise and that they are widely and consistently communicated to all. The committee also monitors and improves the processes of the ethics program and works closely with all parties responsible for supervising and managing the ethics program, including the ethics office, the ethics officer, and the board of directors.

Ethics office: Many enterprises create an ethics office, which is responsible for the day-to-day management and implementation of the enterprise's ethics program. The office provides clarity and guidance on compliance with the code of ethics and the enterprise's policies and procedures regarding reporting and investigation of alleged misconduct. This office normally includes an ethics officer, support staff, and a helpline.

Ethics officer: The position of ethics officer is created to accomplish the day-to-day operations of the business ethics program. The ethics officer may or may not be the person with high-level responsibility for the business ethics program. He or she provides advice on ethical behavior and on how to report ethics concerns, investigates and monitors investigations of possible misconduct, monitors the development of the ethics program, and works with other bodies in the enterprise to promote compliance. The ethics officer ensures that all levels of the organization meet or exceed ethical, legal, and civil society expectations on a day-to-day basis. The ethics officer generally has the right to report directly to both the chief executive officer and the board of directors, and often to the audit committee.

External stakeholders: The external parties that have a stake in an enterprise's success include customers and consumers, suppliers and service providers, civil society organizations, nongovernmental organizations, government agencies, local community representatives, the media, and the environment. External stakeholders share the objective of having business succeed in a manner that strengthens both the economy and civil society. These stakeholders can provide feedback on values and political, economic, and social considerations that an enterprise should integrate into its ethical identity.

Feedback mechanism: A feedback mechanism is a tool that an enterprise may use to obtain timely information pertaining to the implementation and effectiveness of its ethics program. A feedback mechanism could take the form of a survey, a focus group, a one-on-one interview, or a helpline.

Fiduciary duties: Each member of the board of directors of an enterprise is a fiduciary who owes a duty of loyalty and duty of care to the enterprise. The duty of loyalty requires a board member to place the best interests of the enterprise first and to avoid advancing the member's personal, financial, or professional interests at the expense of the enterprise. The duty of care requires a board member to act as a reasonable and diligent businessperson would to help the enterprise create maximum shareholder value with minimum risk.

Focus groups: A focus group is a feedback mechanism that brings together a small group of employees and an outside party to gather information about life in the enterprise. A focus group is a particularly useful device in evaluating a business ethics program. During a focus group, the outside party asks detailed questions and receives in-depth responses from employees about the ethics program.

Good corporate governance: Good corporate governance is the process by which the leadership of an enterprise, especially a limited liability enterprise, sets standards and procedures for employees and agents, fosters reasonable expectations among stakeholders, and meets those expectations. Good corporate governance expresses itself through a sound set of core beliefs, standards and procedures, and expectations. It requires understanding the relevant context of the enterprise, its organizational culture, and its strengths and weaknesses. Good corporate governance exercises those strengths and reforms the weaknesses through infrastructure, including a business ethics program. Good corporate governance is more likely when there is a transparent relationship between the government and the private sector.

Good public governance: Good public governance is the process by which the leadership of a country makes and implements decisions concerning the market. There are eight characteristics of good governance: consensus building, participation of all interest, accountability, transparency, responsiveness, effectiveness and efficiency, equality and inclusiveness, and finally, the rule of law. Good public governance occurs when there is a transparent relationship between the government and the private sector.

Helpline: A helpline or hotline is a secure telephone line that is connected to an ethics office or the office of an ombudsman. Employees use this tool to contact the ethics office or ombudsman to report a violation or receive advice on matters that concern them. A current best practice is that no call to a helpline is refused except for grievance matters under a labor–management bargaining agreement.

Industry standards: Industry standards are standards that different enterprises in a specific industry develop and agree on with one another or that are so common as to be considered a custom of the industry or profession. Such standards go beyond laws and regulations to promote free, fair, and honest competition among the members of the industry.

Integrity pact: An integrity pact is an agreement among a group of businesses that obligates them to participate in a government tender or procurement process in a legal and transparent manner. Under an integrity pact, the parties may pledge not to offer, pay, accept, or seek bribes of any kind during the tender. The key component of an integrity pact is transparency. A business in the pact also abides by any and all sanctions placed on it by the other members of the pact.

Internal stakeholders: The internal parties that have a stake in an enterprise's success include the shareholders, the board of directors, the executive management, and the employees.

Learning organization: A learning organization is an enterprise adept at generating, acquiring, and sharing knowledge about its relevant context, its organizational culture, and the expectations of its stakeholders and at using that knowledge so that its owners, managers, employees, and agents can live the lives they truly want to live.

Money laundering: Under the process of money laundering, one conceals the existence, illegal source, or illegal application of income, and disguises that income to make it appear legitimate. (From Andrew J. Camelio and Benjamin Pergament, "Money Laundering," *American Criminal Law Review* 35, no. 3 (1998); available at *www.questia.com*.)

Ombudsman: The office of ombudsman is designed to be completely independent from enterprise management and to provide a safe place where employees and agents can seek advice and report concerns. The position of an organizational ombudsman in a business ethics program has evolved to be an independent, neutral, and alternative position. The position is independent because the ombudsman is not a part of day-to-day staff or operations management. It is neutral because the ombudsman does not function as an advocate for the enterprise or individual. It is alternative because the ombudsman does not duplicate any other enterprise function, such as investigations. With few exceptions, the ombudsman is authorized only to refer reports of misconduct for investigation with the express consent of the reporting source.

One-on-one interviews: One-on-one interviews of employees are used to secure detailed feedback for enterprise management and to allow management to conduct intensive questioning of individuals that is designed to improve the ethics program. An interview provides a forum in which an employee can identify and address issues that employee surveys may not bring to the surface.

Organizational culture: Organizational culture can be understood in the same way as the culture of a society, nationality, or country. Organizational culture is shaped by the enterprise's origin and history, as well as by the values, norms, and attitudes of its leaders and stakeholders. The culture is reflected in the organization's decision-making and communication procedures, production methods, and policies regarding servicing customers and clients. Organizational culture is the primary predictor of business ethics program success or failure. There are several measurable elements of culture that should be a part of the regular evaluation of the business ethics program by owners and managers.

Parade of horribles: A parade of horribles often consists of news headlines and stories about enterprises that failed and senior executives who went to prison for breaking the law. It is one way to encourage an enterprise and its owners, managers, employees, and agents to embrace the discipline of responsible business conduct. See, for example, *Enron and WorldCom.*

Purpose statement: The fundamental reasons for an enterprise's existence beyond profit are noted in the purpose statement. A purpose, unlike a vision of a desired future, is broad, essential, enduring, and even spiritual. A purpose inspires and guides employees and agents. It is pursued but never fully captured. Researchers suggest that the way to surface the purpose of an enterprise is to describe what the enterprise does, or intends to do, and ask, "Why is that important?" five times.

Relevant context: All enterprises strive to meet enterprise goals and objectives in a context of legal, economic, political, environmental, sociocultural, and technological elements. Each element in an enterprise's relevant context may cause threats, opportunities, demands, constraints, and uncertainties that owners, managers, workers, and agents must recognize and address.

Responsible business conduct: Responsible business conduct reflects an understanding of the relevant context of the enterprise, its organizational culture, and the reasonable expectations of its stakeholders. In one sense, responsible business conduct is very practical and rooted in the particular situation of the individual and enterprise. In another, however, responsible business conduct is a recognition that we are all in this situation together and that one does not cease to be a member of a community simply because one goes into business.

Responsible business enterprise: A responsible business enterprise is a learning organization that is adept at understanding its relevant context, its organization culture, and its core beliefs. From these understandings, the owners, managers, employees, and agents of such an enterprise are able to build an enterprise that has the appropriate standards, procedures, and expectations; has structures and systems; has communication and feedback; and has an enterprise alignment that is able to foster reasonable expectations among its stakeholders and meet those expectations. By meeting reasonable expectations, the responsible business enterprise is able to improve its business performance, to make a profit, and to contribute to the economic progress of its community.

Responsible officer: A responsible officer is a high-level person who is responsible for overseeing the business ethics program. The responsible officer should be an owner, director, or senior manager. This person may or may not be the ethics officer for the enterprise. Indeed, where the enterprise is large or complex, the responsible officer often has executive responsibilities and relies on the ethics officer to run day-to-day operations.

Reward system: Through a system of rewards, an enterprise provides rewards to employees who uphold core values and fulfill ethical goals in their day-to-day activities. These rewards may be formal, taking the form of promotions, pay raises, bonuses, and public recognition. The rewards may also be informal, taking the form of private praise or a special meeting with the president of the enterprise. A reward system reinforces the enterprise's commitment to ethics and encourages its employees and managers to conduct themselves according to the guidelines of the enterprise's code of ethics.

Risk management: The risk management process helps the owners and managers of an enterprise plan, organize, and control the day-to-day operations of the enterprise to minimize risks to capital and earnings. Risk management includes, but is not limited to, the management of risks associated with accidental losses, financial mismanagement, fraud and embezzlement, corruption, loss of reputation, and employee health and safety, as well as other operational risks.

Social capital: Social capital is the mutual trust and shared values among individuals within an organization and between an organization and external stakeholders that enables those parties to work together on a cooperative basis. Social capital accrues through performance at the grassroots level within an enterprise and through the creation of civil society organizations, such as trade groups, business associations, service clubs, charities, and non-governmental organizations.

State capture: State capture is an effort by an enterprise to shape the laws, policies, and regulations of the state to its own advantage by providing illicit, illegitimate, and nontransparent private gains to public officials.

Triple bottom line: Triple bottom line reporting requires enterprises to evaluate their social and environmental performance to the same degree they evaluate and report economic performance.

Values statement: A values statement sets forth in a clear and consistent form the core values that make an enterprise special in the market. Each value is explained in the relevant context and culture of the enterprise. The process of establishing core values requires an enterprise's leaders to consider the values and expectations of internal and external stakeholders.

Vision statement: A vision statement expresses a view of what success for the enterprise will look like. This statement incorporates the enterprise's short- and long-term objectives and provides the enterprise the opportunity to publicly declare its role in the market and in civil society and to set a standard that it can be expected to meet.

Appendix B: Glossary of Business Contract Terms

Acceptance: The unconditional agreement to an *offer*. This creates the contract. Before acceptance, any offer can be withdrawn, but once accepted the contract is binding on both sides. Any *conditions* have the effect of a counteroffer that must be accepted by the other party.

Agent: Somebody appointed to act on behalf of another person (known as the principal). The amount of authority to deal that the agent has is subject to agreement between the principal and the agent. However, unless told otherwise, third parties can assume the agent has full powers to deal.

Arbitration: Using an independent third party to settle disputes without going to court. The third party acting as arbitrator must be agreed by both sides. Contracts often include arbitration clauses nominating an arbitrator in advance.

Breach of contract: Failure by one party to a contract to uphold their part of the deal. A breach of contract will make the whole contract void and can lead to damages being awarded against the party which is in breach.

Collective agreement: Term used for agreements made between employees and employers, usually involving trade unions. They often cover more than one organization. Although these can be seen as contracts, they are governed by employment law, not contract law.

Comfort letters: Documents issued to back up an agreement but which do not have any contractual standing. They are often issued by a parent or associate company stating that the group will back up the position of a small company to improve its trading position. They always state that they are not intended to be legally binding. Also known as *letters of comfort*.

Company seal: An embossing press used to indicate the official signature of a company when accompanied by the signatures of two officers of the company. Since 1989 it has been possible for a company to indicate its agreement without use of the seal, by two signatures (directors or company secretary) plus a formal declaration. However, some companies still prefer to use a seal and the articles of a company can override the law and require a seal to be used.

Conditions: Major terms in a contract. Conditions are the basis of any contract and if one of them fails or is broken, the contract is breached. These are in contrast to *warranties*, the other type of contract term, which are less important and will not usually lead to the breach of the contract but rather an adjustment in price or a payment of damages.

Confidentiality agreement: An agreement made to protect confidential information if it has to be disclosed to another party. This often happens during negotiations for a larger contract, when the parties may need to divulge information about their operations to each other. In this situation, the confidentiality agreement forms a binding contract not to pass on that information whether or not the actual contract is ever signed. Also known as a non-disclosure agreement.

Consideration: In a contract each side must give some consideration to the other. Often referred to as the quid pro quo. Usually this is the price paid by one side and the goods supplied by the other. But it can be anything of value to the other party, and can be negative, for example, someone promising not to exercise a right of access over somebody else's land in return for a payment would be a valid contract, even if there was no intention of ever using the right anyway.

Consumer: A person who buys goods or services but not as part of their business. A company can be a consumer for contracts not related to its business, especially for goods or services it buys for its employees. Charities are also treated as consumers.

Due diligence: The formal process of investigating the background of a business, either prior to buying it, or as another party in a major contract. It is used to ensure that there are no hidden details that could affect the deal.

Employment contract: A contract between an employer and an employee. This differs from other contracts in that it is governed by employment legislation, which takes precedence over normal contract law.

Exclusion clauses: Clauses in a contract that are intended to exclude one party from liability if a stated circumstance happens. They are types of *exemption clauses*. The courts tend to interpret them strictly and, where possible, in favor of the party that did not write them. In customer dealings, exclusion clauses are governed by regulations that render most of them ineffective but note that these regulations do not cover you in business dealings.

Exemption clauses: Clauses in a contract that try to restrict the liability of the party that writes them. These are split into *exclusion clauses* that try to exclude liability completely for specified outcomes, and limitation clauses that try to set a maximum on the amount of damages the party may have to pay if there is a failure of some part of the contract. Exemption clauses are regulated very strictly in consumer dealings but these do not apply for those who deal in the course of their business.

Express terms: The terms actually stated in the contract. These can be the written terms, or verbal ones agreed before or at the time the contract is made (see *implied terms*).

Franchising: Commercial agreements that allow one business to deal in a product or service controlled by another. For example, most car manufacturers give franchises to sell their cars to local garages, who then operate using the manufacturer's brand.

Going concern: Accounting idea that a business should be valued on the basis that it will be continuing to trade and able to use its assets for their intended purpose. The alternative is a break-up basis, which sets values according to what the assets could be sold for immediately, often much less than their value if they were kept in use.

Implied terms: Terms and clauses that are implied in a contract by law or custom and practice without actually being mentioned by any party. Terms implied by custom and practice can always be overridden by *express terms*, but some terms implied by law cannot be overridden, particularly those relating to consumers (see *exemption clauses*).

Incorporate: Inclusion in, or adoption of, some term or condition as part of the contract. It differs from its company law definition where it refers to the legal act of creating a company.

Injunction: A remedy sometimes awarded by the court that stops some action being taken. It can be used to stop another party doing something against the terms of the contract. Injunctions are at the court's discretion and a judge may refuse to give one and award damages instead.

Joint and several liability: Where parties act together in a contract as partners they have joint and several liability. In addition to all the partners being responsible together, each partner is also liable individually for the entire contract. So a creditor could recover a whole debt from any one of them individually, leaving that person to recover their shares from the rest of the partners.

Joint venture: An agreement between two or more independent businesses in a business enterprise, in which they will share the costs, management, profits or benefits arising from the venture. The exact shares and responsibilities will be set out in a joint venture agreement.

Jurisdiction: A jurisdiction clause sets out the country or state whose laws will govern the contract and where any legal action must take place.

Letters of comfort: See *Comfort letters.*

Liability: A person or business deemed liable is subject to a legal obligation. A person/business who commits a wrong or breaks a contract or trust is said to be liable or responsible for it.

Limited liability: Usually refers to limited companies where the owners' liability to pay the debts of the company is limited to the value of their shares. It can also apply to contracts where a valid limitation clause has been included in the terms.

Liquidation: The formal breaking up of a company or partnership by realizing (selling or transferring to pay a debt) the assets of the business. This usually happens when the business is insolvent, but a solvent business can be liquidated if it no longer wishes to continue trading for whatever reason.

Misrepresentation: Where one party to a contract makes a false statement of fact to the other which that other person relies on. Where there has been a misrepresentation, then the party who received the false statement can get damages for their loss. The remedy of rescission (putting things back to how they were before the contract began) is sometimes available, but where it is not possible or too difficult the court can award damages instead.

Nonexecutive director: A director who does not work directly for a company but advises the other directors. Nonexecutive directors have the full powers and authority of any other director and can bind the company to any contract.

Offer: An offer to contract must be made with the intention to create, if accepted, a legal relationship. It must be capable of being accepted (not containing any impossible conditions), must also be complete (not requiring more information to define the offer) and not merely advertising.

Parent company: Where one company owns more than 50% of the voting rights of another company it is the parent of that company, which in turn becomes its subsidiary. It can also occur where the parent has less than 50% but can control the board of directors of the subsidiary; that is, it has the power to appoint and remove directors without referring to other shareholders.

Partnership: When two or more people or organizations join together to carry on a business.

Proxy: A person who acts on behalf of another for a specific purpose, or the form used to make such an appointment. In a company a shareholder can appoint a proxy to attend a meeting and vote on their behalf.

Quorum: The minimum number of people needed at a meeting for it to proceed and make any decisions.

Ratification: Giving authority to an act that has already been done. A company general meeting resolution can ratify an act previously done by the directors; or a principal can choose to ratify the act of an *agent* that was beyond the specified power of the agent.

Repudiation: Has two meanings in contract law. The first is where a party refuses to comply with a contract and this amounts to a breach of contract. The second is where a contract was made by a minor (person under the age of 18), who then repudiates it at or shortly after the age of 18. Then the repudiation *voids* the contract rather than causing a *breach of contract.*

Restrictive covenant: Often included in long-term contracts and contracts of employment to stop the parties working with competitors during the period of the agreement and for some time thereafter. However, unless carefully written, the courts will see them as being a restraint of trade and not enforce them.

Service contract: Directors and officers of a company are usually given service contracts that are different to a contract of service or employment contract. This is because directors and officers are not always employees and the effect of employment law is different.

Shareholders' agreement: An agreement between all of the shareholders about how the company should be run and the application of the rights of the shareholders. This acts as a contract between the shareholders. The company itself is not bound by it, as it is not a party to the agreement.

Subject to contract: Words used on documents exchanged by parties during contract negotiations. They denote that the document is not an offer or acceptance, and negotiations are ongoing. Often the expression *without prejudice* is used when subject to contract is meant.

Trademark: A registered name or logo that is protected by law. Trademarks must be granted through the Patent Office.

Underwriter: A person who signs as party to a contract. Now usually only applied to insurance contracts where the underwriters are those who agree to bear all or part of the risk in return for the premium payments.

Unfair terms: Some terms are made unfair by legislation and will not be enforced by the courts and may even be interpreted against the person who included them in the contract. The legislation mainly protects consumers, but can also apply where there is a business-to-business contract in which one party is significantly more powerful than the other.

Void: A void contract is one that cannot be performed or completed at all. A void contract is void from the beginning (ab initio) and the normal remedy, if possible, is to put things back to where they were before the contract. Contracts are void where one party lacks the capacity to perform the contracted task, it is based on a mistake, or it is illegal.

Warranties: Promises made in a contract, but which are less than a *condition*. Failure of a warranty results in liability to pay damages (see the financial terms below) but will not be a *breach of contract* unlike failure of a condition, which does breach the contract.

Without prejudice: A term used by solicitors in negotiations over disputes where an offer is made in an attempt to avoid going to court. If the case does go to court no offer or facts stated to be without prejudice can be disclosed as evidence. Often misused by businesses during negotiations when they actually mean *subject to contract*.

Appendix C: Glossary of International Trade Terms

A glossary of trade terms used in exporting. This appendix is part of "A Basic Guide to Exporting," (July 7, 2016) provided by the U.S. Commercial Service, to assist companies in exporting.

Advance payment: See *Cash in advance.*

Air waybill: Bill of lading that covers both domestic and international flights transporting goods to a specified destination. It is a nonnegotiable instrument of air transport that serves as a receipt for the shipper, indicating that the carrier has accepted the goods listed therein, and obligates the carrier to carry the consignment to the airport of destination according to specified conditions.

Antidiversion clause: To help ensure that U.S. exports go only to legally authorized destinations, the U.S. government generally requires a Destination Control Statement (DCS) on shipping documents. The DCS must be entered for items subject to the Export Administration Regulations (EARs), except for items designated EAR99 or that are eligible for certain license exceptions.

Antidumping duty: Special duty imposed to offset the price effect of dumping that has been determined to be materially harmful to domestic producers. See also *Dumping.*

Arbitration: Process of resolving a dispute or a grievance outside of the court system by presenting it to an impartial third party or panel for a decision that may or may not be binding.

Bill of lading: Contract between the owner of the goods and the carrier. For vessels, there are two types: a straight bill of lading, which is not negotiable, and a negotiable, or shipper's orders, bill of lading. The latter can be bought, sold, or traded while the goods are in transit.

Carnet: Standardized international customs document known as an ATA (admission temporaire or temporary admission) carnet that is used to obtain duty-free temporary admission of certain goods into the countries that are signatories to the ATA Convention. Under the ATA Convention, commercial and professional travelers may take commercial samples; tools of the trade; advertising material; or cinematographic, audiovisual, medical, scientific, or other professional equipment into member countries temporarily without paying customs duties and taxes or posting a bond at the border of each country to be visited.

Carriage and insurance paid to (CIP): Carriage and insurance paid for delivery to a named destination.

Carriage paid to (CPT): Carriage paid to a named destination. This term is used in place of *cost and freight (CFR)* and *cost, insurance, and freight (CIF)* for all modes of transportation, including intermodal.

Cash in advance (advance payment): Payment from a foreign customer to a U.S. exporter prior to actually receiving the exporter's products. It is the least risky form of payment from the exporter's perspective.

Central America and Dominican Republic Free Trade Agreement (CAFTA-DR): One of a series of free trade agreements involving the U.S. and other countries. Benefits include duty-free or reduced-duty access, better overall market access, treatment equal to local companies, and intellectual property protection.

Certificate of conformity: Signed statement from a manufacturer attesting that a product meets certain technical standards.

Certificate of free sale: Signed statement from the producer or exporter attesting that a product has been commercially sold within the country of origin.

Certificate of origin (COO): Signed statement required in certain nations attesting to the origin of the export item. Certificates of origin are usually validated by a semiofficial organization, such as a local chamber of commerce. A North American Free Trade Agreement (NAFTA) certificate of origin is required for products traded among the NAFTA countries (Canada, Mexico, and the United States) when duty preference is claimed for NAFTA qualified goods.

Commercial invoice: Document prepared by the exporter or freight forwarder and required by the foreign buyer to prove ownership and to arrange for payment to the exporter. It should provide basic information about the transaction, including a description of goods, the address of the shipper and seller, and the delivery and payment terms. In most cases, the commercial invoice is used to assess customs duties.

Confirming house: Company based in a foreign country that acts as a foreign buyer's agent and places confirmed orders with U.S. exporters. The confirming house guarantees payment to the exporters.

Consignment: Delivery of merchandise to the buyer or distributor, whereby the latter agrees to sell it and only then pay the U.S. exporter. The seller retains ownership of the goods until they are sold but also carries all of the financial burden and risk.

Consular invoice: Document required in some countries that describes the shipment of goods and shows information such as the consignor, consignee, and value of the shipment. Certified by the consular official of the foreign country stationed in the United States, it is used by the country's customs officials to verify the value, quantity, and nature of the shipment.

Contract: Written or oral agreement that is legally enforceable.

Copyright protection: Granted to the authors and creators of literary, artistic, dramatic, and musical works, sound recordings, and certain other intellectual works. A computer program, for example, is considered a literary work in the United States and some other countries.

Cost and freight (CFR): Cost and freight to a named overseas port.

Cost, insurance, and freight (CIF): Cost, insurance, and freight to a named overseas post. The seller quotes a price for the goods shipped by ocean (including insurance), all transportation costs, and miscellaneous charges to the point of debarkation from the vessel.

Countertrade: General expression meaning the sale or barter of goods on a reciprocal basis. There may also be multilateral transactions involved.

Countervailing duties: Additional duties imposed by an importing country to offset government subsidies in an exporting country when the subsidized imports provide a measurable benefit to a specific enterprise or industry and cause material injury to domestic industry in the importing country.

Customs-bonded warehouse: Building or other secured area in which dutiable goods may be stored, may be manipulated, or may undergo manufacturing operations without payment of duty.

Customs declaration: Document that traditionally accompanies exported goods bearing such information as the nature of the goods, their value, the consignee, and their ultimate destination. Required for statistical purposes, it accompanies all controlled goods being exported under the appropriate permit.

Customs invoice: Document used to clear goods through customs in the importing country by providing evidence of the value of goods. In some cases, the commercial invoice may be used for this purpose.

Date draft: Document used when the exporter extends credit to the buyer. It specifies a date on which payment is due, rather than a time period as with the time draft.

Destination Control Statement (DCS): Required for all exports from the United States of items on the Commerce Control List that are not classified as EAR99. The statement is added to the commercial invoice.

Direct exporting: Sale by an exporter directly to an importer located in another country.

Distributor: A merchant in the foreign country who purchases goods from the U.S. exporter (often at a discount) and resells them for a profit. The foreign distributor generally provides support and service for the product, relieving the U.S. exporter of these responsibilities.

Dock receipt: Receipt issued by an ocean carrier to acknowledge receipt of a shipment at the carrier's dock or warehouse facilities.

Documentary letter of credit/documentary draft: Document used to protect the interests of both buyer and seller. A letter of credit requires that payment be made on the basis of the presentation of documents to a lender conveying the title and indicating that specific steps have been taken. Letters of credit and drafts may be paid immediately or at a later date. Drafts that are paid on presentation are called sight drafts. Drafts that are to be paid at a later date, often after the buyer receives the goods, are called time drafts or date drafts.

Dumping: Sale of an imported commodity at a lower price in one market than in another—i.e., selling at less than "normal value" on the same level of trade, and in the ordinary course of trade. Dumping is considered an actionable trade practice when it disrupts markets and injures producers of competitive products in the importing country. Article VI of the General Agreement on Tariffs and Trade (World Trade Organization) permits the imposition of special antidumping duties on goods equal to the difference between their export price and their normal value.

E-commerce: Buying and selling over the Internet.

Electronic Export Information (EEI): Formerly known as Shipper's Export Declaration. Document used to control exports and act as a source document for official U.S. export statistics. EEI is required for shipments when the value of the commodities, classified under any single Schedule B number, is more than $2,500. EEI must be prepared and submitted, regardless of value, for all shipments requiring an export license or destined for countries restricted by the Export Administration Regulations.

Export-Import Bank of the United States (Ex-Im Bank): U.S. government organization that provides export finance products to U.S. exporters and foreign buyers of U.S. products.

Export license: Government document that authorizes the export of specific items (including technology), in specific quantities, to a specific destination. May be required for most or all exports to some countries, or for other countries only under special circumstances.

Export management company (EMC): Company that performs the functions that would be typically performed by the export department or the international sales department of manufacturers and suppliers. EMCs develop personalized services promoting their clients' products to international buyers and distributors. They solicit and transact business in the names of the producers they represent or in their own name for a commission, salary, or retainer plus commission. EMCs usually specialize either by product or by foreign market. Because of their specialization, the best EMCs know their products and the markets they serve very well and usually have well-established networks of foreign distributors already in place. This immediate access to foreign markets is one of the principal reasons for using an EMC, because establishing a productive relationship with a foreign representative may be a costly and lengthy process.

Export packing list: List that itemizes the exported material in each package and indicates the type of package, such as a box, crate, drum, or carton. An export packing list is considerably more detailed and informative than a standard domestic packing list. It also shows the individual net, tare, and gross weights and measurements for each package (in both U.S. and metric systems).

Export processing zone (EPZ): Site in a foreign country established to encourage and facilitate international trade. EPZs include free trade zones, special economic zones, bonded warehouses, free ports, and customs zones. EPZs have evolved from initial assembly and simple processing activities to include high-tech and science parks, finance zones, logistics centers, and even tourist resorts.

Export quotas: Specific restrictions or ceilings imposed by an exporting country on the value or volume of certain exports designed, for example, to protect domestic producers and consumers from temporary shortages of the goods affected or to bolster their prices in world markets.

Export subsidies: Government payments or other financially quantifiable benefits provided to domestic producers or exporters contingent on the export of their goods and services.

Export trading company (ETC): Company that acts as an independent distributor, creating transactions by linking domestic producers and foreign buyers. As opposed to representing a given manufacturer in a foreign market, the ETC determines what U.S. products are desired in a given market and then works with U.S. producers to satisfy the demand. ETCs can perform a sourcing function, searching for U.S. suppliers to fill specific foreign requests for U.S. products.

Ex works (EXW): The buyer is responsible for all export procedures, including vehicle loading, transportation, and costs arising after collection of the goods.

Foreign Agricultural Service (FAS): A U.S. Department of Agriculture bureau with programs related to market development, international trade agreements and negotiations, and the collection of statistics and market information. It also administers the USDA's export credit guarantee and food aid programs, and helps increase income and food availability in developing nations.

Foreign Corrupt Practices Act (FCPA): Act making it unlawful for persons or companies subject to U.S. jurisdiction to offer, pay, or promise to pay money or anything of value to any foreign official for the purpose of obtaining or retaining business. It is also unlawful to make a payment to any person while knowing that all or a portion of the payment will be offered, given, or promised, directly or indirectly, to any foreign official for the purposes of assisting the company in obtaining or retaining business. "Knowing" includes the concepts of "conscious disregard" and "willful blindness." The FCPA also covers foreign persons or companies that commit acts in furtherance of such bribery in the territory of the United States.

U.S. persons or companies, or covered foreign persons or companies, should consult an attorney when confronted with FCPA issues.

Foreign-trade zone (FTZ): Domestic U.S. sites that are considered outside U.S. customs territory and are available for activities that might otherwise be carried on overseas for customs reasons. For export operations, the zones provide accelerated export status for purposes of excise tax rebates. For reexport activities, no customs duties, federal excise taxes, or state or local ad valorem taxes are charged on foreign goods moved into zones unless and until the goods or products made from them are moved into customs territory. Thus, the use of zones can be profitable for operations involving foreign dutiable materials and components being assembled or produced in the United States for reexport.

Free alongside ship (FAS): A seller's price for the goods, including the charge for delivery of the goods alongside at the named port of export. The seller handles the cost of wharfage, while the buyer is accountable for the costs of loading, ocean transportation, and insurance. It is the seller's responsibility to clear the goods for export.

Free in: Pricing term that indicates that the charterer of a vessel is responsible for the cost of loading goods onto the vessel.

Free in and out: Pricing term that indicates that the charterer of the vessel is responsible for the cost of loading and unloading goods from the vessel.

Free on board (FOB): An international commercial term (INCO term) that means free on board and is used in international sales contracts. In an FOB contract, a buyer and a seller agree on a designated FOB point. The seller assumes the cost of having goods packaged and ready for shipment from the FOB point, whether it is the seller's own place of business or some intermediate point. The buyer assumes the costs and risks from the FOB point, including inland transportation costs and risks in the exporting country, as well as all subsequent transportation costs, including the costs of loading the merchandise on a vessel. If the contract stipulates "FOB vessel," the seller bears all transportation costs to the vessel named by the buyer, as well as the costs of loading the goods on that vessel. The same principle applies to the abbreviations FOR (free on rail) and FOT (free on truck).

Free out: Pricing term that indicates that the charterer of the vessel is responsible for the cost of unloading goods from the vessel.

Freight forwarder: Agent for moving cargo to an overseas destination. These agents are familiar with the import rules and regulations of foreign countries, the export regulations of the U.S. government, the methods of shipping, and the documents related to foreign trade.

Global Entrepreneurial Ecosystem (GEE): A local community support system for small and medium-size exporters.

Gross domestic product (GDP): The total value of all goods and services produced by a country.

INCO terms: See *Terms of sale.*

Indirect exporting: Sale by the exporter to the buyer through a domestically located intermediary, such as an export management company or an export trading company.

Inspection certificate: Document required by some purchasers and countries to attest to the specifications of the goods shipped. The inspection is usually performed by a third party.

Insurance certificate: Document prepared by the exporter or freight forwarder to provide evidence that insurance against loss or damage has been obtained for the goods.

Intellectual property (IP): Collective term used to refer to new ideas, inventions, designs, writings, films, and so on that are protected by a copyright, patent, or trademark.

International Buyer Program (IBP): U.S. Department of Commerce program that matches U.S. exhibitors at select U.S. trade shows with foreign buyers.

International Trade Administration (ITA): A U.S. Department of Commerce bureau responsible for export promotion programs.

Joint venture: Independent business formed cooperatively by two or more parent companies. This type of partnership is often used to avoid restrictions on foreign ownership and for longer term arrangements that require joint product development, manufacturing, and marketing.

Letter of credit: Instrument issued by a bank on behalf of an importer that guarantees an exporter payment for goods or services, provided that the terms of the credit are met. A letter of credit issued by a foreign bank is sometimes confirmed by a U.S. bank. This confirmation means that the U.S. bank (the confirming bank) adds its promise to pay to that of the foreign bank (the issuing bank). A letter of credit may be either irrevocable, in which case it cannot be changed unless both parties agree, or revocable, in which case either party may unilaterally make changes. A revocable letter of credit is inadvisable as it carries many risks for the exporter.

Licensing: Arrangement in which a company sells the rights to use its products or services but retains some control. Although not usually considered to be a form of partnership, licensing can lead to partnerships.

Market survey: Report that provides a narrative description and assessment of a particular market along with relevant statistics. The reports are often based on original research conducted in the countries studied and may include specific information on both buyers and competitors.

Multilateral development bank (MDB): An institution created by a group of countries to provide development-related financing and professional advising.

NAFTA Certificate of Origin: Used by NAFTA signatories (i.e., Canada, Mexico, and the United States) to determine if goods imported into their countries receive reduced or eliminated duty.

North American Free Trade Agreement (NAFTA): Trade agreement between the U.S., Canada, and Mexico featuring duty-free entry and other benefits for goods that qualify.

Office of the U.S. Trade Representative: U.S. government agency responsible for negotiating trade agreements.

Packing list: See *Export packing list.*

Patent: Right that entitles the patent holder, within the country that granted or recognizes the patent, to prevent all others, for a set period of time, from using, making, or selling the subject matter of the patent.

Piggyback marketing: Arrangement in which one manufacturer or service company distributes a second company's product or service. The most common piggybacking situation is when a U.S. company has a contract with an overseas buyer to provide a wide range of products or services. Often this first company does not produce all of the products it is under contract to provide, and it turns to other U.S. companies to provide the remaining products.

Primary market research: Collection of data directly from a foreign marketplace through interviews, surveys, and other direct contact with representatives and potential buyers. Primary market research has the advantage of being tailored to your company's needs and provides answers to specific questions, but the collection of such data is time consuming and expensive.

Pro forma invoice: Invoice prepared by the exporter before shipping the goods, informing the buyer of the goods to be sent, their value, and other key specifications.

Quotation: Offer by the exporter to sell the goods at a stated price and under certain conditions.

Regional value content (RVC): A technique used to determine whether a product meets a rule of origin.

Remarketer: Export agent or merchant who purchases products directly from the manufacturer, packing and marking the products according to his or her own specifications. Remarketers then sell these products overseas through their contacts in their own names and assume all risks.

Sales representative: Representative who uses your company's product literature and samples to present the product to potential buyers. An overseas sales representative is the equivalent of a manufacturer's representative in the United States. The sales representative usually works on a commission basis, assumes no risk or responsibility, and is under contract for a definite period of time.

Secondary market research: Collection of data from various sources, such as trade statistics for a country or a product. Working with secondary sources is less expensive and helps your company focus its marketing efforts. Although secondary data sources are critical to market research, they do have limitations. The most recent statistics for some countries may be more than two years old, and the data may be too broad to be of much value to your company.

Sight draft: Document used when the exporter wishes to retain title to the shipment until it reaches its destination and payment is made. Before the shipment can be released to the buyer, the original "order" ocean bill of lading (the document that evidences title) must be properly endorsed by the buyer and surrendered to the carrier. It is important to note that air waybills do not need to be presented in order for the buyer to claim the goods. Thus, risk increases when a sight draft is being used with an air shipment.

Small Business Development Center (SBDC): National network of counselors for small enterprises. Offers services that can help first-time exporters.

Tariff: Tax imposed on a product when it is imported into a country. Some foreign countries apply tariffs to exports.

Technology licensing: Contractual arrangement in which the licenser's patents, trademarks, service marks, copyrights, trade secrets, or other intellectual property may be sold or made available to a licensee for compensation that is negotiated in advance between the parties. U.S. companies frequently license their technology to foreign companies that then use it to manufacture and sell products in a country or group of countries defined in the licensing agreement. A technology licensing agreement usually enables a company to enter a foreign market quickly and poses fewer financial and legal risks than owning and operating a foreign manufacturing facility or participating in an overseas joint venture.

Terms of sale: Terms that define the obligations, risks, and costs of the buyer and seller involving the delivery of goods that comprise the export transaction. These terms are commonly known as INCO terms.

Time draft: Document used when the exporter extends credit to the buyer. The draft states that payment is due by a specific time after the buyer accepts the time draft and receives the goods. By signing and writing "accepted" on the draft, the buyer is formally obligated to pay within the stated time.

Trade Fair Certification Program (TFC): A U.S. Department of Commerce program that certifies international trade events so U.S. companies can know ahead of time if an event is high quality and offers opportunities.

Trademark: Word, symbol, name, slogan, or combination thereof that identifies and distinguishes the source of sponsorship of goods and may serve as an index of quality of a particular product.

Trade statistics: Data that indicate total exports or imports by country and by product. They allow you to compare the size of the market for a product in various countries. By looking at statistics over several years, you can determine which markets are growing and which markets are shrinking.

Trading house: Company specializing in the exporting and importing of goods produced or provided by other companies.

U.S. Agency for International Development (USAID): U.S. government agency that procures goods and services from U.S. companies for use in developing countries.

U.S. Central Intelligence Agency (CIA): U.S. government agency tasked with gathering intelligence and statistics. Publishes the *World Factbook*, an important market research resource.

U.S. Commercial Service (CS): The trade promotion arm of the U.S. Department of Commerce's International Trade Administration.

U.S. Department of Agriculture (USDA): U.S. government department responsible for developing and executing federal government policy on farming, agriculture, forestry, and food.

U.S. Department of Commerce (DOC): U.S. government department responsible for promoting domestic economic growth and handling other commerce related responsibilities.

U.S. Small Business Administration (SBA): U.S. government agency that manages programs for U.S. exporters, including finance programs.

U.S. Trade and Development Agency (USTDA): U.S. government agency that provides grants for feasibility studies in developing countries.

Warehouse receipt: Receipt identifying the commodities deposited in a recognized warehouse. It is used to transfer accountability when the domestic carrier moves the export item to the port of embarkation and leaves it with the ship line for export.

Appendix D: Acronyms

AV	adjusted value
B2B	business-to-business
B2C	business-to-consumer
BIS	Bureau of Industry and Security
CAFTA-DR	Central America and Dominican Republic Free Trade Agreement
CDC	Centers for Disease Control and Prevention
CEO	chief operating officer
CIA	Central Intelligence Agency
CIF	cost, insurance, and freight
CIP	carriage and insurance paid to
COO	certificate of origin
COO	chief operating officer
CPT	carriage paid to
CS	U.S. Commercial Service
CTO	chief technology officer
DHL	Formerly DHL Worldwide Express
DOC	U.S. Department of Commerce
DOE	U.S. Department of Energy
DOS	U.S. Department of State
EMC	export management company
ETC	export trading company
Ex-Im Bank	Export-Import Bank of the United States
EXW	ex works
FAS	Foreign Agricultural Service
FAS	free alongside ship
FCA	free carrier
FedEx	Formerly Federal Express
FOB	free on board
FTA	free trade agreement
FTZ	free trade zone
GDP	gross domestic product
GEE	Global Entrepreneurial Ecosystem
IBP	International Buyer Program

ITA	International Trade Administration
LLC	limited liability corporation
LLP	limited liability partnership
MDB	multilateral development bank
NAFTA	North American Free Trade Agreement
NC	net cost
ROI	return on investment
ROO	rule(s) of origin
RVC	regional value content
SBA	U.S. Small Business Administration
SBDC	Small Business Development Center
TANC	Office of Trade Agreements Negotiations and Compliance
TFC	Trade Fair Certification Program
TV	transaction value
UPS	Formerly United Parcel Service
U.S.	United States (of America)
USA	United States of America
USAID	U.S. Agency for International Development
USDA	U.S. Department of Agriculture
USPS	U.S. Postal Service
USTDA	U.S. Trade and Development Agency
USTR	Office of the U.S. Trade Representative
VNM	value of nonoriginating materials
VOM	value of originating materials
VP	vice president
WTO	World Trade Organization

Appendix E: Cybersecurity

BEST PRACTICES FOR VICTIM RESPONSE AND REPORTING OF CYBER INCIDENTS

Version 1.0 (April 2015)

Cybersecurity Unit, Computer Crime & Intellectual Property Section, Criminal Division, U.S. Department of Justice

1301 New York Avenue, N.W., 6th Floor, Washington, D.C. 20530; cybersecurity.ccips@usdoj.gov; (202) 514-1026

Any Internet-connected organization can fall prey to a disruptive network intrusion or costly cyber attack. A quick, effective response to cyber incidents can prove critical to minimizing the resulting harm and expediting recovery. The best time to plan such a response is now, *before* an incident occurs.

This "best practices" document was drafted by the Cybersecurity Unit to assist organizations in preparing a cyber incident response plan and, more generally, in preparing to respond to a cyber incident. It reflects lessons learned by federal prosecutors while handling cyber investigations and prosecutions, including information about how cyber criminals' tactics and tradecraft can thwart recovery. It also incorporates input from private sector companies that have managed cyber incidents. It was drafted with smaller, less well-resourced organizations in mind; however, even larger organizations with more experience in handling cyber incidents may benefit from it.

I. Steps to Take *Before* a Cyber Intrusion or Attack Occurs

Having well-established plans and procedures in place for managing and responding to a cyber intrusion or attack is a critical first step toward preparing an organization to weather a cyber incident. Such pre-planning can help victim organizations limit damage to their computer networks, minimize work stoppages, and maximize the ability of law enforcement to locate and apprehend perpetrators. Organizations should take the precautions outlined below before learning of a cyber incident affecting their networks.

A. Identify Your "Crown Jewels"

Different organizations have different mission critical needs. For some organizations, even a short-term disruption in their ability to send or receive email will have a devastating impact on their operations; others are able to rely on other means of communication to transact business, but they may suffer significant harm if certain intellectual property is stolen. For others still, the ability to guarantee the integrity and security of the data they store and process, such as customer information, is vital to their continued operation.

The expense and resources required to protect a whole enterprise may force an organization to prioritize its efforts and may shape its incident response planning. Before formulating a cyber incident response plan, an organization should first determine which of their data, assets, and services warrants the most protection. Ensuring that protection of an organization's "crown jewels" is appropriately prioritized is an important first step to preventing a cyber intrusion or attack from causing catastrophic harm. The Cybersecurity Framework produced by the National Institute of Standards and Technology (NIST) provides excellent guidance on risk management planning and policies and merits consideration.[1]

B. Have an Actionable Plan in Place Before an Intrusion Occurs

Organizations should have a plan in place for handling computer intrusions before an intrusion occurs. During an intrusion, an organization's management and personnel should be focused on containing the intrusion, mitigating the harm, and collecting and preserving vital information that will help them assess the nature and scope of the damage and the potential source of the threat. A cyber incident is not the time to be

---

[1] The NIST Cybersecurity Framework is available at http://www.nist.gov/cyberframework/upload/cybersecurity-framework-021214.pdf.

creating emergency procedures or considering for the first time how best to respond.

The plan should be "actionable." It should provide specific, concrete procedures to follow in the event of a cyber incident. At a minimum, the procedures should address:

- Who has lead responsibility for different elements of an organization's cyber incident response, from decisions about public communications, to information technology access, to implementation of security measures, to resolving legal questions;
- How to contact critical personnel at any time, day or night;
- How to proceed if critical personnel is unreachable and who will serve as back-up;
- What mission critical data, networks, or services should be prioritized for the greatest protection;
- How to preserve data related to the intrusion in a forensically sound manner;
- What criteria will be used to ascertain whether data owners, customers, or partner companies should be notified if their data or data affecting their networks is stolen; and
- Procedures for notifying law enforcement and/or computer incident-reporting organization.

All personnel who have computer security responsibilities should have access to and familiarity with the plan, particularly anyone who will play a role in making technical, operational, or managerial decisions during an incident. It is important for an organization to institute rules that will ensure its personnel have and maintain familiarity with its incident response plan. For instance, the procedures for responding to a cyber incident under an incident response plan can be integrated into regular personnel training. The plan may also be ingrained through regularly conducted exercises to ensure that it is up-to-date. Such exercises should be designed to verify that necessary lines of communication exist, that decision-making roles and responsibilities are well understood, and that any technology that may be needed during an actual incident is available and likely to be effective. Deficiencies and gaps identified during an exercise should be noted for speedy resolution.

Incident response plans may differ depending upon an organization's size, structure, and nature of its business. Similarly, decision-making under a particular incident response plan may differ depending upon the nature of a cyber incident. In any event, institutionalized familiarity with the organization's framework for addressing a cyber incident will expedite response time and save critical minutes during an incident.

C. Have Appropriate Technology and Services in Place Before an Intrusion Occurs

Organizations should already have in place or have ready access to the technology and services that they will need to respond to a cyber incident. Such equipment may include off-site data back-up, intrusion detection capabilities, data loss prevention technologies, and devices for traffic filtering or scrubbing. An organization's computer servers should also be configured to conduct the logging necessary to identify a network security incident and to perform routine back-ups of important information. The requisite technology should already be installed, tested, and ready to deploy. Any required supporting services should either be acquired beforehand or be identified and ready for acquisition.

D. Have Appropriate Authorization in Place to Permit Network Monitoring

Real-time monitoring of an organization's *own* network is typically lawful if prior consent for such monitoring is obtained from network users. For this reason, before an incident takes place, an organization should adopt the mechanisms necessary for obtaining user consent to monitoring users' communications so it can detect and respond to a cyber incident. One means of accomplishing this is through network warnings or "banners" that greet users who log onto a network and inform them of how the organization will collect, store, and use their communications. A banner can also be installed on the ports through which an intruder is likely to access the organization's system.

A banner, however, is not the only means of obtaining legally valid consent. Computer user agreements, workplace policies, and personnel training may also be used to obtain legally sufficient user consent to monitoring. Organizations should obtain written acknowledgement from their personnel of having signed such agreements or received such training. Doing so will provide an organization with ready proof that they have met legal requirements for conducting network monitoring.

Any means of obtaining legally sufficient consent should notify users that their use of the system constitutes consent to the interception of their communications and that the results of such monitoring may be disclosed to others, including law enforcement.[2] If an organization is a government entity (e.g., a federal, state, or local agency or a state university) or a private entity acting as an instrument or agent of the government, its actions may implicate the Fourth Amendment. Consequently, any notice on the system of such an entity or organization should also inform users of their diminished expectation of privacy for communications on the network.

E. Ensure Your Legal Counsel is Familiar with Technology and Cyber Incident Management to Reduce Response Time During an Incident

Cyber incidents can raise unique legal questions. An organization faced with decisions about how it interacts with government agents, the types of preventative technologies it can lawfully use, its obligation to report the loss of customer information, and its potential liability for taking specific remedial measures (or failing to do so) will benefit from obtaining legal guidance from attorneys who are conversant with technology and knowledgeable about relevant laws (e.g., the Computer Fraud and Abuse Act (18 U.S.C. § 1030), electronic surveillance, and communications privacy laws). Legal counsel that is accustomed to addressing these types of issues that are often associated with cyber incidents will be better prepared to provide a victim organization with timely, accurate advice.

Many private organizations retain outside counsel who specialize in legal questions associated with data breaches while others find such cyber issues are common enough that they have their own cyber-savvy attorneys on staff in their General Counsel's offices. Having ready access to advice from lawyers well acquainted with cyber incident response can speed an organization's decision making and help ensure that a victim organization's incident response activities remain on firm legal footing.

---

[2] More guidance on banners, including a model banners, can be found in our manual on searching and seizing electronic evidence and in a 2009 legal opinion prepared by the Department of Justice's Office of Legal Counsel. *See Searching and Seizing Computers and Obtaining Electronic Evidence in Criminal Investigations* (3d ed. 2009), available at http://www.justice.gov/criminal/cybercrime/docs/ssmanual2009.pdf; and Stephen G. Bradbury, *Legal Issues Relating to the Testing, Use, and Deployment of an Intrusion-Detection System to Protect Unclassified Computer Networks in the Executive Branch*, 33 Op. Off. Legal Counsel 1 (2009), available at http://www.justice.gov/sites/default/files/olc/opinions/2009/01/31/e2-issues.pdf.

F. Ensure Organization Policies Align with Your Cyber Incident Response Plan

Some preventative and preparatory measures related to incident planning may need to be implemented outside the context of preparing a cyber incident response plan. For instance, an organization should review its personnel and human resource policies to ensure they will reasonably minimize the risk of cyber incidents, including from "insider threats." Proper personnel and information technology (IT) policies may help prevent a cyber incident in the first place. For instance, a practice of promptly revoking the network credentials of terminated employees—particularly system administrators and information technology staff—may prevent a subsequent cyber incident from occurring. Furthermore, reasonable access controls on networks may reduce the risk of harmful computer misuse.

G. Engage with Law Enforcement Before an Incident

Organizations should attempt to establish a relationship with their local federal law enforcement offices long before they suffer a cyber incident. Having a point-of-contact and a pre-existing relationship with law enforcement will facilitate any subsequent interaction that may occur if an organization needs to enlist law enforcement's assistance. It will also help establish the trusted relationship that cultivates bi-directional information sharing that is beneficial both to potential victim organizations and to law enforcement. The principal federal law enforcement agencies responsible for investigating criminal violations of the federal Computer Fraud and Abuse Act are the Federal Bureau of Investigation (FBI) and the U.S. Secret Service. Both agencies conduct regular outreach to private companies and other organizations likely to be targeted for intrusions and attacks. Such outreach occurs mostly through the FBI's Infragard chapters and Cyber Task Forces in each of the FBI's 56 field offices, and through the U.S. Secret Service's Electronic Crimes Task Forces.

H. Establish Relationships with Cyber Information Sharing Organizations

Defending a network at all times from every cyber threat is a daunting task. Access to information about new or commonly exploited vulnerabilities can assist an organization prioritize its security measures. Information sharing organizations for every sector of the critical infrastructure exist to provide such information. Information Sharing and Analysis Centers (ISACs) have been created in each sector of the critical infrastructure and for key resources. They produce analysis of cyber threat information that is shared within the relevant sector, with other sectors, and with the government. Depending upon the sector, they may also provide other cybersecurity services. The government has also encouraged the creation of new information sharing entities called Information Sharing and Analysis Organizations (ISAOs) to accommodate organizations that do not fit within an established sector of the critical infrastructure or that have unique needs.[3] ISAOs are intended to provide such organizations with the same benefits of obtaining cyber threat information and other supporting services that are provided by an ISAC.

II. Responding to a Computer Intrusion: Executing Your Incident Response Plan

An organization can fall victim to a cyber intrusion or attack even after taking reasonable precautions. Consequently, having a vetted, actionable cyber incident response plan is critical. A robust incident response plan does more than provide procedures for handling an incident; it also provides guidance on how a victim organization can continue to operate while managing an incident and how to work with law enforcement and/ or incident response firms as an investigation is conducted.[4] An organization's incident response plan should, at a minimum, give serious consideration to all of the steps outlined below.

A. Step 1: Make an Initial Assessment

During a cyber incident, a victim organization should immediately make an assessment of the nature and scope of the incident. In particular, it is important at the outset to determine whether the incident is a malicious act or a technological glitch. The nature of the incident will determine the

---

[3] See, Exec. Order No. 13,691, 80 Fed. Reg. 9347 (Feb. 20, 2015), available at http://www.gpo.gov /fdsys/pkg/FR-2015-02-20/pdf/2015-03714.pdf.

[4] Often in the case of data breaches, organizations may learn that they have been the victim of an intrusion from a third party. For instance, law enforcement may discover evidence while conducting a data breach investigation that other organizations have also been breached, or a cybersecurity company's forensic analysis of a customer's network following a breach may uncover evidence of other victims. Organizations should be prepared to respond to such receiving such notice.

type of assistance an organization will need to address the incident and the type of damage and remedial efforts that may be required.

Having appropriate network logging capabilities enabled can be critical to identifying the cause of a cyber incident. Using log information, a system administrator should attempt to identify:

- The affected computer systems;
- The apparent origin of the incident, intrusion, or attack;
- Any malware used in connection with the incident;
- Any remote servers to which data were sent (if information was exfiltrated); and
- The identity of any other victim organizations, if such data is apparent in logged data.

In addition, the initial assessment of the incident should document:

- Which users are currently logged on;
- What the current connections to the computer systems are;
- Which processes are running; and
- All open ports and their associated services and applications.

Any communications (in particular, threats or extortionate demands) received by the organization that might relate to the incident should also be preserved. Suspicious calls, emails, or other requests for information should be treated as part of the incident.

Evidence that an intrusion or other criminal incident has occurred will typically include logging or file creation data indicating that someone improperly accessed, created, modified, deleted, or copied files or logs; changed system settings; or added or altered user accounts or permissions. In addition, an intruder may have stored "hacker tools" or data from another intrusion on your network. In the case of a root-level intrusion,[5] victims should be alert for signs that the intruder gained access to multiple areas of the network. The victim organization should take care to ensure that its actions do not unintentionally or unnecessarily modify stored data in a way that could hinder incident response or subsequent criminal

---

[5] An intruder with "root level access" has the highest privileges given to a user working with an operating system or other program and has as much authority on the network as a system administrator, including the authority to access files, alter permissions and privileges, and add or remove accounts.

investigation. In particular, potentially relevant files should not be deleted; if at all possible, avoid modifying data or at least keep track of how and when information was modified.

B. Step 2: Implement Measures to Minimize Continuing Damage

After an organization has assessed the nature and scope of the incident and determined it to be an intentional cyber intrusion or attack rather than a technical glitch, it may need to take steps to stop ongoing damage caused by the perpetrator. Such steps may include rerouting network traffic, filtering or blocking a distributed denial-of-service attack,[6] or isolating all or parts of the compromised network. In the case of an intrusion, a system administrator may decide either to block further illegal access or to watch the illegal activity to identify the source of the attack and/or learn the scope of the compromise.

If proper preparations were made, an organization will have an existing back-up copy of critical data and may elect to abandon the network in its current state and to restore it to a prior state. If an organization elects to restore a back-up version of its data, it should first make sure that the back-up is not compromised as well.

Where a victim organization obtains information regarding the location of exfiltrated data or the apparent origin of a cyber attack, it may choose to contact the system administrator of that network. Doing so may stop the attack, assist in regaining possession of stolen data, or help determine the true origin of the malicious activity. A victim organization may also choose to blunt the damage of an ongoing intrusion or attack by "null routing"[7] malicious traffic, closing the ports being used by the intruder to gain access to the network, or otherwise altering the configuration of a network to thwart the malicious activity.

The victim organization should keep detailed records of whatever steps are taken to mitigate the damage and should keep stock of any associated

---

[6] A Distributed Denial of Service (DDOS) attack involves the orchestrated transmission of communications engineered to overwhelm another network's connection to the Internet to impair or disrupt that network's ability to send or receive communications. DDOS attacks are usually launched by a large number of computers infected by malware that permits their actions to be centrally controlled.

[7] A null route directs the system to drop network communications that are destined for a specified IP address on the network, so a system will no longer send any response to the originating IP address. This means the system will continue to receive data from the attackers but no longer respond to them.

costs incurred. Such information may be important for recovering damages from responsible parties and for any subsequent criminal investigation.

C. Step 3: Record and Collect Information

1. Image the Affected Computer(s)

Ideally, a victim organization will immediately make a "forensic image" of the affected computers, which will preserve a record of the system at the time of the incident for later analysis and potentially for use as evidence at trial.[8] This may require the assistance of law enforcement or professional incident response experts. In addition, the victim organization should locate any previously generated backups, which may assist in identifying any changes an intruder made to the network. New or sanitized media should be used to store copies of any data that is retrieved and stored. Once the victim organization makes such copies, it should write-protect the media to safeguard it from alteration. The victim organization should also restrict access to this media to maintain the integrity of the copy's authenticity, safeguard it from unidentified malicious insiders, and establish a chain of custody. These steps will enhance the value of any backups as evidence in any later criminal investigations and prosecutions, internal investigations, or civil law suits.

2. Keep Logs, Notes, Records, and Data

The victim organization should take immediate steps to preserve relevant existing logs. In addition, the victim organization should direct personnel participating in the incident response to keep an ongoing, written record of all steps undertaken. If this is done while responding to the incident or shortly thereafter, personnel can minimize the need to rely on their memories or the memories of others to reconstruct the order of events. As the investigation progresses, information that was collected by the organization contemporaneous to the intrusion may take on unanticipated significance.

---

[8] A "forensic image" is an exact, sector-by-sector copy of a hard disk. Software capable of creating such copies of hard drives preserve deleted files, slack space, system files, and executable files and can be critical for later analysis of an incident.

The types of information that the victim organization should retain include:

- a description of all incident-related events, including dates and times;
- information about incident-related phone calls, emails, and other contacts;
- the identity of persons working on tasks related to the intrusion, including a description, the amount of time spent, and the approximate hourly rate for those persons' work;
- identity of the systems, accounts, services, data, and networks affected by the incident and a description of how these network components were affected;
- information relating to the amount and type of damage inflicted by the incident, which can be important in civil actions by the organization and in criminal cases;
- information regarding network topology;
- the type and version of software being run on the network; and
- any peculiarities in the organization's network architecture, such as proprietary hardware or software.

Ideally, a single, designated employee will retain custody of all such records. This will help to ensure that records are properly preserved and can be produced later on. Proper handling of this information is often useful in rebutting claims in subsequent legal proceedings (whether criminal or civil) that electronic evidence has been tampered with or altered.

3. Records Related to Continuing Attacks

When an incident is ongoing (e.g., during a DDOS attack, as a worm is propagating through the network, or while an intruder is exfiltrating data), the victim organization should record any continuing activity. *If a victim organization has not enabled logging on an affected server, it should do so immediately.* It should also consider increasing the default size of log files on its servers to prevent losing data. A victim organization may also be able to use a "sniffer" or other network-monitoring device to record communications between the intruder and any of its targeted servers. Such monitoring, which implicates the Wiretap Act (18 U.S.C. §§ 2510 et seq.) is typically lawful, provided it is done to protect the organization's rights or property or system users have actually or impliedly consented to such monitoring. An organization should consult with its legal counsel to make sure such monitoring is conducted lawfully and consistent with the organization's employment agreements and privacy policies.

D. Step 4: Notify[9]

1. People Within the Organization

Managers and other personnel within the organization should be notified about the incident as provided for in the incident response plan and should be given the results of any preliminary analysis. Relevant personnel may include senior management, IT and physical security coordinators, communications or public affairs personnel, and legal counsel. The incident response plan should set out individual points-of-contact within the organization and the circumstances in which they should be contacted.

2. Law Enforcement

If an organization suspects at any point during its assessment or response that the incident constitutes criminal activity, it should contact law enforcement immediately. Historically, some companies have been reticent to contact law enforcement following a cyber incident fearing that a criminal investigation may result in disruption of its business or reputational harm. However, a company harboring such concerns should not hesitate to contact law enforcement.

The FBI and U.S. Secret Service place a priority on conducting cyber investigations that cause as little disruption as possible to a victim organization's normal operations and recognize the need to work cooperatively and discreetly with victim companies. They will use investigative measures that avoid computer downtime or displacement of a company's employees. When using an indispensable investigative measures likely to inconvenience a victim organization, they will do so with the objective of minimizing the duration and scope of any disruption.

The FBI and U.S. Secret Service will also conduct their investigations with discretion and work with a victim company to avoid unwarranted disclosure of information. They will attempt to coordinate statements to the news media concerning the incident with a victim company to ensure that information harmful to a company's interests is not needlessly disclosed. Victim companies should likewise consider sharing press releases

---

[9] Some private organizations are regulated by the federal government and may be subject to rules requiring notification if a data breach or other cyber incident occurs. While guidance to such organizations for notifying regulators is beyond the scope of this document, a cyber incident response plan should take into account whether a victim organization may need also to notify regulators and how best to do so.

regarding a cyber incident with investigative agents before issuing them to avoid releasing information that might damage the ongoing investigation.

Contacting law enforcement may also prove beneficial to a victim organization. Law enforcement may be able to use legal authorities and tools that are unavailable to non-governmental entities[10] and to enlist the assistance of international law enforcement partners to locate stolen data or identify the perpetrator. These tools and relationships can greatly increase the odds of successfully apprehending an intruder or attacker and securing lost data. In addition, a cyber criminal who is successfully prosecuted will be prevented from causing further damage to the victim company or to others, and other would-be cyber criminals may be deterred by such a conviction.

In addition, as of January 2015, at least forty-seven states have passed database breach notification laws requiring companies to notify customers whose data is compromised by an intrusion; however, many data breach reporting laws allow a covered organization to delay notification if law enforcement concludes that such notice would impede an investigation. State laws also may allow a victim company to forgo providing notice altogether if the victim company consults with law enforcement and thereafter determines that the breach will not likely result in harm to the individuals whose personal information has been acquired and accessed. Organizations should consult with counsel to determine their obligations under state data breach notification laws. It is also noteworthy that companies from regulated industries that cooperate with law enforcement may be viewed more favorably by regulators looking into a data breach.

3. The Department of Homeland Security

The Department of Homeland Security has components dedicated to cybersecurity that not only collect and report on cyber incidents, phishing, malware, and other vulnerabilities, but also provide certain incident response services. The National Cybersecurity & Communications Integration Center (NCCIC) serves as a 24/7 centralized location for cybersecurity information sharing, incident response, and incident coordination. By

---

[10] For instance, data that are necessary to trace an intrusion or attack to its source may not be obtainable without use of legal process (e.g., a search warrant, court order, or subpoena) that may be unavailable to a private party. Furthermore, some potentially useful intrusion detection techniques require law enforcement involvement. For instance, under 18 U.S.C. § 2511(2)(i) a network owner may authorize law enforcement to intercept a computer trespasser's communications on the network owner's computers during an investigation.

contacting the NCCIC, a victim organization can both share and receive information about an ongoing incident that may prove beneficial to both the victim organization and the government. A victim organization may also obtain technical assistance capable of mitigating an ongoing cyber incident.

4. Other Potential Victims

If a victim organization or the private incident response firm it hires uncovers evidence of additional victims while assessing a cyber incident—for example, in the form of another company's data stored on the network—the other potential victims should be promptly notified. While the initial victim can conduct such notification directly, notifying victims through law enforcement may be preferable. It insulates the initial victim from potentially unnecessary exposure and allows law enforcement to conduct further investigation, which may uncover additional victims warranting notification. Similarly, if a forensic examination reveals an unreported software or hardware vulnerability, the victim organization should make immediate notification to law enforcement or the relevant vendor.

Such notifications may prevent further damage by prompting the victims or vendors to take remedial action immediately. The victim organization may also reap benefits, because other victims may be able to provide helpful information gleaned from their own experiences managing the same cyber incident (e.g., information regarding the perpetrator's methods, a timeline of events, or effective mitigation techniques that may thwart the intruder).

III. What Not to Do Following a Cyber Incident

A. Do Not Use the Compromised System to Communicate

The victim organization should avoid, to the extent reasonably possible, using a system suspected of being compromised to communicate about an incident or to discuss its response to the incident. If the victim organization must use the compromised system to communicate, it should encrypt its communications. To avoid becoming the victim of a "social engineering" attack (i.e., attempts by a perpetrator to convince a target to take an action through use of a ruse or guile that will compromise the security of the system or data), employees of the victim organization should not disclose incident-specific information to unknown communicants inquiring about an incident without first verifying their identity.

B. Do Not Hack Into or Damage Another Network

A victimized organization should not attempt to access, damage, or impair another system that may appear to be involved in the intrusion or attack. Regardless of motive, doing so is likely illegal, under U.S. and some foreign laws, and could result in civil and/or criminal liability. Furthermore, many intrusions and attacks are launched from compromised systems. Consequently, "hacking back" can damage or impair another innocent victim's system rather than the intruder's.

IV. After a Computer Incident

Even after a cyber incident appears to be under control, remain vigilant. Many intruders return to attempt to regain access to networks they previously compromised. It is possible that, despite best efforts, a company that has addressed known security vulnerabilities and taken all reasonable steps to eject an intruder has nevertheless not eliminated all of the means by which the intruder illicitly accessed the network. Continue to monitor your system for anomalous activity.

Once the victim organization has recovered from the attack or intrusion, it should initiate measures to prevent similar attacks. To do so, it should conduct a post-incident review of the organization's response to the incident and assess the strengths and weaknesses of its performance and incident response plan. Part of the assessment should include ascertaining whether the organization followed each of the steps outlined above and, if not, why not. The organization should note and discuss deficiencies and gaps in its response and take remedial steps as needed.

Cyber Incident Preparedness Checklist

Before a Cyber Attack or Intrusion
- Identify mission critical data and assets (i.e., your "Crown Jewels") and institute tiered security measures to appropriately protect those assets.

- Review and adopt risk management practices found in guidance such as the National Institute of Standards and Technology Cybersecurity Framework.
- Create an actionable incident response plan.
  - Test plan with exercises
  - Keep plan up-to-date to reflect changes in personnel and structure
- Have the technology in place (or ensure that it is easily obtainable) that will be used to address an incident.
- Have procedures in place that will permit lawful network monitoring.
- Have legal counsel that is familiar with legal issues associated with cyber incidents
- Align other policies (e.g., human resources and personnel policies) with your incident response plan.
- Develop proactive relationships with relevant law enforcement agencies, outside counsel, public relations firms, and investigative and cybersecurity firms that you may require in the event of an incident.

During a Cyber Attack or Intrusion
- Make an initial assessment of the scope and nature of the incident, particularly whether it is a malicious act or a technological glitch.
- Minimize continuing damage consistent with your cyber incident response plan.
- Collect and preserve data related to the incident.
  - "Image" the network
  - Keep all logs, notes, and other records
  - Keep records of ongoing attacks
- Consistent with your incident response plan, notify—
  - Appropriate management and personnel within the victim organization should
  - Law enforcement
  - Other possible victims
  - Department of Homeland Security
- Do not—
  - Use compromised systems to communicate.
  - "Hack back" or intrude upon another network.

After Recovering from a Cyber Attack or Intrusion
- Continue monitoring the network for any anomalous activity to make sure the intruder has been expelled and you have regained control of your network.
- Conduct a post-incident review to identify deficiencies in planning and execution of your incident response plan.

C-TPAT's Five Step
Risk Assessment

U.S. Customs and
Border Protection

C-TPAT's Five Step Risk Assessment

Table of Contents

Introduction and Concepts 3

    Risk Assessment 6

    Threat Assessment 6

    Vulnerability Assessment 7

    Action Plan 8

    Audit 9

    Recommending a Risk Assessment Process 9

    Documenting the Risk Assessment Process 11

Chapter One — Importers 12

Chapter Two — Brokers 16

Chapter Three — Consolidators 28

Chapter Four — Highway Carriers 32

Chapter Five — Foreign Manufacturers and U.S. Exporters 36

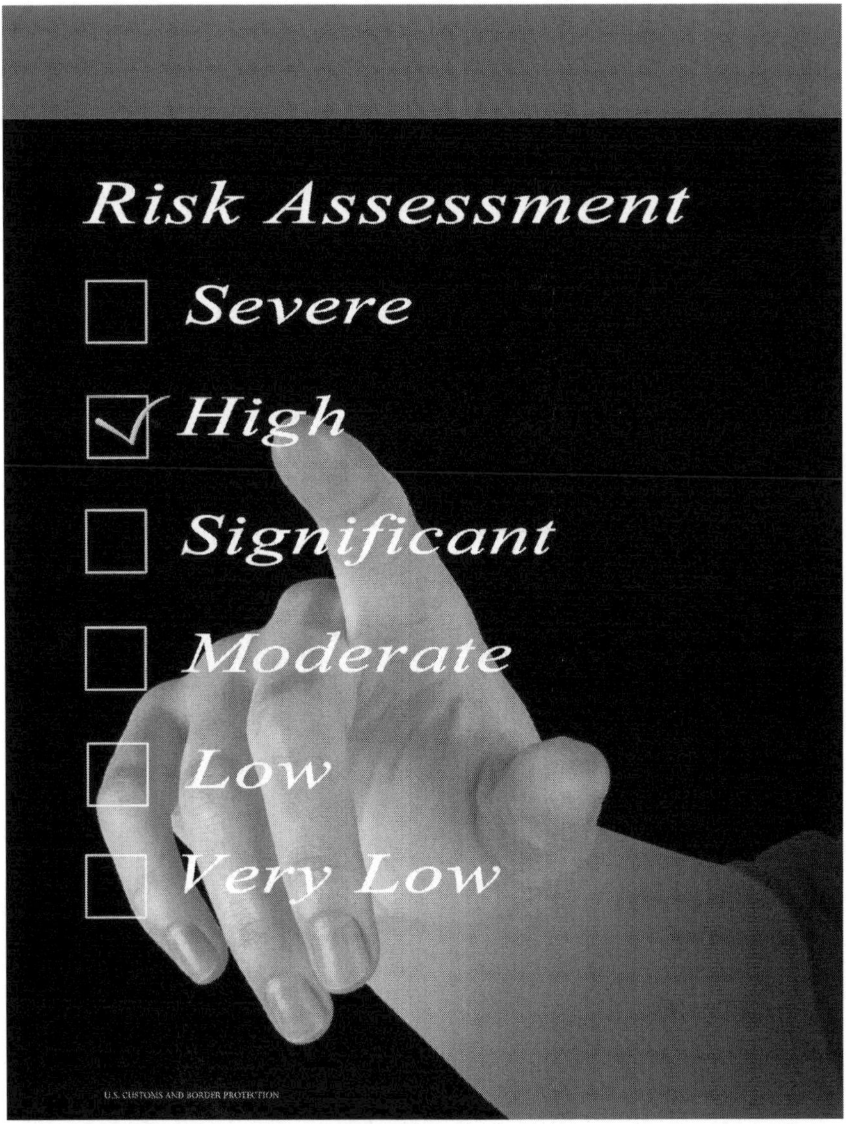
Risk Assessment
Severe
High
Significant
Moderate
Low
Very Low
U.S. CUSTOMS AND BORDER PROTECTION

The Customs-Trade Partnership Against Terrorism (C-TPAT) program is one layer in U.S. Customs and Border Protection's (CBP) multi-layered cargo enforcement strategy. Through this program, CBP works with the trade community to strengthen international supply chains and improve United States border security; in exchange, CBP affords C-TPAT Partners certain benefits, including reduced examination rates and access to the Free and Secure Trade (FAST) lanes.

Launched in November 2001 with seven major importers as a direct result of the tragic events of September 11, 2001, the program now includes more than 10,700 Partner companies, and covers the gamut of the trade community to include importers; exporters; border-crossing highway carriers; rail, air, and sea carriers; licensed U.S. Customs brokers; U.S. marine port authority/terminal operators; U.S. freight consolidators; Mexican and Canadian manufacturers; and Mexican long haul highway carriers. One vitally important aspect of the minimum security criteria Partners must address to maintain the security of their shipments is a documented risk assessment process.

As a voluntary public-private sector partnership program, C-TPAT recognizes that CBP can provide the highest level of cargo security only through close cooperation with the principal stakeholders of the international supply chain. Those companies that become C-TPAT Partners are expected to meet and maintain the security standards of the program. Part of that criteria is the requirement for Partners to conduct and document for C-TPAT's review a risk assessment of their international supply chains. The risk assessment process is critically important as it allows Partners to truly understand their supply chains, where the vulnerabilities lie within those supply chains, and determine what to do in order to mitigate any risks identified.

To assist Partners in creating a robust and effective Risk Assessment process, in 2010 C-TPAT published the "5 Step Risk Assessment Guide." Much time and many world events have occurred since then that necessitate an update and enhancement to the initial guide. Not least among these changes are the creation of the C-TPAT Exporter Entity, and the signing of several additional Mutual Recognition Arrangements. C-TPAT has now signed arrangements with the customs agencies of Canada, the European Union, Japan, Jordan, New Zealand, South Korea, Taiwan, and Israel.

Since its inception in 2001, the C-TPAT program has evolved dramatically. During the revalidation process and when conducting an in-depth review of security breaches, it became apparent the process of conducting a security risk assessment was not being adequately performed, often due to a lack of knowledge on the topic. An analysis of validation results for C-TPAT importers in 2013 revealed 22.6% did not have a documented Risk Assessment process that effectively addressed their international supply chains.

The lack of a documented process generated an Action Required in the Partners' validation reports, and those Partners that did not adequately address this Action Required were subsequently removed from the program. Most C-TPAT Partners are conducting a comprehensive domestic risk assessment of their own facilities and processes in the United States; however, many Partners are not assessing the potential threats and vulnerabilities that may exist within their international supply chain from the point of manufacture/packing/stuffing and at each transportation link within the chain, until the cargo reaches the final point of distribution.

As part of the application process to join the C-TPAT program, applicants must be able to provide a documented process of how the company assesses risk. Due to the unique nature of every Partner's business model, the risk assessments described below are only guides, and all companies should establish a process that conforms to the needs of their business model, and not simply adopt a generic, externally provided model. C-TPAT Partners must conduct a risk assessment at least annually in order to remain in the C-TPAT program.

Even small Partners are required to have a documented Risk Assessment Process. In fact, the smaller a Partner is, the easier it is to conduct a Risk Assessment. If, for example, a small highway carrier with an established business model of hauling from a single manufacturer to a single U.S. importer, and not soliciting other clients or using owner-operator truckers, desires to establish a Risk Assessment process, it should take only several hours to conduct and document an effective process. The key is that Partners are expected to implement a proactive approach and mentality to address risk in their supply chains, and not simply shrug the issue off as being out of their control. Partners should keep in mind they have an important resource to assist them in all security-related issues — their assigned C-TPAT Supply Chain Security Specialist (SCSS).

Other concepts to keep in mind include that quantity does not necessarily define risk. An importer who sources 300 shipments a year from a low risk source in a politically stable country with a low risk of terrorism and smuggling should not disregard the risk of importing two shipments per year from a country that has recently had a violent turnover in government, a high corruption index, or has a current history of a low level of security. As a further example, an importer that receives 80% of its shipments from a specific manufacturer may not have a low risk supply chain if the manufacturer selects foreign ground transportation providers based solely on cost. From week to week or shipment to shipment, a manufacturer who frequently changes carriers is much higher risk than a manufacturer who always uses the same foreign trucker who is certified in an Authorized Economic Operator (AEO) program.

In addition to security, there are other issues that may cause delays in the movement of goods through a company's supply chain. Partners willing to take extra steps to reduce unexpected delays for agricultural issues are encouraged to consider expanding their risk assessments beyond security concerns. The use of wood packaging material (WPM) that is improperly treated and/or shows evidence that pests are present may result in substantial delays and additional costs incurred by the importer, i.e., possible liquidated damages, demurrage charges, costs for remedial mitigated action, and potentially even immediate re-exportation of the shipment.

WPM is defined as wood or wood products (excluding paper products) used in supporting, protecting, or carrying a commodity. Some examples of WPM include, but are not limited to, bins, cases, cratings, load boards, reels, boxes, containers, drums, pallets, skids, bracing, crates, dunnage, pallet collars, etc.

The supply chains with the highest risk of finding imports with non-compliant WPM are metal, stone, food, and finished wood products,

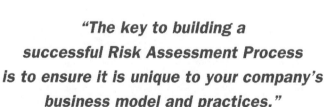

WPM Inspection

along with machinery, electronics, and plants. All imported shipments arriving into the United States using WPM must be properly treated under the International Standards for Phytosanitary Measures (ISPM 15).

C-TPAT has partnered with CBP's Agriculture Programs and Trade Liaison office to help Partners identify and mitigate the risks posed by the use of WPM in their supply chain(s). If your company imports, exports, or transports goods using WPM, please visit the CBP website for more information and training materials.

As part of a C-TPAT Partner's risk assessment process, C-TPAT Partners are not required to gather specific security-related procedures from business partners who have shared their certified C-TPAT or AEO status with the Partner conducting the risk assessment. The fact C-TPAT or a foreign mutually recognized customs program has validated such a Partner's procedures as meeting the minimum security criteria is intended to save time and effort on both Partners' security verification efforts.

While conducting risk assessments, these C-TPAT or AEO certified Partners should be considered low risk, although this does not mean the risk in the partner's involvement in the supply chain should be disregarded. It does mean the business partner is lower risk than other links in the supply chain, and should be treated accordingly.

"The key to building a successful Risk Assessment Process is to ensure it is unique to your company's business model and practices."

The original "5 Step Risk Assessment" guide in 2010 was written with importers in mind, and since the initial publication many questions and suggestions regarding the other types of Partners in the C-TPAT program have been received. Thus, this guide is broken into chapters for different types of business models, though not necessarily by specific C-TPAT entity classifications. This is because some consolidators might have business models similar to importers, while other consolidators might have models similar to brokers. Third Party Logistics operators may have models similar to highway carriers or to consolidators, and exporters may have models similar to foreign manufacturers.

The key to building a successful Risk Assessment Process is to ensure it is unique to your company's business model and practices. Generic, one-size-fits-all, "cookie cutter," externally inflicted procedures can lead to a false sense of security and an eventual breach of security.

As a lead in to the discussion of risk assessments, we will first define some terminology.

Risk Assessment

A Risk Assessment is analyzing external threats against company procedures to identify where vulnerabilities exist, and what procedures can be implemented or improved to reduce such risk.

This may include ensuring (through process improvement, retraining, working with business partners, etc.) that issues identified through analysis and audits as being vulnerabilities are successfully addressed. This may often be something as simple as clarifying a written policy, automating a process, simplifying a form to ensure more effective use of the form, or requiring the security guard to manually hold and examine identification documents (as opposed to viewing ID as a person walks by). A Risk Assessment consists of several components, including a Threat Assessment, Cargo and Data Flow, Vulnerability Assessment, and audits of security procedures. These steps are further delineated on the following pages.

A Risk Assessment should also include how security procedures would be affected by natural and man-made disasters, to include how backup systems will address these vulnerabilities. Such issues include power outages; weather events such as hurricanes; earthquakes; civil unrest; and terrorist events. Partners seeking to reduce the impact of such disasters should have documented business resumption procedures in place that are periodically tested.

You will note throughout the minimum security criteria that expensive technology is not mandatory, for in the end security relies upon the human component. This is why effective personnel screening and security training are critical issues. As an example, no matter how complicated a computer password is required by an Information Technology policy, if employees practice habits such as writing their passwords on sticky notes or "concealing" them underneath keyboards, security is easily breached.

Threat Assessment

A Threat Assessment is simply identifying threats to a supply chain that exist within a country or region, that are external and outside the control of the Partner, to a Partner's business model. Examples include terrorist activity, drug smuggling, hijacking, corruption levels, and human smuggling. Be aware threats in one state or province of a country may differ from threats in other states and provinces within the same country. Below you can see a snapshot of part of a Threat Assessment developed by a C-TPAT Partner for the region (British Columbia) in which they operate. A full, blank version of this document can be found for your use on the public CBP.gov website, under the C-TPAT Resource Library and Job Aids.

Threat Assessment: An assessment of a criminal or terrorist presence within a jurisdiction integrated with an assessment of potential targets of that presence and a statement of probability the criminal or terrorist will commit an unlawful act. The assessment focuses on the criminal's or terrorist's opportunity, capability, and willingness to fulfill the threat.

1 – Low Risk — No recent activity/intelligence information.

2 – Medium Risk — No recent incidents/Some intelligence/information on possible activity.

3 – High Risk — Recent incidents and intelligence/information.

Note: For C-TPAT purposes, a "3" for any Threat Risk Factor below results in a "High Risk" rating for the supply chain.

Partner: SP Trucking

Location: British Columbia

Country/Region: Canada

Threat Risk Factor	Risk Rating	Activity	Source of Information
Terrorism (Political, Bio, Agro, Cyber)	2	Threats posed by terrorism within Canada, particularly the radicalization of domestic extremists, has been clearly demonstrated through...	Canadian Security Intelligence Service www.csis.gc.ca

Threat Assessments should use some type of risk scaling, but this need not be complex. For an importer with dozens of supply chains, a numerical ranking system of 1–10 may be appropriate. For companies with few variances in regions of operations, a limited number of supply chains, and a steady business model, a simple high / medium / low system may be appropriate. The goal is to have a ranked output to determine where your company should focus time, energy, and resources to reduce and mitigate risk.

In the previous Risk Assessment Guide C-TPAT provided numerous internet sites to aid in developing a Threat Assessment. In this edition, internet sites are not being provided as there are literally thousands of useful and informative websites available on this topic. It would thus be presumptive to list only a few of these sites, and considering the extreme variances and complexities within Partners' business models, perhaps counter-effective.

Vulnerability Assessment

A Vulnerability Assessment is identifying weaknesses in a company's security procedures and supply chain that can be used to the advantage of terrorists and other criminals identified in the Threat Assessment. Internal audits and security reviews can be important instruments in identifying vulnerabilities. For example, an internal audit of the company itself (such as an internal audit during the annual security profile review, security questionnaires, and site visits conducted during business partner screening), could go into the overall vulnerability assessment. Corrective actions based on the findings of internal audits and business partner reviews can be implemented as part of the Action Plan. This is how the various actions taken by C-TPAT Partners to address program requirements all interact and overlap to strengthen security overall.

C-TPAT Partners are required to determine and assess the level of risk business partners bring into the supply chain. This is a requirement under the business partner screening section of the minimum security criteria, and information developed as part of that process should be included in determining risk in the appropriate supply chain. Typically, business partners should be analyzed against the appropriate minimum security criteria. For example, the highway carrier minimum security criteria should be used as a tool to assess the practices of, and risk level of, foreign and domestic highway carriers, even if those carriers do not physically cross a border. Similarly, foreign freight forwarders and brokers should be analyzed using the consolidator and/or broker minimum security criteria.

Assigning High Risk Targets

Consider on a personal basis:

You have recently purchased a new vehicle. The vehicle appears as number five on the most frequently stolen vehicle list in the United States for the past two years. This is your Threat Assessment, the external threat to your vehicle over which you have no control. You may need to further research this issue on-line, or by contacting local police departments and insurance companies, to determine if the threat in your area is higher or lower than the national average. Your insurance rate no doubt already includes risk factors of national and local theft rates.

A Vulnerability Assessment is next, which describes where your vehicle is susceptible to theft, and should include issues such as:

- Do you live in an area known for a high vehicle theft rate?

- Do you frequently use street parking at home and at restaurants, or do you lock the vehicle in your garage and only use secure parking lots or valet parking?

- Do you live on an island connected to the mainland via only a single causeway?

- Is it a convertible, with easier access than a traditional hardtop vehicle?

Once these vulnerabilities are identified and documented, you are ready to proceed to the next step, completing an Action Plan that will put into place procedures to reduce or mitigate the threats identified above.

Action Plan

An Action Plan consists of once having identified and documented vulnerabilities, developing and implementing procedures and/or improvements to reduce those vulnerabilities. In severe instances, a company may decide to withdraw from a high risk supply chain. In some instances, additional direct management oversight in daily operations might be deemed adequate to address the risks (e.g., posting an employee who works directly for the importer at a high-risk foreign manufacturer). In others, the implementation of additional overlapping, interlocking procedures or technology might be deemed to adequately address and mitigate the risk.

Using the personal vehicle example above, once having identified when and/or where your vehicle is most at risk of being stolen, what procedures do you put in place to mitigate the threat of theft? Examples might include installation of a theft alarm; installation of a false theft alarm by placing stickers on windows and a flashing red light on the dashboard; installation of a remote engine shutdown system; use of only manually attended parking lots/garages or valet parking at restaurants; use of a steering wheel locking mechanism; or registering and tagging your vehicle with the local police as not being allowed on the road between midnight and five a.m.

An audit of these procedures might include ensuring family discussions with all family members (i.e., periodic security threat and awareness training, or "company musters") on the reasons for, and necessity of, following these procedures, and that all persons understand the ramifications a "family member" (i.e., employee) might face for not following such procedures (resultant loss of use of the vehicle).

Audit

An audit is a periodic documented review to ensure the procedures the company has in place are being conducted and followed through on, as part of regular, every day procedures, and that records are completed and properly filed. Audits may reveal security deficiencies, but do not replace, rather enhance, a company's Vulnerability Assessment. For a sample Audit procedure incorporating the entirety of the minimum security criteria, see the chapter on Brokers.

Recommending a Risk Assessment Process

In order to assist C-TPAT Partners with conducting a risk assessment of their international supply chain(s) in accordance with the C-TPAT minimum security criteria, a Five Step Risk Assessment Process is recommended.

This reference guide contains some of the basic tools, resources, and examples C-TPAT partners should consider using when conducting a risk assessment of their international supply chain(s). The information contained herein is intended to serve as a guide, and is not "all inclusive" of what should be included in an international supply chain security risk assessment. For various free examples of some of these procedures and the suggested evidence of implementation, please see the Resource Library and Job Aids page on CBP.gov.

The Five Step process described below can be used by Partners of all entities to determine what threats exist to their business models, even if a Partner does not physically handle cargo. Those Partners that only handle data are also at risk, for if a terrorist or other criminal seeks access to a cargo shipment, the first thing they require is knowledge of a shipment and the identifying information of the companies involved in the cargo movement.

An example of how the C-TPAT minimum security criteria addresses these issues is under Broker Procedural Security, "Security measures must be in place to ensure the integrity of any data or documents relevant to security of processes, transportation, handling, and storage of cargo in the supply chain."

While many Partners use a numerical rating system to assess risk, an alternative method can be used. It is up to each Partner to determine how risk will be assessed. The threat and vulnerability factors described in this document should be used to determine the level of risk, which should be described appropriately (e.g., high, medium, or low; acceptable or unacceptable; pass or fail, etc.). A complex rating system may be used, but is not appropriate for all business models.

Partners should be aware that Incoterms have little to do with security assessments for terrorism and criminal activity. Incoterms are primarily directed towards cost, ownership, and insurance purposes. A terrorist willing to explode a device within a U.S. harbor, or a human trafficker impersonating a legitimate shipment through identity theft, cares not for legitimate ownership and insurance claims. The C-TPAT Partners responsible for the importation and exportation of goods across U.S. borders, no matter where the actual transfer of ownership occurs, are ultimately responsible for the security of that shipment, regardless of the Incoterms. The acknowledgment of this fact, and the willingness to be proactive and energetic in addressing supply chain security, is what separates C-TPAT Partners from those who are not Partners. Companies that feel the requirements of the C-TPAT minimum security criteria are too burdensome are not suited for the C-TPAT Program. For exporters particularly, it is critical shipments are protected from threats to U.S. allies to whom shipments are destined. The reputation of the entire U.S. business community rests on exporters being proactive and conscientious of their responsibilities concerning supply chain security. It is thus critical for the survival of all C-TPAT Partners to be aware, and selective of, its business partners.

The Five Step Risk Assessment Process includes:

1. **Mapping Cargo/Data Flow and Control and Identifying Business Partners** (whether directly or indirectly contracted) and how cargo moves throughout the supply chain to include modes of transportation (air, sea, rail, or truck) and nodes (country of origin, transit points).

2. **Conducting a Threat Assessment** focusing on Terrorism, Contraband Smuggling, Human Smuggling, Agricultural and Public Safety Threats, Organized Crime, and conditions in a country/region which may foster such threats, and ranking those threats.

3. **Conducting a Vulnerability Assessment in accordance with the C-TPAT Minimum Security Criteria.** A vulnerability assessment includes identifying what the Partner has that a terrorist or criminal might desire. For brokers this might be data; for importers, manufacturers, and exporters, this might be access to cargo and company information. Then, identifying weaknesses in company procedures that would allow a terrorist or criminal to gain access to these processes, data, or cargo.

4. **Preparing a Written Action Plan to Address Vulnerabilities.** This includes mechanisms to record identified weaknesses, who is responsible for addressing the issues, and due dates. Reporting results to appropriate company officials and employees on completed follow up and changes is also essential.

5. **Documenting the Procedure for How Risk Assessments are Conducted, to include Reviewing and Revising the Procedure Periodically.** The process itself should be reviewed and updated as needed at least annually, and a Risk Assessment should be conducted — and documented — at least annually, more frequently for highway carriers and high risk supply chains.

It is understood that some C-TPAT Partners have numerous supply chains, which may present a major task when conducting a comprehensive security risk assessment of their international supply chains. Therefore, it is recommended that C-TPAT Partners first identify their "High Risk" supply chains by conducting a threat assessment at the point of origin/region and where the cargo is routed/transshipped, and then conducting a comprehensive security vulnerability assessment of those supply chains. Subsequently the Partner should address the supply chains identified as medium and then low risk. This is to ensure the assumptions made in identifying risk levels as medium or low are in fact accurate. Companies that seek to elevate their security procedures to a Tier III status would be expected to complete threat, vulnerability, and risk assessments on all partners and supply chains.

Documenting the Risk Assessment Process

The five-step process above is generic in nature to allow its application to all business entities and models. A sample Risk Assessment Procedure, as described in Step Five above, is displayed here. A company's documented risk assessment process (e.g., policies and procedures) should contain, at minimum, the following information:

1. Date the Risk Assessment Process was established by the Partner, and latest revision date.

2. Identify company personnel responsible for keeping the process up-to-date, including "back-up" personnel.

3. When or how often a Risk Assessment must be conducted (e.g., annually, quarterly (recommended especially for highway carriers); a new business partner in a supply chain; threat conditions change in a country or region).

4. Required frequency of review and update to the actual Risk Assessment procedure (e.g., annually, quarterly, etc.).

5. How Threat Assessments of international supply chains are to be conducted.

6. How Vulnerability Assessments on the International Supply Chain are to be conducted (e.g., verification of C-TPAT/PIP/AEO Status, site visits by Quality Assurance Managers, analysis of completed security questionnaires).

7. How follow-up is conducted on "action items" (e.g., site visits to address vulnerabilities, termination of contracts).

8. Procedure for training key individuals who are responsible for the Risk Assessment Process, to include regional employees who frequently visit foreign sites for other purposes (e.g., quality assurance managers, sales representatives).

9. Internal management oversight and accountability for ensuring the process is carried out consistently and effectively.

Verifying Radioactive Isotopes Are As Manifested

Chapter One

For importers, the first step in a Risk Assessment is identifying all business partners involved in the knowledge and movement of cargo from point of origin to destination. If an importer cannot identify all steps and business partners in the movement of cargo from origin to destination in the U.S., the importer will not be able to control the security of each step in the supply chain. A sample spreadsheet delineating business partners involved in the movement of cargo from point of manufacture to destination in the U.S. is shown below. Note some supply chains may contain more steps than shown in the example, and some will contain fewer steps.

A modifiable version of the below document for Everything Importers is available on the public CBP.gov website, under the C-TPAT Resource Library and Job Aids.

Supply Chain Step	Type of Service Provided	Details About Business Partner	Issues to Consider
Foreign Manufacturer Information	Manufacturer	ABC Manufacturer 183 Jalan Bukit Bintang, Kuala Lumpur, Malaysia. Provides importer approximately 63% of imports.	Not eligible for C-TPAT; country has no AEO program
Highway Carrier (for both FCL and LCL)	Moves cargo from factory to consolidator and port of export	Super Secure Freight, Lebuh Relau, 11360 Bayan Lepas, Kuala Lumpur, Malaysia	Not eligible for C-TPAT; country has no AEO program
Consolidation Facility	Physical location where LCL freight is stuffed into container	FastCon, Building 62, Predak Commercial Zone, Kuala Lumpur, Malaysia	Not eligible, but visited by a C-TPAT team 12/12/2013. Report on file with importer, no Actions Required

Supply Chain Step	Type of Service Provided	Details About Business Partner	Issues to Consider
Highway Carrier	Moves cargo from consolidator to port of export	Reliable Haulers, 168 Jalan Imbi, Kuala Lumpur, Malaysia	Not eligible for C-TPAT; country has no AEO program
Freight Forwarder	Processes paperwork for cargo export, including ISF	Global Freight Coordinators, No 32, 1st Floor, BBandung Lepas, Kuala Lumpur, Malaysia	Not eligible for C-TPAT; country has no AEO program
Port of Export	Stores and handles cargo prior to lading	Pelabuhan Klang, Malaysia	Meets ISPS requirements
Ocean Carrier	Moves cargo from port to port	Excellent Ocean Carriers, 626 Joro Blvd, Pelabuhan Klang, Malaysia	C-TPAT status verified in Portal.
Transhipment Port	Stores and handles cargo in between vessel movements	Kaohsiung, Taiwan	Taiwan AEO Certified, Certificate in Portal Document Exchange
Ocean Carrier	Moves cargo from port to port	Pacific Swells, 5th Floor, No. 2, Chung Cheng 3rd Rd., Xin-Xing District, Kaohsiung City, Taiwan	C-TPAT status verified in Portal.
Ocean Terminal in US	Location of unlading	LA/Long Beach, CA	C-TPAT status verified in Portal.
US Import Broker	Files US import documentation	Paperwork Professionals, 555 Imperial Highway, Suite 816, Los Angeles, CA 90211	C-TPAT status verified in Portal.
Terminal Operator	Handles and stores cargo after unlading	Smith Terminal Facilities, Pier Z, Los Angeles, CA 90809	C-TPAT status verified in Portal.
Domestic Drayage	Trucks cargo from ocean terminal to consolidator or ultimate destination	Porter Transportation, 301 Normandie, Torrance, CA 90518	Not eligible, completed security questionnaire for this year on file

Supply Chain Step	Type of Service Provided	Details About Business Partner	Issues to Consider
Deconsolidator	Cuts seal and unloads container prior to domestic delivery of cargo.	Ochoa Warehousing, 201 Del Amo, Wilmington, CA 90512	Has no bond with CBP, thus not eligible. Security site visit conducted in past three months, results analyzed and on file. Three Actions Required. Uses outsourced day laborers; high risk.
Domestic Drayage	Trucks cargo from ocean terminal to consolidator or ultimate destination	Parsons Parcels and Trucking, 689 Opp St., Los Angeles, CA 90613	Not eligible, completed security questionnaire on file from last month.
Importer	This is our company.	Everything Importers, Address of Receiving Facility	This is our company, see latest Internal Audit on security procedures.

Container Inspections Should Detect Altered Container Frames

Chapter Two

For brokers that do not handle cargo, the primary item they possess and need to safeguard is information. If a terrorist desires to conceal weapons or people in a shipment, the first thing they need is specific knowledge of the shipment. C-TPAT has identified at least two occasions of identity theft targeting brokers, one the theft of identity of a client-importer of the broker to smuggle trademark violation merchandise, and the other an attempt at financial fraud.

For brokers that physically handle cargo, the choice for a risk assessment may be a combination of the broker and consolidator, or even importer, risk assessment processes. When determining how to create a Risk Assessment Process, brokers should consider their business model first. For a broker, steps one through three of the five step process could vary widely depending on the company's business model.

1. Cargo Mapping

- Cargo handler — similar to importer, with addition of broker example
- Non-cargo handler — use broker example

2. Vulnerability

- Cargo handler — similar to importer, with addition of broker example
- Non-cargo handler — use broker example

3. Threat

- Cargo handler — similar to importer, with addition of broker example
- Non-cargo handler — use broker example

4. Action Plan

5. Documented Procedure

The primary security task for brokers is to control who has access to their data and their clients' data. A full assessment of risks to the data can be identified through an internal audit that includes all aspects of the minimum security criteria, to determine both if procedures are adequate and if security procedures are being followed by employees. By controlling who the broker does business with and who has access to its facilities and data systems, the broker can control who can access its information.

"The primary security task for brokers is to control who has access to their data and their clients' data."

The first step in a risk assessment process for brokers includes an audit of documentation to ensure security procedures are followed on a daily, systemic basis, and that adherence to these standards is adequately documented. Persons conducting audits on various processes should not be those responsible for conducting the work regularly, but someone from another division or assignment. Results of the audits should be documented, to include possible vulnerabilities identified, and suggestions on how to improve and revise procedures.

The process used to conduct the first full risk assessment audit should be documented for future use. The process should be conducted on a scheduled basis, and should include the persons responsible for the completion of the project and those tasked with its parts.

All security-related procedures that have not yet been documented should be documented as part of the first assessment. All procedures and policies should have issuance and revision dates. A broker must consider all aspects of the minimum security criteria.

A more detailed checklist of items that should be reviewed, documented, and followed up on by the broker may be found at the end of this chapter.

Please remember that under the broker minimum security criteria, business partners are broken into two categories: Importer Clients and Service Providers.

An Importer Client is a company that approaches the broker and offers to pay the broker for services rendered to assist in clearing cargo with CBP.

A Service Provider is a business partner selected by the broker to supply services to the broker. Examples of the latter include a domestic drayage company; a de-consolidator; or a freight forwarder.

A visual for possible variations in screening these classes of partners is displayed here:

Importer Clients	Service Providers
C-TPAT status queried, verified, and documented?	C-TPAT status queried, verified, and documented?
Status in foreign program queried, verified, and documented?	Status in foreign program queried, verified, and documented?
Status within ISO 28000 queried, verified, and documented?	Status within ISO 28000 queried, verified, and documented?
Credit checks verified and documented?	Credit checks verified and documented?
Business References verified and documented?	Business References verified and documented?
Original Power of Attorney on file?	Membership in professional organizations verified and documented? (e.g., American Trucking Association)
	Status with U.S. government programs verified and documented? (TSA, IATA, FMC, etc.)
	Written statement (security questionnaire, letter of affirmation, etc.) that non-C-TPAT company is meeting minimum security criteria?
	Site visit for security purposes documented?
	Follow up action plan documented?
	Resolution of action items documented?

At the end of this chapter is a sample listing of some, but not all, of the items a broker might include on its Internal Audit Checklist to ensure employees are conforming to company security procedures. The items are broken down into these general C-TPAT criteria sections:

- **Business Partners**

- **Container and Trailer Security**

- **Procedural Security**

- **Physical Security**

- **Physical Access Controls**

- **Personnel Security**

- **Security Training and Threat Awareness**

- **Information Technology Security**

Audit Checklist

Business Partners

☐ Do all C-TPAT Partners show "certified" in the portal? If not, why not?

☐ If a previous C-TPAT partner now shows "not certified," have the remaining steps in the business partner screening process been conducted and documented?

☐ For all non-C-TPAT business partners, are records up to date with documented evidence of the required additional screening? This might include copies of current PIP/AEO certificates; completed copies of Security Questionnaires; documented reviews and analysis of completed Security Questionnaire; documented site visits; documented follow up on weaknesses; results of background queries, such as Specially Designated National queries, and industry certifications.

☐ Have "extra scrutiny triggers" for the screening of business partners been reviewed and updated?

☐ Has the company's Preferred Provider List been rescreened and updated?

☐ Has the updated list been disseminated to employees and old lists destroyed?

☐ Has Outreach/Training on the C-TPAT program been conducted with non-C-TPAT partners?

☐ Has the Outreach/Training been documented for each company?
If yes, in what manner? (On-site, telephonic, web-based, etc.).

☐ What topics were covered in the Outreach/Training (e.g., tracking and monitoring, conveyance inspections, seal procedures, notification to our company and customs/law enforcement with discrepancies, access controls, internal conspiracies, challenging strangers)?

☐ Have all business partners (both importer clients and service providers) been provided with the broker's contact information for security inquiries?

☐ Has the broker's website been updated with C-TPAT information and valid links to CBP.gov?

☐ What actions were taken to improve processes in this security category?

Procedural

- [ ] **Powers of Attorney** — Does our company have original, current powers of attorney for each active importer client?

  - [ ] If no, what follow up actions are to be taken?

- [ ] **Importer Security Filing** — What score did our company receive on its latest Importer Security Filing Progress Report?

  - [ ] How can this score be improved upon, if necessary?

  - [ ] How and what information was requested from importer clients whose track record requires improvement?

  - [ ] Who was tasked with this improvement?

  - [ ] Have the improvements been completed?

- [ ] **Entry filing** — What is the date of the last audit of entries filed with CBP?

  - [ ] What issues were identified that could be improved upon?

  - [ ] Who was tasked with this improvement?

  - [ ] What steps were taken to complete these improvements?

  - [ ] Have the improvements been completed?

- [ ] **Visitor and Driver Logs** — A manual review of all Visitor and Driver logs must be conducted.

  - [ ] What were the results?

  - [ ] Were all entries complete and legible?

  - [ ] What patterns of concern emerged?

  - [ ] Are there additional items it would make sense to add to the logs?

  - [ ] What actions can be taken to improve the logs?

Below, please find an example of the business processes typically provided by brokers to their client-importers. This Procedural Security breakdown is displayed below to assist brokers in drilling down to determine the level of security procedures in place to protect data.

Supply Chain Step	Type of Service Conducted by Our Company	Process	Risks Identified	Actions Taken to Mitigate Risks
Receipt of entry processing information	Documentation: Receiving in advance of arrival	Brokerage and Import Managers monitor the documentation transfer	Data leakage	Employees of both Departments sign non-disclosure statements. IT Firewall, Anti-virus, Anti-spyware software installed Training computer users on internet threats, to include phishing emails, and how to identify and report suspicious IT activity
Verification of import documents	Verification of Commercial Invoice information and other relevant import data	Brokerage Manager monitors the documentation verification	Overlooking inadequate, or not recognizing tampered documentation	Training appropriate employees on recognizing suspicious shipment and document indicators. Regular Audits and corrective actions
Obtaining and validating Power of Attorney (POA)	Having valid Power of Attorney	Brokerage Manager monitors the POA validation	Mistaken validation	Regular sampling and checking of validated POAs
Verification of description for proper classification	Verification of description for correct classification of imported goods	Brokerage Manager monitors the verification and classification	Misclassification, especially of suspicious goods	Training appropriate employees on recognizing suspicious shipment and document indicators Regular sampling and checking of Schedule B numbers against product descriptions
Contact CBP Website	Perform Bond Query	Brokerage Manager monitors the Bond Query process	Phishing through company internet access and email	IT Firewall, Anti-virus, Anti-spyware software installed Training computer users on internet threats, to include phishing emails, and how to identify and report suspicious IT activity
Contact CBP Website	Processing CBP entry and receive immediate electronic CBP release	Brokerage Manager monitors the CBP release	Phishing through company internet access and email	IT Firewall, Anti-virus, Anti-spyware software installed Training computer users on internet threats, to include phishing emails, and how to identify and report suspicious IT activity
Contact CBP Website	Print CBP Forms	Entry processing	Storage of blank forms	All forms kept in locked cabinets or only available electronically on computer

Supply Chain Step	Type of Service Conducted by Our Company	Process	Risks Identified	Actions Taken to Mitigate Risks
Arranging Pickup and Delivery	Arrange pick-up and delivery by approved Trucker upon arrival of freight	Quality Assurance Department monitors the selection of Truckers	Selection of trucker not on approved list Use of outdated approved list	Ensure employees trained to use truckers only on current list posted on intranet (no hardcopies that may be outdated allowed)
Instructing selected Trucker	Notify Trucker to validate container number, inspect container and perform View, Verify, Tug, and Twist seal inspection	Brokerage Compliance Department monitors the notification to Truckers	Improper communication to the selected Trucker	Periodic audit of notification e-mail messages
Pick Up and Deliver Shipment	Dispatch trucker for Pickup and Delivery of shipment	Dispatching Brokerage Staff	Diversion of products for introduction/ removal of unauthorized materials	Use of escort, GPS and driver who calls dispatcher often to update on movements until delivery. Dispatcher who logs contacts with driver and conducts real-time comparisons to GPS data/ driver calls. Audits of tracking and monitoring records for anomalies
Contact with Consignee	Verify delivery and obtain Proof of Delivery	Brokerage Manager monitors the process	Modification of documentation to conceal wrong doing	Regular checking by Brokerage Manager
Contact CBP	Submission of entry summary for final reconciliation by CBP	Brokerage Manager monitors the process	Concealing wrong doing	CBP reconciliation detects anomalies
Closing and filing	Closing entry files and filing them away for records	Brokerage Manager monitors the process	Ensure prevention of leakage of documents	Regular documented auditing by Brokerage Manager
Destruction of Records	Destroying entry files, commercial invoices, email printouts, etc.	Use of on-site contract shredding truck	Ensure documents are actually destroyed and not diverted during process	All destruction is conducted under direct supervision of brokerage employee

Physical Security

If the company has a security alarm system:

☐ What was the date of the last system test?

☐ What were the results?

☐ What possible improvements were identified?

If the company has a video surveillance system:

☐ What was the date of the last system test?

☐ Does review of night time video show adequate lighting in place?

☐ Were repairs made immediately upon discovery of a malfunction?

☐ Was a verification conducted to ensure that security cameras remained pointed on key areas?

☐ Are cameras not easily accessible in order to prevent tampering?

☐ Are recordings stored in a secure location?

☐ Describe what issues were identified and actions taken to address issues:

☐ What actions were taken to improve processes in this security category?

Access Controls

Access Device Logs

☐ Did a review of the issuance/retrieval of access device logs reveal any discrepancies? (e.g. any ex-employees still shown as having keys, ID cards, alarm codes?)

☐ Was a physical inventory of all access devices conducted?

☐ If yes, what issues of concern were found?

☐ What actions were taken to resolve these issues?

☐ What actions were taken to prevent recurrences?

☐ Building Inspections

☐ Are building inspection logs complete?

☐ Were identified issues resolved?

☐ How can the process to ensure building integrity be improved?

☐ What actions were taken to improve processes in this security category?

Personnel

Review all personnel files of persons hired and separated since last assessment.

☐ Did the review show any documents or data missing or incomplete?

☐ Were I-9 forms complete?

☐ Were all new hires queried through the E-Verify system?

☐ What patterns emerged concerning missing documents or data?

☐ What actions were taken to prevent recurrences?

☐ What actions were taken to improve processes in this security category?

Security Awareness and Training

☐ Has security training been updated since the previous iteration?

☐ Have all employees received mandatory training for their job position?

☐ If no, has make-up training been scheduled?

☐ What security topics were covered, and was training tailored to the responsibilities/jobs of the employees?

Below find a sample log that can be kept to ensure each employee receives the necessary job-specific training.

Employee Name	Job Title	C-TPAT Program Criteria	17-Point Inspections	Documenting Inspections	Challenging Strangers	Abnormal Shipments	Reporting Suspicious Activities	Conducting Site Security	IT Security	Mail / Package Safety
Woods, Porter	Operations Clerk	[Date]	N/A	N/A	[Date]	[Date]	[Date]	N/A	[Date]	[Date]
Adams, John	Dispatcher	[Date]	[Date]	[Date]	[Date]	[Date]	[Date]	N/A	[Date]	[Date]
Fraser, Alex	Mechanic	[Date]	[Date]	[Date]	[Date]	N/A	[Date]	N/A	N/A	N/A
Foss, Joseph	Driver	[Date]	[Date]	[Date]	[Date]	[Date]	[Date]	[Date]	N/A	N/A

N/A — Not applicable, this employee does not perform this activity/task.

[Date] — Last date this training was completed by this employee.

All training should be refreshed periodically, *at least* annually.

Information Technology (IT)

☐ Has the IT service provider been rescreened since the initial contract was signed?

☐ How frequently are firewall, anti-virus, and anti-spyware software updated?

☐ Was a security intrusion test performed to determine the effectiveness of protections?

☐ What were the results?

☐ What can be improved?

☐ How frequently are system backups conducted?

☐ Are backups stored in secure location?

☐ If cloud storage is used, was business partner screening conducted on the provider?

☐ Has IT retraining been conducted and documented?

☐ What actions were taken to improve processes in this security category?

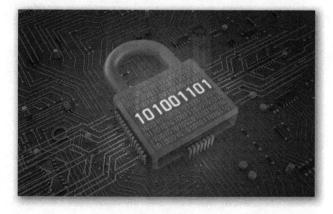

Chapter Three

Consolidator Partners in the C-TPAT program are not required to physically handle cargo, or even be involved in the import process. Consolidators who otherwise meet the C-TPAT eligibility requirements may be involved solely in the export business. Thus, many potential business models for C-TPAT consolidators exist. When determining how to create a Risk Assessment Process, consolidators should consider their business model first. For a consolidator, steps one through three of the five step process could vary widely depending on the company's business model.

1. Cargo Mapping

- Cargo handler (foreign or domestic) — similar to importer and exporter
- Non-cargo handler — similar to broker

2. Vulnerability

- Cargo handler (foreign) — similar to foreign manufacturer
- Cargo handler (domestic) — similar to importer and exporter
- Non-cargo handler — similar to broker

3. Threat

- Cargo handler (foreign) — similar to foreign manufacturer
- Cargo handler (domestic) — similar to importer and exporter
- Non-cargo handler — similar to broker

4. Action Plan

5. Documented Procedure

If the company does not physically handle freight, instead functioning primarily as a freight forwarder or "paper" consolidator, the Broker Risk Assessment model may best apply. If the consolidator is physically handling imported freight, the importer model may apply, with modifications. For export-only consolidators, a risk assessment process closer to that of a U.S. exporter may apply. For consolidators that also control the operations at a foreign facility for cargo moving to the U.S., concepts from the foreign manufacturer risk assessment process may be most applicable.

Obviously, consolidators are not typically in the business of selecting foreign manufacturers or foreign incountry transportation providers. Manufacturers are typically selected by the consolidator's client-importer, and foreign in-country transportation providers are often selected by the consolidator's foreign business partner agents. To address this lack of control over selecting business partners, it is extremely important for consolidators to address risk by selecting quality foreign agents, and to have strong and proactive outreach and education programs on C-TPAT and equivalent AEO programs. "Pushing out" the C-TPAT minimum security criteria to all levels of the supply chain through outreach and education, including to third and fourth level business partners, is a critical minimum security criteria element for all C-TPAT Partners, and becomes especially important when Partners have limited ability to select transportation providers in foreign countries. The best-case scenario is to require all partners in all links in the supply chain to be AEO or C-TPAT certified.

As an example of the dangers of using generic, "cookie cutter" risk assessments, consider a consolidator that does not handle cargo and has a single office located in a high-rise office building, but has elected to use a generic risk assessment process provided by an external advisor. The only valuable item such a consolidator possesses is information, but the generic process adopted from their advisor is actually formulated for importers who physically handle their own cargo.

Now consider these vulnerabilities:

■ A third-party janitorial service, selected by the building landlord, has metal keys allowing access for cleaning on Sundays when the consolidator's office is closed.

■ The consolidator has no alarm system to record when the third party employees, who are completely unknown and unscreened by the consolidator, actually enter and exit the office space.

■ The consolidator assumes the janitors access the office only on Sunday evenings, but have no method to verify this.

■ No video camera system exists for the consolidator's managers to review each morning to determine who was in the office after hours, and what they were doing.

■ The office photocopier's electronic records are not reviewed to determine if photocopies are made outside normal office hours.

■ The consolidator's IT contractor conducts no special checks or reports to determine if the company's IT system has been accessed or used outside normal business hours.

While the company has established a Risk Assessment process, it does not fit the company's business model and can lead to a false sense of security and eventual data theft. Is this the type of business partner with whom you would willingly put your personal bank account or company identity information at risk?

Chapter Four

Cross-border highway carriers' business models have some similarities to brokers, in the sense both brokers and carriers are hired by importers or manufacturers to provide services to these clients. However, while brokers need only protect a set location or locations, carriers, by their very nature, must be able to protect stationary facilities and moving conveyances.

For highway carriers, a supply chain might be displayed as the sample below.

Supply Chain Step	Type of Activity	Details About Partner	Issues to Consider
Foreign Manufacturer	Trailer storage, trailer loading	ABC Manufacturer, 123 Chavez, Tijuana, Baja California, provides 53% of shipments we move to US.	C-TPAT Certified, Physical security around truck and trailer (fences, gates, guards); restricted access to loading dock; secure overnight storage
Transport to border	Movement of cargo from manufacturer to border. Loaded trailers never taken to our storage yard.	This is our company. Internal procedures, especially as related to tracking and monitoring, must address vulnerabilities.	Tight and overlapping tracking and monitoring of trucks must be in place, with direct management oversight and written procedures for when things go wrong.
Export broker	Company that provides border crossing paperwork and may transmit data to government agencies.	Mexico broker. Knows about shipment and details in advance.	Are Personnel and IT security at a high level?
Port of Entry to US	Wait time	What is typical wait and release time at each port of entry?	How exposed is conveyance while waiting in line?
US Import broker	Company that provides border crossing paperwork and may transmit data to CBP.	US broker. Knows about shipment and details in advance.	Are Personnel and IT security at a high level?
Transport to destination in US	Movement of cargo from border to destination/transfer yard.	This is our company. Internal procedures, especially as related to tracking and monitoring, must address vulnerabilities. Reporting delays and suspicious activities critical for driver.	Tight and overlapping tracking and monitoring of trucks must be in place, with direct management oversight and written procedures for when things go wrong.

Once locations and movements are identified, the regional Threat Assessment can be applied against these steps in the carrier's daily activities to determine where weaknesses and vulnerabilities exist. Once these vulnerabilities are identified, an Action Plan to address such issues can be documented. A highway carrier's risk assessment will have more to do with addressing internal processes and vulnerabilities at points of loading, as opposed to correcting weaknesses in clients' internal processes, as the highway carrier is the service provider. Nevertheless, there may come a time when a client's processes are so high risk the highway carrier may determine for its own safety to stop conducting business with that client.

Highway carriers that handle less than trailer load freight and a spoke and hub consolidation network will have a different set of issues to address than in the example above. Similarly, carriers using a pick up and deliver ("milk run") business model will have a more complex series of issues to consider.

Risk factors for Highway Carriers

The history of highway carriers in the C-TPAT Program has demonstrated the issues below as being repetitive contributors to security breaches. Therefore, each step in a carrier's supply chain and business model should be analyzed for weaknesses in these areas:

- Loose tracking and monitoring of conveyances in transit;

- No overlapping or layered verifications of conveyance monitoring (e.g. no GPS to go with radio communications with drivers, no unannounced following of conveyances by managers, no escorts or convoys in use, etc.);

- Weak oversight at office of tracking and monitoring procedures (e.g. dispatcher over-burdened, improperly trained, not rotated randomly to avoid collusion with drivers)

- Use of subcontractors;

- No direct management oversight in day-to-day operations;

- Inappropriate delegation of authority to employees (e.g. allowing dispatchers to choose or approve clients and other business partners);

- No or weak use of GPS and geo-fencing;

- Infrequent visits to business partners at point of loading to discuss and inspect security;

- Security where loaded and empty conveyances and tractors are stored overnight;

- If drivers must leave vehicle to pick up paperwork en route;

- Time elapsed since last full investigation/check of driver (not simply DOT drug tests)

- Employee turnover rate at business partners; and

- No C-TPAT/PIP/NEEC participation, even though eligible.

Chapter Five

Where a manufacturer outsources or contracts elements of their supply chain, such as another facility, warehouse, or other elements, to include transportation, the manufacturer must work with these business partners to ensure pertinent security measures are in place and are adhered to throughout their supply chain. The supply chain for C-TPAT purposes is defined from point of origin through to point of distribution.

Manufacturers and exporters are often responsible for selecting the carriers for freight destined to the port of export, and frequently across the border to destination as well. Other partners in the export chain might also be selected by the manufacturer or exporter, such as freight forwarders, brokers, consolidators, etc. As selecting these service providers is the responsibility of manufacturers and exporters, so too is screening these business partners to ensure such partners are meeting the C-TPAT minimum security criteria. The easiest method, of course, is to select partners who are C-TPAT Partners and/or members of other governments' supply chain security programs. If a business partner has no such certification, then the manufacturer or exporter must conduct security assessments of all such business partners in the supply chain.

The table on the following pages is an example of how a manufacturer exporting to the U.S. might document their supply chain.

Compartment in Trailer Floor

U.S. CUSTOMS AND BORDER PROTECTION

Supply Chain Step	Type of Service Provided	Details About Business Partner	Issues to Consider
Manufacturer	Manufacturing/Exporter	This is our company, Francisco Javier Clavijero	C-TPAT Certified
Highway Carrier (for both FCL and LCL)	Moves cargo from factory to port of export	Pedro Thomas Ruiz de Velasco	C-TPAT Status Verified in Portal
Export Broker	Processes paperwork for cargo export	José Guadalupe Posada	NEEC Eligible, application in process
U.S. Port of Entry	Wait time	What is typical wait and release time?	How exposed is conveyance while waiting in line?
U.S. Broker	Files import documentation at destination	Jose Mendoza Brokers	Not C-TPAT, but eligible. Why not C-TPAT? Investigation and Security Assessment must be conducted. Are Personnel and IT security at a high level?
Transport to destination in U.S.	Movement of cargo from border to destination/ transfer yard.	This is our company. Internal procedures, especially as related to tracking and monitoring, must address vulnerabilities. Reporting delays and suspicious activities critical for driver.	Tight and overlapping tracking and monitoring of trucks must be in place, with direct management oversight and written procedures for when things go wrong.
Importer/Consignee	U.S. Importer client	Agerholm Importers 524 Mesquite Drive, Laredo, Texas	C-TPAT Status Verified in Portal

Export Examination

Below is an example of how a U.S. exporter might document their supply chain.

Supply Chain Step	Type of Service Provided	Details About Business Partner	Issues to Consider
Manufacturer	Exporter	This is our company, Henderson Manufacturers	C-TPAT Status Verified in Portal
Highway Carrier (for both FCL and LCL)	Moves cargo from factory to port of export	Wilson Trucking, 231 Dean Forest Rd., Savannah, GA	Not eligible. Security Assessment for this year on file. Working with company to activate five minute pings and geo-fencing on GPS system.
Freight Forwarder	Processes paperwork for cargo export	Global Freight Coordinators, 21 Bay St., Savannah, GA	Not eligible, but could be if they obtained CBP bond. Outreach to partner should be conducted to encourage C-TPAT participation.
Port of Export	Stores and handles cargo prior to lading	Georgia Port Authority	C-TPAT Status Verified in Portal
Ocean Carrier	Moves cargo from port to port	Excellent Ocean Carriers	C-TPAT Status Verified in Portal
Transhipment Port	Stores and handles cargo in between vessel movements	Izmir, Turkey	No, but could apply to C-TPAT
Ocean Carrier	Moves cargo from port to port	Mersin Carriers	Not eligible
Port of Entry at Foreign	Location of unlading	Constanta, Romania	No, but could apply to AEO. Romanian client asked to conduct outreach and encourage membership.
Foreign Broker	Files import documentation at destination	Torenescu Brothers	No, but could apply to AEO. Romanian client asked to conduct outreach and encourage membership.
Terminal Operator	Handles and stores cargo after unlading	Constanta Government Terminal	No, but could apply to AEO. Romanian client asked to conduct outreach and encourage membership.
Foreign Drayage	Trucks cargo from ocean terminal to destination	Ponta Transport	Not eligible, completed security questionnaire for this year on file
Foreign Consignee	This is our client.	Basescu Importers	AEO Certified, Certificate on file in Document Exchange

 U.S. Customs and
Border Protection

U.S. Customs and Border Protection
Office of Field Operations
C-TPAT Program
1300 Pennsylvania Avenue, NW
Washington, DC 20229

(202) 344-1180
industry.partnership@dhs.gov

Please visit the CBP and C-TPAT Web sites at
www.cbp.gov
www.cbp.gov/ctpat

CBP Publication No. 0206-0814
August 2014

Appendix G: Conflict Minerals Reporting Form

CFSI website: (www.conflictfreesourcing.org)
Training and guidance, template, Conflict-Free Smelter Program compliant smelter list.

Introduction

This Conflict Minerals Reporting Template (Template) is a free, standardized reporting template created by the Electronic Industry Citizenship Coalition® (EICC®) and the Global e-Sustainability Initiative (GeSI). The Template facilitates the transfer of information through the supply chain regarding mineral country of origin and smelters and refiners being utilized and supports compliance to legislation*. The template also facilitates the identification of new smelters and refiners to potentially undergo an audit via the Conflict-Free Smelter Program**.

The CMRT was designed for downstream companies to disclose information about their supply chains up to but not including the smelter. If you are a 3TG smelter or refiner, in accordance with the CFSP protocols, we recommend you enter your own name in the smelter list tab.

When filling out the form, none of the cell entries should start will "=" or "#."

---

* In 2010, the U.S. Dodd-Frank Wall Street Reform and Consumer Protection Act was passed concerning "conflict minerals" originating from the Democratic Republic of the Congo (DRC) or adjoining countries. The SEC published final rules associated with the disclosure of the source of conflict minerals by U.S. publicly traded companies (see the rules at http://www.sec.gov/rules/final/2012/34-67716 .pdf). The rules reference the OECD Due Diligence Guidance for Responsible Supply Chains of Minerals from Conflict-Affected and High-Risk Areas,
(http://www.oecd.org/daf/inv/mne/GuidanceEdition2.pdf), which guides suppliers to establish policies, due diligence frameworks and management systems.
** See information on the Conflict-Free Sourcing Initiative (www.conflictfreesourcing.org).

```
-----------------------------------------------------------------------
Instructions for completing Company Information questions (rows
8-22).
Provide comments in ENGLISH only
-----------------------------------------------------------------------
Note:  Entries with (*) are mandatory fields.
-----------------------------------------------------------------------
1. Insert your company's Legal Name.  Please do not use
abbreviations. In this field you have the option to add other
commercial names, DBAs, etc.
-----------------------------------------------------------------------
2. Select your company's Declaration Scope.  The options for scope
are:

A.  Company-wide
B.  Product (or List of Products)
C.  User-Defined

For "Company-wide", the declaration encompasses the entirety of a
company's products or product substances produced by the parent
company. Therefore if the user is reporting 3TG data at the company
level, they will be reporting conflict minerals data on all products they
manufacture.

For Scope selection of Product (or List of Products), a link to the
worksheet tab for Product List will be displayed.  If this scope is
chosen, it is mandatory to list the Manufacturer's Product Number of
the products covered under the Scope of this Declaration in Column B
of the Product List worksheet. It is optional to list the Manufacturer's
Product Name in Column C of the Product List worksheet.

For Scope selection of "User Defined", it is mandatory that the user
describes the scope to which the 3TG disclosure is applicable. The
scope of this class shall be defined in a text field by the supplier and
should be easily understood by customers or the receivers of the
document. As an example, companies may provide a link to clarifying
information.

This field is mandatory.
-----------------------------------------------------------------------
3. Insert your company's unique identifier number or code (DUNS
number, VAT number, customer-specific identifier, etc.)
-----------------------------------------------------------------------
4. Insert the source for the unique identifier number or code ("DUNS",
"VAT", "Customer", etc).
-----------------------------------------------------------------------
```

5. Insert your full company address (street, city, state, country, postal code). This field is optional.

6. Insert the name of the person to contact regarding the contents of the declaration information. This field is mandatory.

7. Insert the email address of the contact person. If an email address is not available, state "not available" or "n/a." A blank field may cause an error in form implementation. This field is mandatory.

8. Insert the telephone number for the contact. This field is mandatory.

9. Insert the name of the person who is responsible for the contents of the declaration information. The authorizer may be a different individual than the contact person. It is not correct to use the words "same" or similar identification to provide the name of the authorizer. This field is mandatory.

10. Insert the title for the Authorizing person. This field is optional.

11. Insert the email address of the Authorizing person. If an email address is not available, state "not available" or "n/a." A blank field may cause an error in form implementation. This field is mandatory.

12. Insert the telephone number for the Authorizing person. This field is mandatory.

13. Please enter the Date of Completion for this form using the format DD-MMM-YYYY. This field is mandatory.

14. As an example, the user may save the file name as: companyname-date.xls (date as YYYY-MM-DD).

Instructions for completing the seven Due Diligence Questions (rows 24–65).
Provide answers in ENGLISH only

These seven questions define the usage, origination and sourcing identification for each of the metals. The questions are designed to collect information about the use of 3TG in the company's product(s) to allow for the determination of regulatory applicability. Responses to these questions shall represent the 'Declaration Scope' selected in the company information section.The responses to the questions in this section can be used to determine applicability and completeness of 3TG reporting.

For each of the seven required questions, provide an answer for each metal using the pull down menu selections.The questions in this section must be completed for all 3TG. If the response for a given metal to questions 1 and/or question 2 is positive, then the subsequent questions shall be completed for that metal and the following due diligence questions (A to J) shall be completed about the company's overall due diligence program.

1. This is the first of two questions for which the response is used to determine whether the 3TG is within the scope of conflict minerals reporting requirements. This question relies upon the guidance provided by the SEC in the final rules regarding the determination if a 3TG is "necessary to the functionality" of a product. The SEC guidance is based upon the presumption that a company in the supply chain for a product would not intentionally add a 3TG to that product or any of a product's sub-components if that 3TG was not necessary to the product's generally expected function, use, or purpose. This response to this question serves to exclude any trace level contaminants such as tin in steel.

This question asks if any conflict minerals are used as raw material, component or additive in a product that you manufacture or contract to manufacture (including raw material and components). Impurities from raw materials, components, additives, abrasives, and cutting tools are outside the scope of the survey.

This question shall be answered for each 3TG. Valid responses to this question are either "yes" or "no". This question is mandatory.

Some companies may require substantiation for a "No" answer that should be entered into the Comment Field.

2. This is the second of two questions for which the response is used to determine whether the 3TG is within the scope of conflict minerals reporting requirements as described in the SEC's final rules regarding the determination if a 3TG is "necessary to the production" of a product. This question is separate and independent from the question and response to question 1. This query is intended to identify 3TGs which are intentionally used in the manufacturing process of a product and where some amount of the 3TG remains in the finished product. These 3TGs likely were not intended to become part of the final product nor are they likely "necessary to the functionality" of the product but are only present as residuals of the manufacturing process. In many cases, the manufacturer may have attempted to remove or facilitate consumption of the 3TG during the manufacturing process, however, some amount of the 3TG remains. Should the 3TG, which is used during the manufacturing process, be completely removed during that process, the response to this question would be "no."

This question shall be answered for each 3TG. Valid answers to this question are either "yes" or "no". This question is mandatory.

3. This is a declaration that any portion of the 3TGs contained in a product or multiple products originates from the DRC or an adjoining country (covered countries).

The answer to this query shall be "yes", "no", or "unknown". Substantiate a "Yes" answer in the comments section.

This question is mandatory for a specific metal if the response to Question 1 or 2 is "Yes" for that metal.

4. This is a declaration that identifies whether 3TGs contained in the product(s) necessary to the functionality of that product(s) originate from recycled or scrap sources.

The answer to this query shall be "yes", "no", or "unknown". This question is mandatory for a specific metal if the response to Question 1 or 2 is "Yes" for that metal.

A "Yes" answer means that 100% of the 3TG comes from recycled or scrap sources. A "No" answer means that some of the 3TG does not come from recycled or scrap sources. An "Unknown" answer means that the user does not know whether or not 100% of the 3TG comes from recycled or scrap sources.

5. This is a declaration to determine whether a company has received conflict minerals disclosures from all direct suppliers reasonably believed to be providing 3TGs contained in the products covered by the scope of this declaration. Permissible responses to this question are:

- Yes, 100%
- No, but greater than 75%
- No, but greater than 50%
- No, but greater than 25%
- No, but less than 25%
- None

This question is mandatory for a specific metal if the response to Question 1 or 2 is "Yes" for that metal.

6. This question verifies if the supplier has reason to believe they have identified all of the smelters providing 3TGs in the products covered by this declaration. The answer to this question shall be "yes" or "no", along with a comment in certain cases, e.g. list of smelters. This question is mandatory for a specific metal if the response to Question 1 or 2 is "Yes" for that metal.

7. This question verifies that all of the smelters identified to be providing any of the 3TGs contained in the products covered by the scope of this declaration have been reported in this declaration. The answer to this question shall be "yes" or "no" along with a comment in certain cases, e.g. list of smelters. This question is mandatory for a specific metal if the response to Question 1 or 2 is "Yes" for that metal.

Provide comments in the Comment sections as required to clarify your responses.

Instructions for completing Questions A.–J. (rows 69–87).
Questions A. through J. are mandatory if the response to Question 1 or 2 is "Yes" for any metal.
Provide answers in ENGLISH only

The OECD Due Diligence Guidance for Responsible Supply Chains of Minerals from Conflict-affected and High-risk Areas (OECD Guidance) defines "Due Diligence" as "an on-going, proactive and reactive process through which companies can ensure that they respect human rights and do not contribute to conflict". Due diligence should be an integral part of your company's overall conflict free sourcing strategy. Questions A. thru J. are designed to assess your company's conflict-free minerals sourcing due diligence activities. Responses to these questions shall represent the full scope of your company's activities and shall not be limited to the 'Declaration Scope' selected in the company information section.

A. Please answer "Yes" or "No". Provide any comments, if necessary.

B. Please answer "Yes" or "No" If "Yes", provide the web link in the comments section.

C. Please answer "Yes" or "No". Provide any comments if necessary. See Definitions worksheet for definition of "DRC conflict-free".

D. This is a declaration to determine whether a company requires their direct suppliers to source 3TG from validated, conflict free smelters. The answer to this query shall be "yes" or "no". This question is mandatory.

E. Please answer "Yes" or "No" to disclose whether your company has implemented conflict minerals sourcing due diligence measures. This declaration is not intended to provide the details of a company's due diligence measures - just that a company has implemented due diligence measures. The aspects of acceptable due diligence measures shall be determined by the requestor and supplier.

Examples of due diligence measures may include: communicating and incorporating into contracts (where possible) your expectations to suppliers on conflict-free mineral supply chain; identifying and assessing risks in the supply chain; designing and implementing a strategy to respond to identified risks; verifying your direct supplier's compliance to its DRC conflict-free policy, etc. These due diligence measure examples are consistent with the guidelines included in the internationally recognized OECD Guidance.

F. This is a declaration to disclose whether a company requests their supplier to fill out a conflict minerals declaration. The answer to this query shall be "yes" or "no" along with a comment in certain cases, i.e., to provide the format used for collecting information. This question is mandatory.

G. Please answer "Yes" or "No". Provide any comments, if necessary.

H. Please answer "Yes" or "No". In the comments section, you can provide additional information on your approach. Examples could be:

"3rd party audit" – on-site audits of your suppliers conducted by independent third parties.
"Documentation review only" – a reviewof supplier submitted records and documentation conducted by independent third parties and, or your company personnel.
"Internal audit" - on-site audits of your suppliers conducted by your company personnel.

I. Please answer "Yes" or "No". If "Yes", please describe how you manage your corrective action process.

J. Please answer "Yes" or "No". The SEC conflict minerals disclosure requirements apply to US exchange-traded companies that are subject to the US Securities Exchange Act. For more information please refer to www.sec.gov.

Instructions for completing the Smelter List Tab.
Provide answers in ENGLISH only

Note: Columns with (*) are mandatory fields

This template allows for smelter identification using the Smelter Reference List. Columns B,C,D and E must be completed in order from left to right to utilize the Smelter Reference List feature.
Use a separate line for each metal/smelter/country combination

1. Smelter Identification Input Column – If you know the Smelter Identification Number, input the number in Column A (columns B, C, D, E, F, G, I, and J will auto-populate). Column A does not autopopulate.

2. Metal (*)   -   Use the pull down menu to select the metal for which you are entering smelter information. This field is mandatory.

3. Smelter Reference List(*) – Select from dropdown. This is the list of known smelters as of template release date. If smelter is not listed select 'Smelter Not Listed'. This will allow you to enter the name of the smelter in Column D. If you do not know the name or location of the smelter, select 'Smelter Not Yet Identified.' For this option, columns D and E will autopopulate to say, 'unknown.' This field is mandatory.

4. Smelter Name (*)– Fill in smelter name if you selected "Smelter Not Listed" in column C. This field will auto-populate when a smelter name in selected in Column C. This field is mandatory.

5. Smelter Country (*) – This field will auto-populate when a smelter name is selected in column C. If you selected "Smelter Not Listed" in column C, use the pull down menu to select the country location of the smelter. This field is mandatory.

6. Smelter Identification – This is a unique identifier assigned to a smelter or refiner according to an established smelter and refinery identification system. It is expected that multiple names or aliases could be used to describe a single smelter or refiner and therefore multiple names or aliases could be associated to a single 'Smelter ID'.

7. Source of Smelter Identification Number – This is the source of the Smelter Identification Number entered in Column F. If a smelter name was selected in Column C using the dropdown box, this field will auto-populate.

8. Smelter Street – Provide the street name on which the smelter is located. This field is optional.

9. Smelter City – Provide the city name of where the smelter is located. This field is optional.

10. Smelter Location: State/Province, if applicable – Provide the state or province where the smelter is located. This field is optional.

11. Smelter Contact Name – The Conflict Minerals Reporting Template (CMRT) is circulated among companies in the requesting company's supply chain to ensure compliance with the OECD Due Diligence Guidance for Responsible Supply Chains of Minerals from Conflict-Affected and High-Risk Areas and the U.S. Securities and Exchange Commission Final Rule on conflict minerals.

If the template is circulated in a country where laws protecting personal information exist, sharing personal contact information in the CMRT may violate related regulations. Therefore, it is recommended that the requesting company take precautions such as obtaining the contact person's permission to share the information with other companies in the supply chain when completing "Smelter Contact Name" and the "Smelter Contact Email" columns.

If you have permission to share this information, please fill in the name of the Smelter Facility Contact person who you worked with.

12. Smelter Contact Email – Fill in the email address of the Smelter Facility contact person who was identified as the Smelter Contact Name. Example: John.Smith@SmelterXXX.com. Please review the instructions for Smelter Contact Name before completing this field.

13. Name of Mine(s) – This field allows a company to define the actual mines being used by the smelter. Please enter the actual mine names if known. If 100% of the smelter's feedstock originates from recycled or scrap sources, enter "Recycled" or "Scrap" in place of the name of the mine and answer "Yes" in Column P.

"RCOI confirmed as per CFSI" may be an acceptable answer to this question.

CFSI website: (www.conflictfreesourcing.org)
Training and guidance, template, Conflict-Free Smelter Program compliant smelter list.

Introduction

This Conflict Minerals Reporting Template (Template) is a free, standardized reporting template created by the Electronic Industry Citizenship Coalition® (EICC®) and the Global e-Sustainability Initiative (GeSI). The Template facilitates the transfer of information through the supply chain regarding mineral country of origin and smelters and refiners being utilized and supports compliance to legislation*. The template also facilitates the identification of new smelters and refiners to potentially undergo an audit via the Conflict-Free Smelter Program**.

The CMRT was designed for downstream companies to disclose information about their supply chains up to but not including the smelter. If you are a 3TG smelter or refiner, in accordance with the CFSP protocols, we recommend you enter your own name in the smelter list tab.

When filling out the form, none of the cell entries should start will "=" or "#."

---

* In 2010, the U.S. Dodd-Frank Wall Street Reform and Consumer Protection Act was passed concerning "conflict minerals" originating from the Democratic Republic of the Congo (DRC) or adjoining countries. The SEC published final rules associated with the disclosure of the source of conflict minerals by U.S. publicly traded companies (see the rules at http://www.sec.gov/rules/final/2012/34-67716.pdf). The rules reference the OECD Due Diligence Guidance for Responsible Supply Chains of Minerals from Conflict-Affected and High-Risk Areas, (http://www.oecd.org/daf/inv/mne/GuidanceEdition2.pdf), which guides suppliers to establish policies, due diligence frameworks and management systems.
** See information on the Conflict-Free Sourcing Initiative (www.conflictfreesourcing.org).

Neither EICC nor GeSI makes any representations or warranties with respect to the List or any Tool. The List and Tools are provided on an "AS IS" and on an "AS AVAILABLE" basis. EICC and GeSI hereby disclaim all warranties of any nature, express, implied or otherwise, or arising from trade or custom, including, without limitation, any implied warranties of merchantability, non-infringement, quality, title, fitness for a particular purpose, completeness or accuracy.

To the fullest extent permitted by applicable laws, EICC and GeSI renounce any liability for any losses, expenses or damages of any nature, including, without limitation, special, incidental, punitive, direct, indirect or consequential damages or lost income or profits, resulting from or arising out of the User's use of the List or any Tool, whether arising in tort, contract, statute, or otherwise, even if shown that they were advised of the possibility of such damages.

In consideration for access and use of the List and/or any Tool, THE USER hereby agrees to and does (a) release and forever discharge EICC and GeSI, as well as their respective officers, directors, agents, employees, volunteers, representatives, contractors, successors, and assigns, from any and all claims, actions, losses, suits, damages, judgments, levies, and executions, which the User has ever had, has, or ever can, shall, or may have or claim to have against EICC and/or GeSI, as well as their respective officers, directors, agents, employees, volunteers, representatives, contractors, successors, and assigns, resulting from or arising out of the List or any Tool or use thereof, and agrees to (b) indemnify, defend and hold harmless EICC and GeSI, as well as their respective officers, directors, agents, employees, volunteers, representatives, contractors, successors, and assigns, from any and all claims, actions, losses, suits, damages, judgments, levies, and executions resulting from or arising out of the USER'S use of the List or any Tool.

If any part of any provision of these Terms and Conditions shall be invalid or unenforceable under applicable law, said part shall be deemed ineffective to the extent of such invalidity or unenforceability only, without in any way affecting the remaining parts of said provision or the remaining provisions of these Terms and Conditions.

By accessing and using the List or any Tool, and in consideration thereof, the User agrees to the foregoing.

Revision 4.20 November 30, 2016

Appendix H: Professionalism Service Managers at U.S. Customs and Border Protection

Professionalism Service Managers (PSMs) are the primary point of contact to address concerns or comments about the inspections process of international travelers. The following is a list from www.cpb.gov.

Name	Phone Number	Ports of Entry	State(s)
Leopoldo Reyes	(907) 983-3144	Anchorage	AK
Shannon Chaney	(310) 665-4633	Los Angeles International Airport	CA
Darryl Tamayo	(562) 366-5772	L.A./Long Beach Seaport	CA
Kenia Diaz	(760) 768-2633	Calexico	CA
William Renold	(619) 685-4309	San Diego Airport/Seaport	CA
David Vallego	(760) 572-7260	Andrade	CA
Rosa Preciado, Terri L. Lopez	(619) 690-8973	San Ysidro	CA
Andrew Rushing	(619) 671-8262	Otay Mesa	CA
Antonio Garcia	(619) 938-8331	Tecate	CA
Vanessa Butler	(415) 782-9418	San Francisco	CA
Ramon Gonzalez	(303) 342-7400	Denver	CO
Patricia Coggins	(215) 863-4244	Wilmington, Pittsburgh, Philadelphia	DE, PA
James Prestridge	(305) 874-4300	Miami	FL
Mashika L. Acosta	(407) 825-4777	Orlando	FL
John J. Ortiz	(954) 634-1905	Port Everglades/ Ft. Lauderdale	FL
Joseph Hill	(305) 296-0303	Key West	FL
Gerardo L. Martinez	(561) 848-6922, ext. 372	West Palm Beach	FL
Randy Pryor, Shana Wells	(404) 765-2248	Atlanta	GA

(Continued)

Name	Phone Number	Ports of Entry	State(s)
Michael Stroud	(912) 966-0557	Brunswick, Savannah	GA
James H. Lee	(808) 237-4610	Honolulu	HI
Mark Hanson	(406) 791-6116	Area Port of Great Falls	MT
Sean Gillis	(773) 894-2900	Chicago–O'Hare/Midway, Green Bay, Peoria, Quad Cities, Milwaukee, Racine, Rockford, Rosemont	IL, WI
Lawrence Byrd	(617) 568-1810	Boston, Providence	MA
Paula Moragne	(410) 962-8179	Baltimore	MD
Michael Hodson	(207) 771-3629	Bangor, Houlton, Ft. Fairfield, Madawaska, Fort Kent, Van Buren, Calais, Vanceboro, Lubec/Eastport, Jackman, Bridgewater	ME
Robert Steger	(734) 941-6180, ext. 244	Detroit	MI
Tom Coffield	(701) 825-5619	International Falls, Baudette, Roseau, Pinecreek, Lancaster, Grand Portage, Hannah, Warroad	MN
Brian Nevanen	(612) 727-3415, ext. 2340	Minneapolis	MN
Melvyn Verbeck	(314) 428-2662, ext. 227	St. Louis	MO
Mark Hanson	(406) 791-6116	Bozeman, Helena, Kalispell, Sweetgrass, Turner, Opheim, Great Falls, Chief Mountain, Piegan, Scobey, Raymond, Willow Creek, Roosville, Wild Horse, Morgan, Great Falls	MT
Elliot Ortiz	(702) 730-6100, ext. 6037	Las Vegas	NV
Miguel Mercado	(718) 553-1648	New York (JFK)	NY
Keith Wagner	(973) 297-6504	New York, Newark	NY, NJ
Kevin Packwood	(518) 298-8319	Albany, Champlain, Trout River	NY
David S. Scott	(315) 769-3091, ext. 7031	Alexandria Bay, Ogdensburg, Massena	NY
Robert E. Ramsey	(716) 843-8401	Buffalo	NY

(Continued)

Name	Phone Number	Ports of Entry	State(s)
Heather Kennedy	(980) 235-1600	Charlotte, Wilmington, Raleigh-Durham, Morehead City, Winston-Salem	NC
Tom Coffield	(701) 825-5619	Grand Forks, Fargo, Portal, St. John, Antler, Sherwood, Noonan, Hansboro, Westhope, Carbury, Walhalla, Dunseith, Neche, Maida, Pembina, Ambrose, Northgate, Sarles, Fortuna	ND
Susan P. Anderson	(216) 267-3600, ext. 1	Ashtabula/Conneaut, Cincinnati, Louisville, Indianapolis	OH
Janis Robinson	(503) 326-3498	Portland	OR
Patricia Coggins	(215) 863-4244	Philadelphia, Pittsburgh, Wilmington	PA
Brett Mueller	(843) 745-2680	Charleston, Greenville, Columbia, Myrtle Beach, Georgetown	SC
Kirk Gomes	(972) 870-7531	Dallas	TX
Alicia Tellez	(281) 230-4727	Houston Service Port and Airports	TX
Pablo Cavazos	(713) 454-8002	Houston/Galveston Airport	TX
Mario Holguin	(915) 730-7145	El Paso	TX
Sharon Ansick	(830) 306-4339	Del Rio	TX
Esteban Garcia	(956) 843-5751	Hidalgo/Pharr/Anzalduas	TX
Jaime A. Gonzalez	(830) 752-3560	Eagle Pass	TX
Everardo Villarreal	(956) 548-2744, ext. 1502	Brownsville	TX
Javier A. Pena	(956) 523-7379	Laredo	TX
Walter J. Seibert	(956) 693-5773		
James Heil	(340) 774-4554	St. Thomas, USVI	USVI
Ricardo Simmons	(340) 773-1490	St. Croix, USVI	USVI
Tod Phillabaum	(802) 873-3219	Derby Line	VT
Matthew Nebesnik	(802) 868-2778	Highgate Springs	VT
Kevin Coy	(802) 527-3300	St. Albans	VT
Douglas Callen	(703) 661-7127	Washington-Dulles	VA
Frederick Eisler	(757) 266-7427	Norfolk, Richmond	VA

(*Continued*)

Name	Phone Number	Ports of Entry	State(s)
Kenneth Longshore	(360) 332-3118	Blaine, Sumas, Lynden, Danville, Bellingham, Point Roberts, Anacortes, Oroville, Laurier, Ferry, Metaline Falls, Nighthawk, Frontier, Boundary, Friday Harbor, Roche Harbor	WA
Richard Hammond	(206) 553-7960	Seattle, Port Angeles, Everett, Spokane, Aberdeen	WA
Mayra Alicea	(787) 253-4511	Puerto Rico	PR
Greg Grumbs	(905) 676-2606, ext. 194	Toronto	Canada
Robert M. Havens	(670) 288-0028	Saipan	MP
Mark Pablo	(671) 642-7611	Guam (Tamuning)	GU

Index

A

AAEI, *see* American Association of Exporters and Importers (AAEI)
ACE, *see* Automated Commercial Environment (ACE)
Acronyms, 247–248
Adidas, 99
AIG, 190
Airforwarders Association (AfA), 212
Alibaba, 135
Amazon, 135
American Association of Exporters and Importers (AAEI), 211–212
Anheuser-Busch InBev, 39
Antibribery, *see* Foreign Corrupt Practices Act (FCPA), antibribery provisions of
ARM Manufacturing, Ohio/Kobe Japan, 2011, tsunami, 19
Arms Export Control Act (AECA), 168
AstraZeneca, 39
ATA carnets, 172–173, 21, 235
Automated Commercial Environment (ACE), 161

B

Bankruptcy of major carrier, 129–132
Bering Communications, California/Sudan, 2015, political risk, kidnap and ransom, IT security, 21
Best practice strategy, structuring of, 197–218
  credits, 218
  effective corporate compliance program, elements of, 208–211
  resources, 211–217
  step 1 (determine a point person), 198–199
  step 2 (obtain senior management support and authorization), 199–200
  step 3 (create a committee of stakeholders), 200–201
  step 4 (perform an assessment), 202–203
  step 5 (come up with a plan of attack), 203–204
  step 6 (develop resources), 204
  step 7 (outreach to all fiefdoms), 204–205
  step 8 (create SOPs), 205–206
  step 9 (start internal training programs), 206–207
  step 10 (ascertain audit capability), 207–208
Binding ruling process, 147
BIS, *see* Bureau of Industry and Security (BIS)
Blue Tiger International, 99
Bonded warehouses, 120–121
Branding (corporate), 101–102
Bureau of Industry and Security (BIS), 161, 164
Business Action to Stop Counterfeiting and Piracy (BASCAP) initiative (ICC), 71
Business contract terms, glossary of, 229–234
Business terms, glossary of, 219–228

C

Cargo insurance, 117, 190; *see also* Marine insurance
Cargo Loss Control, 190
Cash-in-advance, 83
CBP, *see* U.S. Customs and Border Protection (CBP)
Chipotle, 98
Commerce Control List (CCL), 160
Commercial Crime Services (ICC), 71
Confiscation, expropriation, nationalization, and deprivation (C, E, N, and D), 28–29

Conflict minerals, 46–48
  Conflict Minerals Report, 50–53
  contracting to manufacture, 48–49
  origin of, 49–50
  reporting form, 311–321
  SEC rules on disclosing use of, 48, 311
Container Security Initiative (CSI), 72–73
Contracting to manufacture (company),
      48–49
Contract management (international), 77–82
  contract administration, 81
  contract closeout, 81–82
  process, 78–82
  procurement planning, 79
  recommendations, 78
  solicitation planning, 79–80
  source selection, 80–81
Contract Management Maturity Model
      (CMMM), 82
Contract repudiation, 29
Corporate reputation branding and
      marketing, 101–102
Council of Supply Chain Management
      Professionals (CSCMP), 216
Counterfeit products, 106
Crime and fiduciary liability insurance,
      194–195
CSI, *see* Container Security Initiative (CSI)
C-TPAT (Customs-Trade Partnership
      Against Terrorism) five step risk
      assessment, 267–310
  brokers, 285–295
  consolidators, 297–298
  foreign manufacturers and U.S.
      exporters, 305–307
  highway carriers, 301–302
  importers, 281–283
  introduction and concepts, 271–279
  risk assessment, 270
  table of contents, 269
Cultural issues in global trade,
      management of, 13–18
  business culture, 14
  considering cultural factors, 14–18
  domestic customers, 15
  exchange of business cards, 16
  gift giving, 16
  negotiation, 18
  punctuality, attitudes toward, 17

Currency, 89–92
Currency inconvertibility, 30
Customhouse brokers, 149–152
Cyber liability insurance coverage, 195–196
Cybersecurity, 249–265
  after a computer incident, 263–265
  incident response plan, execution of,
      255–262
  steps to take before intrusion or attack
      occurs, 249–255
  what not to do following a cyber
      incident, 262–263
Cyberspace, safeguarding and securing (U.S.
      government program for), 62–71
  business need for coverage, 67–70
  cyber insurance, 68
  cyber liability claims examples, 65–67
  Cybersecurity Partners Local Access
      Plan, 63
  Cybersecurity Workforce Initiative, 64
  EINSTEIN, 63
  fighting commercial crime, 70–71
  Information Sharing and Analysis
      Centers, 64
  interagency collaboration, 64
  National Cyber Incident Response
      Plan, 64
  National Cybersecurity Awareness
      Month, 64
  National Cybersecurity and
      Communications Integration
      Center, 63
  National Cybersecurity Protection
      System, 62–63
  Stop.Think.Connect, 64
  technological development and
      deployment, 64
  U.S. Computer Emergency Readiness
      Team (US-CERT), 63

D

Data theft, 67
Default, 30
Defense Trade Controls (DTC), 161
Deferred prosecution agreement (DPA), 43
Defining the global supply chain and
      enterprise risk management, 1–24
  case studies in global risk, 18–24

cultural issues in global trade,
management of, 13–18
enterprise risk management, 4–8
key challenges in global supply chain,
10–11
overview, 1–3
risk defined, 11–13
risk and spending in global supply
chain, 9–10
Deneson Products Corporation, Florida/
Venezuela, 2014, cargo risk, 22–23
Denied party screening, 164
Dodd-Frank Act, 47, 48
DPA, *see* Deferred prosecution agreement
(DPA)
DTC, *see* Defense Trade Controls (DTC)
Dumpster diving, 66
Durkee Foods, Netherlands/New Orleans,
2005, hurricane, 20–21

E

EARs, *see* Export Administration
Regulations (EARs)
ECCN, *see* Export Control Classification
Number (ECCN)
E-commerce (global), 132–137
EINSTEIN, 63
Electronic Export Information (EEI),
160–161
Embargoed country screening, 164–168
Embraer, 39
Employee, rogue, 66
Enterprise risk management (ERM), 4–8
Export Administration Regulations
(EARs), 159
Export Control Classification Number
(ECCN), 160
Export factoring, 86–87
Export supply chain, 157–172
breakdown of consolidated screening
list, 168–169
Commerce Control List, 160
consularization and legalization, 169–170
denied party screening, 164
Electronic Export Information, 160–161
embargoed country screening, 164–168
Export Administration Regulations, 159
free trade affirmations, 171

getting paid, 172
government agencies responsible
for exports, 158
International Traffic in Arms
Regulations, 158–159
preshipment inspections, 170–171
record-keeping requirements, 163
Schedule B number/Harmonized Tariff
number, 162–163
U.S. Principal Party in Interest,
161–162
valuation, 163

F

FCPA, *see* Foreign Corrupt Practices Act
(FCPA)
Finance, risk management and, 82–92
consignment, 85
currency, 89–92
documentary collections, 84
export working capital financing, 86
forfaiting, 87
international payment terms, 83–89
letters of credit, 83–84, 85–86
open account, 85
Foreign Corrupt Practices Act (FCPA),
antibribery provisions of, 37–46
antibribery compliance program,
reasons for having, 45–46
corporate compliance program, 41–44
Department of Justice, overview from,
40–41
example cases, 39–40
highlights, 38
Foreign exchange (FX) risk (currency), 89
Foreign sanctions evaders (FSEs), 169
Foreign Trade Association (FTA), 213
Foreign trade zones (FTZs), 119–120
Forfaiting, 87
Free of particular average (FPA), 185
Free trade agreements (FTAs), 121, 171

G

GlaxoSmithKline, 39
Global e-commerce, 132–137
Global Energies, New Jersey/China, 2016,
Foreign Corrupt Practices Act, 22

Global Intellectual Property Academy
(GIPA), 103
Global Purchasing Group, 215
Global risk, case studies in, 18–24
ARM Manufacturing, Ohio/Kobe
Japan, 2011, tsunami, 19
Bering Communications, California/
Sudan, 2015, political risk, kidnap
and ransom, IT security, 21
Deneson Products Corporation, Florida/
Venezuela, 2014, cargo risk, 22–23
Durkee Foods, Netherlands/New
Orleans, 2005, hurricane, 20–21
Global Energies, New Jersey/China,
2016, Foreign Corrupt Practices
Act, 22
Rathen Industries, New York/Russia,
2014, trade compliance, 19–20
Global risk management, 25–60;
see also Insurance (international)
and global risk management
conflict minerals, 46–53
Foreign Corrupt Practices Act and
antibribery, 37–46
global supply chain risk verticals, 25–27
personnel, 53–60
political risk, 27–30
receivable management, 30–31
security and terrorism, 31–36
"supply chain focus," 26–27
Global supply chain
areas of opportunity in, 9
conflict minerals entering, 47
cost reduction, 127
disruptions, 128
driving risk and spending from, 9–10
FTZs in, 119
green initiatives built into, 94
key challenges in, 10–11
security, 153
Global trade risks, 61–107
contract management, 77–82
corporate reputation branding and
marketing, 101–102
currency, 89–92
cyberspace, safeguarding and securing
(U.S. government program for),
62–71
finance, 82–92

geophysical, environmental,
sustainability, 92–101
going green, 94–101
intellectual property rights, 101, 103–107
international payment terms, 83–89
technology and cyber issues, 61–71
U.S. Customs and Border Protection's
security programs, 71–77
Glossary
business contract terms, 229–234
business terms, 219–228
international trade terms, 235–246
Green initiatives, 94–101

H

Hacking
of Democratic National Committee,
61–62
organization victimized by, 263
of small business, 66
Harmonized Tariff Schedule of the United
States (HTSUS), 142
Harris Corporation, 39
Hartford, 190

I

ICC, *see* International Chamber of
Commerce (ICC)
Importer Security Filing (ISF), 76–77
Import supply chain, 138–157
bonds, 156
country of origin marking, 143
customhouse brokers, 149–152
duties and fees, 138–142
harmonized tariff classification,
142–143
internal supervision and control, 152
invoice requirements, 154–155
reasonable care standard, 144–149
record retention, 156–157
supply chain security, 153–154
Inconvertible currencies, 30
INCO Terms, 109–115
basic history, 110
revision of terms, 111
rules, 111–112, 113–115
significant revisions, 110–111

Information Sharing and Analysis Centers (ISACs), 64, 255
Information Sharing and Analysis Organizations (ISAOs), 255
Institute of Supply Management (ISM), 216
Insurance
    cargo, 117, 190; *see also* Marine insurance
    credit (export), 86
    cyber, 68
    kidnap and ransom, 21
    marine, *see* Marine insurance
    trade credit, 30
Insurance (international) and global risk management, 181–196
    commercial insurances overview, 192–193
    crime and fiduciary liability insurance, 194–195
    cyber liability insurance coverage, 195–196
    international directors and officers liability insurance, 196
    liability insurance, 194
    marine insurance, 117, 181–192
    property insurance, 193–194
    resources for international insurances, 196
Intellectual property rights (IPRs), 101, 103–107
International Chamber of Commerce (ICC), 70, 71, 110
International contract management, *see* Contract management (international)
International directors and officers liability insurance, 196
International Plant Protection Convention (IPPC), 170
International SOS, 53, 55
International trade terms, glossary of, 235–246
International Traffic in Arms Regulations (ITAR), 158–159, 168
IPRs, *see* Intellectual property rights (IPRs)
ISACs, *see* Information Sharing and Analysis Centers (ISACs)
ISAOs, *see* Information Sharing and Analysis Organizations (ISAOs)
ISF, *see* Importer Security Filing (ISF)

ISM, *see* Institute of Supply Management (ISM)
ITAR, *see* International Traffic in Arms Regulations (ITAR)

J

JPMorgan, 39

K

Kelly Global, 185
Kidnap and ransom exposures, 59
K&R (kidnap and ransom) insurance, 21

L

Landed costs, 178–179
Laptops, stolen, 65
Letters of comfort, 229
Letters of credit (LCs), 83–84
Liability insurance, 194
Lloyds of London, 190
Logistics, 119–132
    bankruptcy of major carrier, 129–132
    bidding, 121–124
    bonded warehouses, 120–121
    foreign trade zones, 119–120
    free trade agreements, 121
    freight, 124–127
    reducing supply chain costs, 127–129
    sea–air combination, 128
    summary of considerations, 173–180

M

Marine insurance, 181–192
    cancellation, 192
    consolidation and deconsolidation, 186–187
    domestic transit, 187
    effective dates, 186
    exclusions, 188–192
    geographic areas covered, 183
    interruptions in transit, 187–188
    key considerations, 182–183
    limits of liability, 184
    modes of transit covered, 183–184
    named insured, 183
    special terms, 185

storage/warehousing, 186
terrorism, 186
underwriting terms, 185
valuation, 184
war and SRCC coverage, 185–186
Marketing (corporate), 101–102
Merchandise processing fees (MPFs), 120

N

NAFTA, *see* North American Free Trade
    Agreement (NAFTA)
National Cyber Incident Response Plan, 64
National Cybersecurity Awareness
    Month, 64
National Cybersecurity and
    Communications Integration
    Center, 63
National Cybersecurity Protection
    System, 62–63
National Institute of World Trade
    (NIWT), 214
New York District Export Council
    (NYDEC), 214
Non-disclosure agreement, 230
Nongovernmental organizations (NGOs),
    101
Non-prosecution agreement (NPA), 43
Non-SDN Iranian Sanctions Act List
    (NS-ISA), 169
North American Free Trade Agreement
    (NAFTA), 121, 171
Nu Skin Enterprises, 39
NYDEC, *see* New York District Export
    Council (NYDEC)

O

Och-Ziff, 39
Office of Foreign Asset Controls (OFAC), 164
Organization for Economic Co-operation
    and Development (OECD), 50, 52
Other government agency (OGA), 152

P

Palestinian Legislative Council (PLC)
    List, 169
Panasonic, 98

Personnel exposures, 53–60
    examples, 53–59
    kidnap and ransom exposures, 59
    training, 60
Political risk, 27–30
    confiscation, expropriation,
        nationalization, and
        deprivation, 28–29
    contract repudiation, default,
        currency inconvertibility, and
        devaluation, 29–30
    financial losses and, 27
Professionalism Service Managers (PSMs),
    323–326
Property insurance, 193–194

Q

Quid pro quo, 230

R

Rathen Industries, New York/Russia,
    2014, trade compliance, 19–20
Receivable management, 30–31
Request for proposal (RFP), 122
RIMS, 4
Risk, definition of, 11–13
Risk and Insurance Management Society
    (RIMS), 217
Risk management, *see* Global risk
    management
Roanoke, 190

S

Schedule B number/Harmonized Tariff
    number, 162–163
SDGT, *see* Specially designated global
    terrorist (SDGT)
SEC, *see* U.S. Securities and Exchange
    Commission (SEC)
Sectoral Sanctions Identifications (SSI)
    List, 169
Securities and Exchange Act of 1934, 48
Security and Accountability for Every
    Port Act of 2006, 73
Security and terrorism, 31–36
    corporate terrorism best practices, 35–36
    physical assets, 31–32

preventing terrorist attacks, 32–33
rules for preventing and countering
terrorism, 33–35
Shareholder value, 8, 46, 224
Sight drafts, 238
Small- and medium-sized enterprises
(SMEs), 89
Solid wood packing material (SWPM)
certificates, 170
Sony Pictures Entertainment, 69–70
SOPs, *see* Standard operating procedures
(SOPs)
SOW, *see* Statements of Work (SOW)
Specially designated global terrorist
(SDGT), 169
Special purpose vehicles (SPVs), 42
Spyware virus, 66
Squirepb.com, 52
SRCC, *see* Strikes, riots, and civil
commotions (SRCC)
SSI List, *see* Sectoral Sanctions
Identifications (SSI) List
Standard operating procedures (SOPs), 40
Starbucks, 99
Statements of Work (SOW), 79
Stop.Think.Connect, 64
Strikes, riots, and civil commotions
(SRCC), 185
Supply chain and logistics, 109–180
ATA carnets, 172–173
export supply chain, 157–172
global e-commerce, 132–137
import supply chain, 138–157
INCO terms, 109–115, 174–175
insurance, 175
landed costs, 178–179
logistics, 119–132, 173–180
sourcing and purchasing, 115–119
supply chain security, 153–154
tracking of shipments, 177
trade compliance, 137–172, 179–180
SWPM certificates, *see* Solid wood packing
material (SWPM) certificates

T

Technology and cyber issues (global trade
risks), 61–71
Terrorism, *see* Security and terrorism

TIA, *see* Transportation Intermediaries
Association (TIA)
Trade compliance, 137–172
export supply chain, 157–172
import supply chain, 138–157
Trade credit insurance, 30
Trademark law, 104–105
Trade risks, *see* Global trade risks
Trade terms, *see* International trade terms,
glossary of
Transportation Intermediaries
Association (TIA), 213
Travelers, 190

U

United States Chamber of Commerce
(USCC), 215
United States Council for International
Business (USCIB), 214–215
United States Munitions List (USML),
158
U.S. Computer Emergency Readiness
Team (US-CERT), 63
U.S. Customs and Border Protection
(CBP), 143, 161
Professionalism Service Managers at,
323–326
security programs, 71–77
U.S. Export-Import Bank, 86, 87
U.S. Principal Party in Interest (USPPI),
161–162
U.S. Securities and Exchange Commission
(SEC), 39
conflict minerals, rules on disclosing
use of, 48, 311
focus on company self-policing, 43
U.S. Small Business Administration, 86

V

Verticals, 25

W

Work Breakdown Structures (WBS), 79

Z

Zurich, 190

About the Author

 **Thomas A. Cook** is the managing director of Blue Tiger International (bluetigerintl.com), a premier international business consulting company on supply chain management, trade compliance, purchasing, sales and business development, global trade, and logistics.

Cook was the former CEO of American River International in New York and Apex Global Logistics Supply Chain Operation in Los Angeles.

He has mote than 30 years of experience in assisting companies all over the world managing their global operations.

He is a member of the New York District Export Council, sits on the boards of numerous corporations, and is considered a leader in the business verticals he works in.

Cook has been engaged by the American Management Association since 1981. He has been a course developer and leader/instructor in a host of areas, such as, but not limited to, project management, import and export, global supply chain, purchasing, risk management, negotiation skills, sales, marketing, and business development.

He has now authored more than 19 books on global trade and is in the middle of an eight-book series titled The Global Warrior: Advancing on the Necessary Skill Sets to Compete Effectively in Global Trade. He has also authored books on sales management, customer service, purchasing, and growth in world markets.

Cook has been or is involved with a number of organizations in education and training in a number of industry verticals, such as, but not limited to, the Institute of Supply Management, Council of Supply Chain Management Professionals, Transportation Intermediaries Association, Airforwarders Association, U.S. Chamber of Commerce, Department of Commerce, Conference Board, State University of New York (SUNY), Dale Carnegie, California State University–Long Beach, and New York Institute of Technology. Cook is also the director of the National Institute of World Trade (niwt.org), a 30-year-old educational and training organization based in New York.

He has been a lecturer and program adviser at Stony Brook University on Long Island and an adjunct professor at the Fashion Institute of Technology.

Cook is a former U.S. Naval and Merchant Marine Officer. He holds a BS and MS degree in business from SUNY Fort Schuyler, Maritime College.

Cook has created a veterans foundation, Soldier On (soldieronathome .org) on Long Island benefiting wounded combat veterans and helping with the development of specialized dogs utilized in the treatment of post-traumatic stress disorder (PTSD).

Cook can be reached at tomcook@bluetigerintl.com or 516-359-6232.

Tom is also the founder of the "Soldier on at Home" organization, assisting wounded combat veterans and dogs along with funding dog training for Veterans with PTSD. www.soldieronathome.org.